D0771717

THE SECULAR ENLIGHTENMENT

The Secular Enlightenment

MARGARET C. JACOB

PRINCETON UNIVERSITY PRESS

PRINCETON & OXFORD

Published by Princeton University Press
41 William Street, Princeton, New Jersey 08540
6 Oxford Street, Woodstock, Oxfordshire OX20 1TR

press.princeton.edu

LCCN 2018946123
First paperback printing, 2021
Paperback ISBN 978-0-691-21676-8
Cloth ISBN 978-0691-16132-7

British Library Cataloging-in-Publication Data is available

Editorial: Rob Tempio and Matt Rohal
Production Editorial: Sara Lerner
Jacket/Cover Design: Leslie Flis
Jacket/Cover Credit: Johannes Jelgerhuis (1770–1836), *The Shop of the Bookdealer, Pieter Meijer Warnars on the Vijgendam in Amsterdam.*
Prisma Archivo / Alamy Stock Photo
Production: Erin Suydam
Publicity: Jodi Price
Copyeditor: Jennifer Harris

This book has been composed in Arno Pro

Printed in the United States of America

To Jacob Soll, Matt Kadane, and the future

CONTENTS

IMAGES

ACKNOWLEDGMENTS

LET ME BEGIN with sadness. Two friends and mentors were sorely missed at the completion of this book: Joyce Appleby and Helli Koenigsberger—both died in the period of its being written. I miss them.

Happily many debts were accumulated that can now be acknowledged: John Zammito, Geoffrey Symcox, Matt Kadane, Jake Soll, my graduate students, and as always my partner of thirty years, Lynn Hunt. All read, corrected, admonished, and generally made the life of researching and writing so much more rewarding than it might otherwise be. The wonders of the UCLA library and the University of California system can best be appreciated in the endnotes. The staffs of the History Department and the library are always efficient and kind. Various research assistants worked with alacrity, and I want to thank Paul Cella and Grace Ballor for being exceptionally helpful.

THE SECULAR ENLIGHTENMENT

Prologue

THE ENLIGHTENMENT was an eighteenth-century movement of ideas and practices that made the secular world its point of departure. It did not necessarily deny the meaning or emotional hold of religion, but it gradually shifted attention away from religious questions toward secular ones. By seeking answers in secular terms—even to many religious questions—it vastly expanded the sphere of the secular, making it, for increasing numbers of educated people, a primary frame of reference. In the Western world, art, music, science, politics, and even the categories of space and time had undergone a gradual process of secularization in the sixteenth and seventeenth centuries; the Enlightenment built on this process and made it into an international intellectual cause. By asserting this expansion of secularity, I do not mean to downplay the many religious manifestations found in the age. This book does not claim that religion was en route to being cast aside like bad bacteria waiting to be knocked out by an antibiotic of deism or atheism.

The chapters ahead do claim that attachment to the world—the here and the now—to a life lived without constant reference to God, became increasingly commonplace and the source of an explosion of innovative thinking about society, government, and the economy, to mention but a few areas of inquiry. In attaching to the world, many people lost interest, or belief, in hell. Its proprietor, the devil, still haunted popular beliefs but was no longer invoked on a daily basis by the literate and educated.

Areas of human behavior once explained by concepts like miracles or original sin now received explanations inspired by physical science or the emerging studies of social and economic relations. Space and time were cleared of their Christian meaning, and people became more concerned with reorganizing the present and planning for the future than in their fate after death. They could enter churches not to pray but to admire the architecture, spend Sunday mornings reading a newspaper, cast a cold eye on clergy of every persuasion, and read risqué books to their heart's content.[1] The secular-minded and literate could pursue their economic or commercial success, become innovative in science or technology, take up the liberal professions, work long hours in business or household, and imagine their successes or failures as the reward for their actions or the result of blind economic or social forces.

In a secular setting, the purpose of human life takes shape without necessary reference to a transcendent order; temporal well-being is the end being sought, now more readily managed by the increasing use of pocket watches. Where once the deeply religious monitored time to identify their shortcomings and assess their chances at salvation, the secular man lived a punctual life that found pleasure in work or social life. The secular woman, when not caring for home and domestic life, read novels, entertained in gatherings with an agenda—the abolition of the slave trade, the news from France or America—and died without fear of what might come next. Fathers and mothers sought to educate children so that they might find temporal happiness.

It is one thing to say that increasingly secular values and pursuits can be observed in the course of the eighteenth century; it is another to assert that a teleological process took hold particularly in the Western world and it is here to stay. Most recently, such an assertion allows its believers to look down upon Islam, for example. It also assumes that nation-states making it first to the finish line of secularization would be immune to the dark forces of totalitarianism or fascism.[2]

In this book, readers will hear a cacophony of rich voices new to the age. We will be introduced to freethinkers, low and high Anglican churchmen, Hobbes, Spinoza, Locke, Newton, moderate Scots Presbyterians, French materialists, Rousseauian idealists, pornographers, Lutheran pantheists, and deeply anticlerical Catholics. As a result of their writings about politics, society, or religion, after 1750 a new generation of Europeans and American colonists could imagine entirely human creations such as republics and democracies. So much of this creative energy occurred in cities—hence the focus in many chapters on major urban settings. They did not cause the Enlightenment, but they facilitated its birthing.

Sometimes the signs of secularity, of living in the here and now, were subtle. Around the middle of the seventeenth century, Dutch professors of astronomy stopped teaching astrology. It was still widely practiced, yet, ever so gradually, in most annual Dutch almanacs its importance dwindled. About the same time, in the lifetime of Spinoza (d. 1677), few of his contemporaries could understand, let alone accept, his identification of God with Nature. Fast-forward to the 1780s in both England and Germany, where thinkers with obviously religious sentiments like the Lutheran Johann Herder, or the poet of Dissenting (non-Anglican, Protestant) background, Samuel Taylor Coleridge, could imagine a universe infused with the divine. In three generations, one of the foundations of Christian meta-physics, the absolute separation of Creator from Creation, of spirit from matter, had disaggregated.

The disaggregation could also be symbolic. A French masonic ceremony of the late 1770s occurred in its "Sanctuary." There we find the throne of the master of the lodge and next to it on the altar three silver candlesticks, the book of statutes and rules of the lodge, the "book of the gospel, a compass, a mallet," and in pride of place "reposes, displayed, the new Constitutions from the Grand Orient of France."[3] Were these masonic brothers in Strasbourg mocking the accoutrements of the Catholic Church? Or using them to signal the importance they attached to their legal status within the fraternity? The setting was adorned with sky-blue serge, braids and ribbons of gold, silver and jewels. It belonged to a lodge of merchants who lost little love for their aristocratic brothers largely found in other lodges. The orator of the occasion noted the bravery of the French soldiers fighting in the American Revolution. He also said that brothers meet under "the living image of the Grand Architect of the Universe." Somewhere, in this mélange of symbols and talk about the Grand Architect, lurks the residue of the Christian heritage common to all the brothers, but did one of them actually have to believe in it? Readers can make up their own minds.

Last, what to make of the Christian heritage? As early as the 1720s, an entirely new approach to religion emerged among a circle of exiled French Huguenot writers, German publishers, and engravers resident in the Dutch Republic. Overwhelm-ingly, the literature about Christianity and all the other religions had praised and privileged the first, even mocked the alterna-tives. Time out of mind, Jews and Christians waged polemical warfare in multiple texts, while Catholics and Protestants had been at one another's throats since the 1520s. None of them liked Muslims. Then a set of large, engraved French volumes, Picart and Bernard's *Religious Ceremonies of the World*, began to appear from 1723 onward, and it sought to treat all the religions of the world evenhandedly.[4] The volumes would remain in print in multiple editions, in the major languages, well into the nineteenth century. The impulse to develop such a treatment can best be described as secular; it focused on people's religious customs and ceremonies, not on the truth or falsity of their beliefs. By comparing in this way, the volumes helped establish the category of "religion," itself an offshoot of secular thinking. Religion was now a cultural practice that varied across time and space; it could be explained in secular terms.

This book tries to understand the major intellectual currents of the century that gave birth to the label "secular." In the writing of history, in many European languages, the number of Enlightenments has now proliferated: the Radical Enlightenment, the Moderate Enlightenment, the Religious Enlightenment, even the Catholic Enlightenment. I too am guilty. *The Radical Enlightenment: Pantheists, Freemasons and Republicans* (1981) was my creation.[5] It is surely blatantly presumptuous in the area of title making to bring forward yet another one, the Secular Enlightenment. At least this title possesses a historical lineage that goes back to the writings of Ernst Cassirer in the 1930s and includes, in our own time, Peter Gay, Franco Venturi, Daniel Roche, and John Marshall. Here, I seek to add a contribution to their legacy.

1

The Setting

SPACE EXPANDED AND FILLED ANEW

BETWEEN 1500 AND 1700, Westerners discovered two new worlds: one in the heavens, the other on earth. These discoveries coincided with and helped further a vast expansion of commerce that brought yet more peoples and places into the Western orbit. Celestial and terrestrial space were reconfigured. Making sense of these monumental discoveries required new thought and language.

Christianity had to rise to the intellectual challenge presented by the new spatial reality. The findings of the new science displaced the earth from the center of the universe and thereby raised doubts about all traditional explanations. The discovery of new continents and peoples had an even more immediate effect. Why did the new peoples being discovered believe what they believed, having never heard the Christian message? Some could be converted; others not so readily. Missionaries discovered an almost unimaginable variety of beliefs and soon began to debate the meanings of this diversity. Did everyone have a notion of God, or were some newly discovered peoples natural atheists? The Greek and Roman authorities long revered in Europe had not the slightest inkling of the existence of the Americas. Western peoples could no longer rely on the coherence and order long provided by Christian theology. In this way, the new spatial realities provided the setting wherein enlightened ideas first emerged.

Physico-theology was one of the first attempts to give coherence to the physical reality of a mathematically knowable world. Its conserving goal was to augment piety and exalt the Grand Architect, to redefine the coherence and order of Christianity. The new physics of the seventeenth century—heliocentric, mechanical, and mathematical—could reinforce the theology of order and providential design. Science in the service of Christian orthodoxy became a goal championed particularly by English natural philosophers, Francis Bacon, Robert Boyle, and most remarkably Isaac Newton (figure 1). They aimed physico-theology against the new heresies of the age: atheism, deism, and materialism. In doing so, they fashioned what became a moderate version of enlightened ideas that embraced science, eschewed doctrinal quarrels among Christians, and endorsed religious toleration.[1] The voices of physico-theology constituted the chorus that emanated from the liberal segment of the Church of England. Thanks in good part to Samuel Clarke, Newton's friend and interpreter, this segment exerted influence everywhere in Protestant Europe through personal contacts and translated sermons.

By the end of the war-torn seventeenth century, more than a science-based Christian orthodoxy was needed. The political crises of the century—revolution in three kingdoms of the British Isles, the removal of Spanish authority in the northern Netherlands, the devastation in Central Europe caused by the Thirty Years War—required new responses to political reality. Hobbes, Locke, the English republican and Commonwealth

FIGURE 1. Isaac Newton, whose science became one of the anchors for enlightened thought. (ID# 1775740). Courtesy of Bridgeman Images.

men, and not least, in the Dutch Republic, Grotius and Spinoza attempted to redefine the political order and, in the process, confounded aspects of Christian orthodoxy. They laid the foundation upon which enlightened approaches to society and government would rest. Each in his way refused to endorse monarchical absolutism and the divine rights of kings. They invested the power of the state in social arrangements that offered security, the protection of property, and justice in return for the consent (however tacit) of the governed. Even Hobbes rested state power on a contract among the people to embrace the mortal god, Leviathan.

Aside from war and revolution, there were still other challenges to spatial order and coherence. The spread of money had the effect of revolutionizing the production and consumption of all commodities, creating new transactions, histories, and affairs. In European society, new forms of urban association emerged, and these conferred upon participants, as John Dewey wrote many centuries later, the means "of unlocking energies hitherto pent in."[2] In short, faced with new dynamics and social arrangements, Europeans and later American colonists responded with language that reordered their understanding of spatial reality. To give but one example, late in the eighteenth century Thomas Jefferson broke out of the classical republican vision he inherited to argue that rather than being small, a republic could stretch across an entire Continent, from sea to shining sea.

Space conquered and negotiated by the imperialist impulse introduced unprecedented power relations between subject and conqueror. The European nation-states and then the newly created American state possessed sophisticated armaments and armies, ships and horses—accompanied by disease and the will to enslave. Their sometimes brutal actions, when reported, forced European minds in the direction of distant peoples and customs that needed to be understood. Whether the Spanish absolutist monarchy or the Dutch republican government undertook or endorsed imperialist ventures to extend their power, every occasion required knowledge of the spaces, peoples, and heavens. Never before in Western history had such an expansion of spatial knowledge been both possible and necessary.

Therein lay the roots of the Enlightenment: the unintended consequence of commercial and state-sponsored expansion. Paradoxically, as the power of absolute monarchies and the clergy that supported them grew in Europe—augmented as they were by global conquest—inventive responses to new spatial realities multiplied. Their combined weight secularized space and removed not only its boundaries but also its supernatural powers. They undermined belief in heaven and hell and the authority of absolutist regimes. By the 1770s, major theorists from the Scottish school in Edinburgh to the French *philosophes* in Paris furthered the corrosive process by providing new vocabularies that denigrated empires, state-supported orthodoxies, and the clergy who benefited from them.

The combined impact of the subversive literature that began in the 1650s and continued into the 1790s ultimately delegitimized courts and monarchs. From the clandestine literature, early in the century to the abbé Raynal, Diderot, Rousseau, the abolitionists in its last quarter, and Herder and Kant in the 1790s, every support for unchecked authority in church and state, as well as empire, had been challenged, mocked, dismissed, or decried as immoral.

Early in the period, travel literature, complete with engravings, told of new peoples in the Americas and Africa about whom both the Bible and ancient writings had been entirely silent. Their novelty was matched only by the strangeness of their behavior. The Spanish conquerors found indigenous people in what we now know as Mexico who practiced human sacrifice, wore little clothing, and occasionally ate their victims.[3] The space opened by new peoples and continents fired

FIGURE 2. De Bry's depiction of cannibalism. Theodore de Bry (1528–98)
(ID# 164722). Courtesy of Bridgeman Images.

imperialist fantasy, to be sure. Just as important in the *longue
durée*, imperial space also licensed bold and heterodox freethinking in the service of trying to make sense out of the previously unimaginable.

Images of these new Amerindians were widely circulated by
German and Dutch printing houses, among which the de Bry
family in Frankfurt produced the most striking and bloodcur-
dling (figure 2). Such imagery only emphasized the challenge
faced by the Iberian Church and monarchy, whose declared purpose was the conversion and "civilizing" of the indigenous peoples. The ultimate irony of the European expansion into global
space—accompanied by such sanctimonious intentions—lay

FIGURE 3. Ferdinand Alvarez de Toledo eating a child. Courtesy of Wikimedia.

in the gradual undermining of European religious certainty and political authority. It became possible in Dutch propaganda, for example, to depict the Spanish authorities as tyrants and baby-eating cannibals (figure 3). Anti-authoritarian responses to European conquest and exploitation emerged only gradually as people tried to make sense out of the recently discovered earthly and heavenly spaces.

No less exotic than the Americas, China and Africa also entered European consciousness, but they elicited wildly different responses. By and large, the Chinese were respected for the longevity of their civilization, and freethinkers even compared Buddhism to the natural religion that they espoused. Such was the approach taken by Bernard Picart, engraver, and Jean Frederick Bernard, writer and publisher of the first even-handed attempt to understand all of the known religions of the world, *Ceremonies et coutumes religieuses de tous les peuples du monde* (1723–43) (figure 4).[4]

Africa was actually far less known than North and Central America, yet even there Picart and Bernard tried to understand the religions of people never personally experienced. Illustrations of ceremonies in honor of their deities appear along with pages describing birth and death ceremonies. The Picart-Bernard effort became justly famous as the first attempt to relativize all religions. This conclusion was the exact opposite of what the Christian missionaries at work on every continent had intended.

After roughly the year 1600, literate Westerners (and many of the illiterate) knew that vast, new, and inhabited continents filled large portions of the globe. Thinking about the world outside Europe had commenced irretrievably. But the expansion of space did not stop there. Looking into the heavens entailed new knowledge about their structure—even if thousands still doubted the Copernican system that placed the sun at the center of the universe. Also by 1700, the highly educated knew that there now existed a mathematical law to explain how the force of universal gravitation ordered the heavens and made them knowable. The almanacs might still talk about the role played by the stars in determining human fate, but followers

FIGURE 4. Frontispiece to the *Ceremonies et coutumes*, illustrating all the world's religions, with only the Catholic Church being depicted in a negative light.

of Newtonian science thought little about such influences for which no solid proof existed. At one time, heavenly space possessed the power to influence the health and well-being of mortals. After 1687, space in the *Principia* is empty and neutral, as desacralized as Henry VIII's former monastic lands.[5]

The macrocosm of global and heavenly space framed the growing diversity of public space in the microcosm of European cities.[6] The "public sphere," "civil society," and "sociability" are all terms used to describe the relatively new spatial associations available to urban dwellers. Drawn to cities by ever-expanding markets, merchants, lawyers, stockbrokers, ladies of the *salon*, denizens of coffee shops and cafés stayed to see and be seen, and to read the burgeoning supply of newspapers and journals. They invented and filled urban spaces separate from court and king as well as from family dwellings (figure 5). When so occupied, they said their efforts aimed to correct "the want of a regular and publick encouragement of learning." Small societies would publish books by their members, enhance their profits, all the while instituting "a republic of letters for the promoting of arts and sciences."[7]

By midcentury, a London social life could revolve solely around eating clubs and the pub life that went with them. In the 1770s, John Wilkes dined nightly with the governing elite of the city and frequently, as his diary notes, at a "Tavern with the supporters of the Bill of Rights." The Beef Steak Club, the Irish Club, and the Antigallican Club helped fill the spatial vastness of Wilkes's London, where Benjamin Franklin occasionally joined in the festivities.[8] By the second half of the century, if not well before, the task of policing and spying on this or any other great metropolis had become formidable. The city also offered a visual feast for the curious, as brilliantly captured by artist and engraver William Hogarth (figure 6).

FIGURE 5. Early eighteenth-century example of casual sociability.
Bernard Picart (ID# 516565). Courtesy of Bridgeman Images.

FIGURE 6. Hogarth's representation of the foibles of Londoners. *Gin Lane*, William Hogarth (1697–1764) (ID# 265846). Courtesy of Bridgeman Images.

Most aptly named, *The Spectator* burst upon the London literary scene in 1711 and was an instant success. The journalist as spectator saw himself as living "in the World, rather as a Spectator of Mankind, than as one of the Species; by which means I have made myself a Speculative Statesman, Soldier, Merchant, and Artisan." He dared to take on so many roles in part because he claimed to have visited every city in Europe.[9] His *métier* as gossiper, raconteur, and man-about-town signaled a new urban vitality. Not surprisingly, the Dutch cities were among the first to imitate the originally English genre of spectatorial literature.[10] So too, new world cities like Boston sported imitations that claimed to be the work of a society of gentlemen. There, in 1727, the journal *Proteus Echo* sought to satisfy the curiosity of "All Mankind," for they "burn with an unquenchable Ardour after Knowledge." It sought to provide "Publick usefulness."[11]

Cities were also the natural habitat of publishers and would-be philosophes. In the period after 1650, cities from Amsterdam to Paris, Edinburgh to London grew in size and continued to do so throughout the century. In the seventeenth century, Naples was also one of the largest cities in Europe, and we know that in this period Italian bookshops, cafés, and even hat shops bristled with anti-clerical and anti-doctrinal gossip (figure 7). The Inquisition barely kept up with the irreverent banter to be found in such public spaces.[12]

The reality of global space framed not only civil society but also the imaginary realm of mercantile life. The central lobby of the Amsterdam City Hall, built between 1648 and 1665, contains a marble floor in which images of the two hemispheres of the world are inlaid in copper. Statues grace the scene and lay out themes such as "Peace," "Providence," and "Righteousness." The mercantile elite of the city walked upon this floor while discussing news and global trade.

Less grand in size or aspirations, other cities throughout Europe with more than 30,000 people—like Newcastle, The Hague, or Berlin—became more numerous. Strasbourg, Danzig, and Breslau sported around 40,000, and Vienna had about 100,000. If the curious could afford books and find coffee houses where the like-minded gathered in relative anonymity—only cities of

FIGURE 7. A rowdy version of eighteenth-century socializing.
(ID# 2987207). Courtesy of Bridgeman Images.

a decent size provided such haunts—amid the chatter people might begin to think new and unorthodox thoughts. A circle that met in The Hague in 1710 called itself a chapter of "the Knights of Jubilation," and its publishing members brought to the public the clandestine treatise that named Jesus, Moses, and Mohammed as the three great impostors. The denizens of urban space flouted the authorities and in plain sight invented the clandestine. The genre became the venue for the most radical ideas of the age.

About the same year in both London and Paris, cabarets and clubs sprang up where men made marriages together; the spying authorities called their occupants by the derogatory term "sodomites." The Parisian coterie took women's names and fashioned ceremonies for "la Reception des Prozelites."[13] Other far more respectable Paris cafés offered elegant and decorously furnished settings to entice the wealthy and aristocratic.[14]

Elite French women disdained smoking, and hence it was banned in the elegant cafés of the capital. English and Dutch public houses evinced no such inhibition and also provided newspapers to be read by patrons. In that first decade of the new century, London taverns existed where working women supped and engaged in ribald banter.[15] Among literate, more leisured women, novels and journals offered access to the empathy and polite knowledge that came to be associated with enlightened culture.

By 1700, urban spaces offered unprecedented displays of the outrageous, daring, and free. In Amsterdam, hundreds of free blacks originally from Africa, mostly men, congregated.[16] By 1730, male homosexuality, real or imagined, led to a vast persecution in which hundreds of men were queried or prosecuted, and on occasion executed. In Amsterdam between 1730 and 1732, thirty-five men were summoned, tortured, and banished for what the "confession books" labeled as "anaal contact."[17]

The expanding commerce in goods and staples matched a growing consciousness of the once unspoken, or unimagined, or feared. There was no choice but to take in the possibility of an infinite universe and within it an earth inhabited by new and previously unimagined peoples. Few urban places escaped access to the new science and, armed with it, theorists debated the original nature of humankind, the process by which civilizing occurred, the nature of authority, and the terms under which obedience to it was due. Some people came to the cities in search of the new literature that tried to explain a vastly altered spatial universe.

Is it little wonder, then, that any urban space could nurture freethinking? A small city like Namur, in the highly censored Austrian Netherlands (that is, Belgium), had about a dozen bookstores. When the authorities raided them in 1730, they found what they labeled "bad books": French translations of works by John Locke and Machiavelli, along with the anonymous and risqué. A decade later, when a local merchant-tanner died, his library was found to contain works by Voltaire, as well as fashionable encyclopedias of the era.[18]

Meanwhile, outside Paris in 1728, a hapless priest got himself arrested for claiming that Jesus, Moses, and Mohammed had been impostors.[19] The claim was old news by the time the curate got hold of the *Traité des trois imposteurs*, if that is what he was reading. As was so often the case in the stories told by the authorities, the heretical required its own social space. They claimed that the curé had made himself the head of an assembly of like-minded followers. In faraway Saxony, a good ten years earlier, the authorities had been searching the bookstores in the hope of confiscating the very same tract.[20] Around 1710, as we now know, deists and pantheists in the Dutch Republic—self-described knights or, as they said, "brothers"—had written all or part of it, and their publisher associates put it out in a now rare edition of 1719. Around 1700, writing in Latin, another bold spirit probably at work in Halle made the same argument. To this day, we are not sure about the author's identity.

If Namur was bad, Paris was far worse. Throughout the eighteenth century, the police hunted and sometimes caught the purveyors of books "against religion, the state and good morals." This illicit commerce provided the infrastructure wherein enlightened ideas found expression. In 1704, one Antoine Galoche fell into the hands of the authorities and his police file singled out his traffic in a new genre of literature, pornography. Books with titles such as *Venus in the Cloister* clearly announced their subject matter. In the 1740s, a gang of seven engraved, circulated, and sold works about the phallic god Priapus and salacious stories about "Dom Bougre," a clerical practitioner of buggery.[21] Other dealers caught in the police net went to prison with the verdict that they were peddling "works injurious to the government." Still others specialized in satires against the king, Louis XV, and his mistress. One denizen of the prisons said, "the king is an imbecile and a tyrant." Even a captain in the king's cavalry was caught distributing "very indecent libels" against his majesty and his mistress.[22]

In the 1740s, the French police spied upon the new forms of sociability—in one case imported from Britain. From London, the freemasons moved on to the Continent, first to Rotterdam by 1720 and then to The Hague and Paris. Known or unknown to the authorities, the masonic *Constitutions* of 1723 advised the brothers that "in ancient Times Masons were charg'd in every Country to be of the Religion of that Country or Nation, whatever it was, yet 'tis now thought more expedient only to oblige them to that Religion in which all Men agree." Hardly a ringing endorsement of religious orthodoxy! Masonic principles were universal and global: "we are also of all Nations, Tongues, Kindreds, and Languages, and are resolv'd against all Politicks, as what never yet conduc'd to the Welfare of the Lodge."[23]

The French authorities found the freemasons suspicious because their rituals made them look like a new religion and because they had attracted aristocratic membership. The new fraternity with its universalist claims could be plotting a cabal against the government; hence their literature had to be confiscated and the distributor put behind bars. One of the earliest French members we can actually find is identified as "a Negro in the King's Guard." He broke bread with other brothers in a Paris lodge.[24] It had become fashionable for monarchs to display the sweep of their global power by using Africans as soldiers or valets; this one was a trumpeter.

By the 1730s, the lodges had made their way to Russia, where they played an important role in the movement toward the light.[25] As in Sweden, the Russian lodges functioned as areas where influence could be exerted on government officials. The lodges also facilitated British influence in Russia, and in the early years Jacobites played a significant role in the spread of masonic practices. By the reign of Catherine the Great, the Viennese lodges were also places where progressive intellectuals congregated with aristocrats and court officials.

Some masonic lodges created a new cosmopolitan space. They brought veritable strangers together who crossed class and race boundaries—at least for those who could afford the dues. Many French lodges gradually began to admit Protestants, although Jews and Muslims were never welcomed. That intolerance was not the case in London or Amsterdam. By the 1780s, French lodges for men and women placed images of four women within the heart of the lodge. They represented the four parts of the world—Africa, America, Asia, and Europe. The global reach, however oppressive it was for non-Westerners, also allowed Europeans to imagine themselves as true world citizens.[26]

The lodges remained suspect in Catholic Europe well into the second half of the century. In Strasbourg in 1757, the authorities shut down a lodge on the grounds that it was a hotbed of licentious behavior. The same happened to lodges even in Protestant Switzerland. After the pope condemned membership in the lodges in 1738, men were denied absolution in confession for being members. Condemnation did not stop Catholics from belonging, and priests who joined were described as "enlightened."[27] In the 1760s, 40 percent of Dublin freemasons were Catholics.[28]

Many lodges put great emphasis on Christian behavior and described themselves as "schools of virtue."[29] The virtue being sought was closer, however, to the ideals of classical republicanism than to the traditional teaching of the churches. Masonic virtue focused on a robust public spiritedness, on attention to internal governance, and on the ideal of friendship as the social cement of the lodges, hence of the larger society.[30] By the 1780s, French lodges sent representatives to Paris, where they voted not by estates but by one man, one vote.

Urban spaces could also offer new religious opportunities and hence dangers for any government. Very early in the century, the French army had routed Protestants living in the south, in an area known as the Cevennes. Out of that persecution came a millenarian group, the French prophets, who made their way through the cities of Western Europe prophesizing the demise of Louis XIV and the coming end of the world. Freethinkers in the Dutch Republic were horrified by their antics, but in London, Isaac Newton came out to see them and to consult with their scribe (who wrote down the prophecies). He was Newton's close friend, the Swiss Protestant Fatio de Duillier.[31] While Newtonian science became a springboard for enlightened approaches to religion, the master himself remained very much a seventeenth-century Protestant given to millenarian sentiments, convinced that the pope was the anti-Christ. Yet it was Newtonian space, empty, capable of geometrical exposition as it was understood in the eighteenth century, that came to prevail.

The prophets assumed that time would come to an end and so too would space. They took aim against the anti-Christ and avoided Paris for obvious reasons. There too, various other forms of what the age called "enthusiasm" could readily be found in the capital. The *convulsionnaires* assembled around the tomb of a dead priest in the parish of Saint-Médard. He was believed to work miracles, and followers displayed signs of being possessed by his powers. They would have been harmless enough, except for the fact that clergy who were attracted to an

austere reform of Catholicism known as Jansenism also looked
for divine intervention to prove the justness of their cause.
The monarchy saw such clergy as a threat, and the papacy condemned Jansenism in a bull of 1713. The Jansenists took up the
cause of the Saint-Médard priest and his followers. The curious
German Lutheran traveler Hermann Reimarus lamented, "we
now have fanatics, inspirationists, convulsionnaires, just as the
Ancients had their sibyls and pythians."[32] Once possessed by
spiritual forces, whether in Paris or the Cevennes, enthusiasts
posed a threat to established authority that it, in turn, was keen
to condemn.

Undeterred, the Jansenists and their supporters produced
books that flourished in the same semi-clandestine market used
by the freethinkers and pornographers. Arrests were swift, and
they reveal that the same people, including priests, could be distributing pro-Jansenist tracts along with the heretical and salacious.[33] Cities permitted strange bedfellows and easily gave the
authorities the message that all illegal actors—pornographers,
freethinkers, Jansenists, even freemasons—could make
common cause and work to undermine both church and state.
The irreligious knew that convulsionnaires and Jansenists were
their enemies, but remarkably the police kept their files in the
same dossier. Ever vigilant for conspiracies, they even imagined
that the freemasons had their own pope, as reported by anonymous informants.[34]

By the 1770s, the patience of the French censors wore thin.
They longed for an opportunity to strike at this Dutch-centered
international commerce in forbidden books: "it is time to set
an example in this republican nation, one that is capable of
intimidating the unfortunates who seek refuge there in the
hope of impunity."[35] On this occasion, the provocation grew
out of information gathered after the arrest and interrogation

of the widow Stockdorff, who also traded in the Dutch Republic. After journeying eight days from Strasbourg to Paris in the company of two abbés, the widow proceeded to seek out every materialist and pornographic work on the market. We know about her activities because the police had been following her and made a copy of her shopping list. She engaged in an international traffic that included various French and Dutch cities; hence the frustration of the authorities. In the 1770s, nothing came of the censor's threat against the widow and the Dutch Republic. A very different French force entered the Republic in 1795, when the Revolutionary army invaded Amsterdam. They were met with jubilation by the city's main masonic lodge, and all assembled sang "La Marseillaise."

In the decades before 1789, associational life everywhere in Europe, both licit and semi-clandestine, expanded. In Britain and Ireland, the freemasons were only one of several types of new associations that flourished in the capital as well as in the provinces. In the Dutch Republic, eating and drinking clubs for elites competed for attention with societies dedicated to useful reforms. By the 1770s, the societies dedicated to *het Nut* ("the useful") had metastasized and boded ill for the *stadtholder* ("head of state") and oligarchs who governed the localities and the Republic. In the German states where literacy was less common, the universities still dominated the public sphere, and within them clubs and cliques were the norm. Just about every enlightened thinker from Lessing to Herder and Kant found a home in one or another university and club setting. Only the Prussian court in Berlin offered a viable and fashionable alternative.[36] It became a refuge for French philosophes on the run and intellectuals like Voltaire.

The space filled by voluntary association, in which strangers could become acquaintances, also included the courts of Europe. In Vienna earlier in the century, Prince Eugene of Savoy retired after a successful military career in the Low Countries fighting against France. His court became a magnet for travelers, bibliophiles, freethinkers, and religious reformers from all over Europe. The Italian Lodovico Antonio Muratori (d. 1750) brought a reformed Catholicism to Eugene's court, and from that entrée stemmed one source for the reforming efforts later in the century of the Austrian emperor, Joseph II.[37]

Despite never having left Europe, Eugene owned a globally focused library of over 15,000 books and manuscripts. It contained an almost priceless "Blue Atlas" that in forty-six folio pages displayed the entire world. It was complemented by a vast collection of travel literature to places like Russia and the Levant. In addition, Eugene possessed histories of the Scandinavian lands, Russia, Hungary, Croatia, the Near East, east and south Asia, Africa, and the Americas. Eugene also specialized in religious and theological literature, with a polyglot Bible, works by and about the early Protestant reformers, a translation of a Chinese work about Confucius, but also works by known freethinkers like John Toland.

All the major seventeenth-century philosophers and men of science had a place in Eugene's library, as did important travel accounts of Turkey, Persia, the Indies, the Americas, Lebanon, and Syria (by Jean Baptiste Tavernier, Louis Hennepin, Jean Baptiste Labat, Joseph Lafitau, Garciliaso de la Vega, and Jean La-Roque). Prince Eugene could also consult medical texts by European and Arabic doctors. Both new worlds—on earth and in the heavens—resided in his palace in Vienna.[38]

Fittingly, the first global atlases described "the theatre of the earthly orb," an unprecedented stage upon which anyone in principle could be an actor.[39] Many of these books had been made for the new European nation-states or the trading companies that now traveled the world. They were practical manuals that also provided the occasion for flights of fancy, some of them quite naughty.

The old Paris national library used to keep an especially judgmental category of books in *le cabinet d'enfer*—the "collection from hell." Overwhelmingly, the category contained pornographic works, some making plentiful use of the travel guides and manuals. The librarian who created it may have assumed that the souls of readers would wind up there some day. The particularly outrageous *Histoire du Prince Apprius* (that is, Priapus) in 1729 claimed to be drawn from "the splendors of the world since Creation." The book said that it originated from a manuscript in the library of the king of Prussia and was published in Constantinople. Not a word of that was true. The kingdom described in the history was fancifully inhabited by buggers, tribades (lesbians), "batdaches" (male prostitutes), and knights of the Manchette, a common term used for male homosexual gatherings. "The tribades are a visionary nation, incomprehensible, loving pleasure to excess." The *Histoire* created an imaginary world with sexual mores totally opposite from what could be tolerated on earth.[40]

The possibilities were endless. The discontented found in travel literature a mirror with which to reflect on their world by invoking an imaginary new one, a distant utopia. For example, the *Nouveau Voyage de la terre austral* (1693) said that all the androgynous Australians are born with two sexes inside them, and the word "father" is unknown to them. Hence mothers and children are not subordinated to fathers, and "the great empire that man has usurped over woman, has been rather the effect of an odious tyranny and not a legitimate authority."[41] When tyranny comes under attack, its gendered definition could be broadened fairly easily to include all male authority figures. In addition, once the high and mighty can be seen to be libertines, why not invest whole peoples with the power of sexual license? Travel east or west, even to Africa, the pundits said; there love is made freely, without shame.[42]

The essence of humankind, according to the Australians, is liberty. They are also vague about God: "they believe that this incomprehensible being is all there is and they give him all the veneration imaginable." They never, however, talk about religion. The old Australian guide, le vieillard philosophe, then explains that the universe is composed of atoms in motion, nothing more. In the journey to an imagined new world, the old philosopher tells us, in effect, that passage from deism to materialism, thanks to the new science, has become virtually effortless.

At precisely the same moment, an anonymous Englishman journeying to Tartary—at least in his imagination—in 1689 discovered "Death to be nothing else but a Cessation from the Motions of Action and Thought." The Tartars clearly do not believe in an afterlife. If anyone asks the traveler his religion, he should say that he is a shepherd.[43] The subgenre of utopian travel literature, specifically intended to teach irreligion and open up new vistas of disbelief, originated among countless anonymous authors writing from late in the seventeenth century.

Even in parts of Eastern Europe without an imperial stake in global exploration, imaginary travel opened up rich possibilities. For most Europeans, Tartary was beyond the pale. It began roughly with Russia and went on ever eastward. There was, however, an east that was closer, which Western Europeans both then and now describe as Eastern Europe. In Vienna, Eugene of Savoy stood close to its gateway. By the eighteenth century, this part of Europe had come to be regarded as backward in both literacy and numeracy. This had not always been the case.

The cities of Poland and Lithuania in the sixteenth century possessed wages and a level of prosperity (as measured in the height of people) comparable to that of England. But gradually serfdom was imposed, and by 1700 there existed far less literacy and numeracy than in Western Europe. With literacy rates well below 10 percent, the possibility of creating a vibrant marketplace for ideas such as could be seen in London, Amsterdam, or Paris simply did not exist in these eastern and central areas of Europe.[44] But ideas move. Indeed, it was Protestant Germans who first brought enlightened ideas into Polish territory. That said, the Poles were fully capable of producing their own libertines and atheists. The early Enlightenment can be found in cities from Dublin to Cracow and beyond.[45]

Even the vast dispersal of Armenian traders everywhere in Europe and India did not exempt them from the influence of the Enlightenment. This took the form first of the creation of a periodical Armenian press in Madras. *Azdarar* (*Monitor*) appeared there in 1794 and was soon followed by other periodicals in Venice and Constantinople. Equally important, a discernibly republican line of thought, influenced by the writings of Locke and Montesquieu, surfaced in these texts. The secularization of Armenia was a process that developed largely in the nineteenth century, but it was facilitated by the late eighteenth-century move toward mass literacy and the literature that catered to it.[46]

As we discovered in France and Italy, the reach of censorship had its limits. Even the Spanish could barely keep up with the import and export of forbidden books. By the 1780s, they could be found in Buenos Aires—at least so the Spanish Inquisition believed. On one occasion, it rummaged through five boxes of books being sent from Madrid to Buenos Aires and there found a treasure trove of the forbidden.[47] If the Inquisition could not stop such traffic, then no one was safe.

The certainty of royal and ecclesiastical absolutisms crumbled in the face of the late-century democratic revolutions and the principles they articulated. The Enlightenment made that articulation possible partly through an anonymous, seditious, pornographic, and illicit trade that no eighteenth-century government ever managed to stop. Through it, the mechanical philosophy, and the infinite universe filled with atoms that it postulated, became an avenue to materialism. The peoples of our earth and their oppression demanded explanation, a new language and new theories to explain their situation. Major and minor philosophes rose to the challenge. Rather than embrace inferiority as explanatory, the Scottish philosophers saw stages of human progress; English reformers proclaimed the abolition of slavery, while French philosophes like Rousseau became dreamers of democracy. Not all of these reformers were materialists. Yet none of them invoked divine providence or the hand of God to explain the effects of imperialism, or the nature of monarchical authority, or the equality and human rights demanded now for all the peoples of the world.

By 1700, the Enlightenment had taken shape and came to rest in the urban spaces of Western Europe. An infinity of possible explanations for how society and government should operate, how the excesses of power should be trimmed, if not eliminated, beckoned for anyone gifted at using pen and paper. Men, and the occasional woman, joined the enterprise as critics, satirists, and theorists. Most lacked funding, and the hunt was on to find patrons. Voltaire landed at the Berlin court of Frederick the Great, enjoyed himself, and came eventually to see the king and his army as predatory. The less famous like Picart and Bernard made a decent living as publishers and engravers. Toland acted as a spy for the Whig party and lay on his deathbed in 1722 too poor to pay his doctor. It is nothing short of remarkable that

2

Time Reinvented

THE INTELLECTUAL and cultural shift described as the Enlightenment happened in only one century, and as such may be described as rapid for its time. The "for its time" part is the hardest for twenty-first-century people to understand. When the period opened in the 1680s, time was understood very differently than it is today. In addition, change in daily events—in comings and goings—would feel to us painstakingly slow. Everything took longer. The passage from one place to another, whether on land or water, took roughly the same time whether on a canal boat in the Dutch countryside or on a repaired English turnpike. A good speed consisted of 4 or 5 miles an hour; on the open sea, a boat from Dover to Calais made the 20-mile crossing in three hours and thirty-five minutes.[1] By 1770, going 14 miles by coach could take as little as one hour and thirty-five minutes, or as much as three.[2] In the last quarter of the century, British sailing ships made technological improvements that shortened their time at sea. Only very late in the eighteenth century did steam-driven transportation become possible, and its speed can be associated only with nineteenth-century travel. Western European people or colonial Americans, traveling in the eighteenth century, ambled through time, but this should not suggest a temporality without change, static, or even boring. Indeed, it was quite the reverse.[3]

In just a hundred years, three generations of eighteenth-century Euro-Americans questioned all inherited orthodoxies, and they did so within the framework of putting in place a new, secular understanding of time. They moved from Christian to modern time as we know it. They did not do this in some sort of lock-step progression. Believers in Christian time could be found early and late in the century (not to mention today), yet expressions of secular time being lived became more commonplace and expected. Part of the explanation for this shift occurred well before the eighteenth century, in the sixteenth-century Protestant Reformation. Its effect was felt all over Christian Europe: in England, the king closed the monasteries and seized their land; in the Low Countries, a Protestant revolt against Catholic Spain created the Dutch Republic; and in the German-speaking lands, religious warfare erupted. Dramatic change made the difference between the present time and the past more vivid, yet the overall structure of the time available on earth held.[4]

The eighteenth century opened with many ordinary people as well as the highly educated believing that human time and the age of the earth coincided and would come to encompass about 6,000 years. Philosophers like Isaac Newton (d. 1727) assumed that God created the earth around 4004 BCE and would end it similarly, although the exact date was known definitively only by Him. Newton's friend, the philosopher John Locke, thought that "the world was created about september" of that year.[5] Newton's best and cautious guess put the end around 2060—that is, one generation from now. In the ensuing conflagration, he wrote, "the wicked (probably) to be punished thereby." The key to finding the hidden meaning of human time lay largely in the prophetic books of the Bible, although other learned, generally Protestant commentators on those mysteries could also be consulted. The meaning of the end of time, for Newton and many Protestant millenarians, rested on the certainty that at the sounding of the trumpet mentioned in the Bible, "the Kingdoms of this world are become the Kingdoms of our Lord and of his Christ & he shall reign for ever and ever." Thus would the thousand years of Christ's reign on earth dramatically begin and our world end—forever. Religious time would end abruptly just as it had begun.[6]

Christian time as Newton understood it belonged to anyone who could read and afford a pocket almanac. That is, anyone Protestant. By and large, they, and not Catholics, revered the biblical timeline to be inferred from almanacs published generally in Protestant countries.[7] Almanacs done in Catholic France, for instance, did not lay emphasis on the beginning of the world and certainly not on its end. Rather, their chronology began with the birth of Christ, and the days of the year were often assigned their particular saint. They seldom went into predictions of future events, and Christianity began with the first pope, Peter, and stood proven by an unbroken succession of popes and dogmas. At century's end, Spanish almanacs in Lima, Peru, still gave the date of the beginning of the world, the birth year of Christ, and then all the saints with their days properly noted. There was no hint as to when the new world of the Americas, or the old one of Europe, would end, as millenarians believed had been prophesized. From their very beginning late in the fifteenth century, Spanish almanacs had apportioned time by the saints' days and offered no prediction about the end of time.[8]

Nothing as dramatic happened in the calendars of eighteenth-century Protestants, although the French revolution brought temporary upheavals in several Protestant regions. For many decades, Protestant almanacs began generally at 4004 BCE and took the reader up to the present, then added prognostications about the future. As early as the late sixteenth century, Dutch Protestant almanacs attacked the Catholic reliance on saints' days as having no foundation in the Bible. Yet despite these disputes, by 1700 both Catholic and Protestant sensibilities made Christian time and ordinary experience vastly different, although the Protestant understanding of time included a willingness to predict its end. Belonging to the realm of the sacred, Christian time was divinely appointed and its end assured. Earthly time just flowed slowly, marked generally by personal events or matters of state, the birth or death of a king, a battle won or lost, or a religious feast.

At first, even the unorthodox whose religiosity might be suspect failed to tackle the presumed age of the world. Anonymous French astrologers published almanacs with predictions, yet they also gave the correct saint for every day in the year. A risqué almanac of masonic origin also listed all the saints associated with each day of the year. Neither astronomy nor astrology challenged the roughly 6,000 years believed to be available to humankind.

Although their practices were controversial, astrologers excelled at predictions about the future. Their presumed accuracy held up better in some places than in others. By the mid-seventeenth century, Dutch almanacs, as well as Dutch academic teaching of astronomy, left out astrological training and hence the ability to predict. Thus, in the republic the demise of astrology occurred more rapidly than in England or much of the American colonies.[9] In Scotland well into mid-eighteenth century, the Christian understanding of time held the potential to explain political upheaval. The supporters of the British monarchy defined their Jacobite enemies as the Anti-Christ and thus proclaimed the godliness of the Hanoverian cause.[10]

Only in the 1780s did political turmoil finally undo Christian temporality. Its standard French Catholic version locked time into the liturgical calendar, but the most avid supporters of the French Revolution rebelled against the entire construct. Three years before a select committee devised a new calendar fit for free and equal citizens, anonymous, anti-Christian, and revolutionary voices proclaimed 1789 "the first year of the reign of reason and liberty." In less than one century after Newton's death, in certain settings, the Christian understanding of time had been debunked and by some, discarded.

In the years before the French Revolution, new versions of time multiplied. Almanacs sprang up that called themselves "profane" and for every day of the year gave the name not of a saint but of a famous person, who either was born or died on that day, and who should be remembered. In March, the reader might begin on the first day honoring Moses, and then go on to think about Michelangelo, remember the Ides of March (15th) when Brutus murdered Caesar, and among the moderns take note of Turgot, Toland, Newton, Wollaston, and Descartes. In April, Jesus Christ and Hobbes got their days. May offered Albert Durer, Campanella, and Voltaire, while June honored Anthony Collins, Leibniz, and J.-J. Rousseau, among others. The saints quite simply disappeared, by and large replaced by an international cast of learned thinkers, artists, and notorious freethinkers.

The Parlement of Paris condemned the profane book to be burned and found its contents and grouping of famous men "scandalous" and "monstrous." Clearly, it asserted, the whole secular exercise had been inspired by "materialism" and would lead to "atheism." Both are "isms" to which we will return on multiple occasions; indeed, given their importance they will receive a separate section of chapter 4. Regardless of its intellectual pedigree, the anonymous author of the 1788 calendar said that it offered "an edifice of peace" where people of any religion can find a day to their own liking. Quite suddenly, time had been rendered neutral and an entirely human invention without biblical justification. To accomplish this feat, original thinkers and artists replaced the saints.[11] The idea of naming intellectuals or artists did not make it into the entirely secular calendar that was finally adopted. Instead, it favored a celebration of nature and the ancients.

For twelve years from 1793 onward, the French nation abided by a new calendar that erased Christian time entirely. Republican or revolutionary time could only be a human invention, a bold proclamation of secular time. One reformer in 1790 had lobbied for beginning the year with January as the month of Voltaire, "this immoral genius who had presaged the revolution."[12] The idea did not stick, but for many the experience of revolution never faded. Recollecting French events in that year, a young English enthusiast remembered the intensity of his feeling for time itself: "there are two things which particularly strike me on recalling the above time to my recollection, first the very short time which passed in 1790 which to my memory was years, altho in truth only a few months, secondly the talk of cutting off heads which I too well remember."[13] He watched revolutionary festivals of reason in the provinces where leaders denounced "the Harlequinades of the priests . . . [and] said there was neither heaven nor hell, neither resurrection, angel or spirit." Then this young, somewhat mystified Englishman was blessed by the goddess of Reason.[14] At century's end, a brave new world emerged and Christian time was but one of its many casualties. The long nineteenth century witnessed numerous attempts to reform time, to make it uniform, broadcast by tower clocks, measurable on land and at sea.[15]

By 1800 and not just in France, time became an entirely human invention without end, open to the narratives of every individual life. By the 1770s in the American colonies, almanacs as a lived category. Hardly a proponent of religious orthodoxy, Hobbes could declare God to be the arbiter of right reason, and then say "for the *Secular Lawes*, I mean those which concern justice, and the carriage of men towards men." He relegated religion to its own circumscribed sphere.[20] He could further assure his readers that if anyone displayed repugnancy at being asked to obey both God and man, that anxiety "is to be removed by the distinction between the points necessary, and not necessary to Salvation . . . *in secular matters* deriv'd from him who had the Soveraigne power, whether he were one Man, or an Assembly of Men, that the same *in spirituall matters* depended on the authority of the *Church*."[21] In Hobbes's mind a clear divide existed between the secular and the sacred. There were many reasons why contemporaries called Hobbes a heretic—even worse an atheist—and one of them concerned the sharp divide he postulated between the secular and the sacred.

When the imagined atheist Hobbes made the distinction between the sovereign realms of the secular and the ecclesiastical, he put the pious into a fighting mood. By contrast, in the hands of authors noted for their piety making the distinction produced, as far as we know, little reaction. It was just part of received language. The Dutch writer and translator associated with the separation of the worldly and the churchly, Simon de Vries, was also a harsh critic of the Cartesian and devil-denier Balthazar Bekker. Who better to understand the difference between the secular and the spiritual than an orthodox writer professing to know the nefarious dealings of Satan himself?[22] Thinkers on either side of the looming divide between the pious and the enlightened had accepted the reality of separate temporal spheres.

The majority of Protestant almanacs before about 1750 gave the age of the world with dates that the great Isaac Newton would have approved. English annual almanacs appeared as early as 1572, and as late as the 1750s they gave the chronology of time since the beginning of the world, the year of the almanac being, for example, 5,581 years since the beginning of time, and 3,934 years since Noah's Flood, noting that the reign of Queen Elizabeth began 62 years ago—that is, in 1559; in short, the almanac belonged to the year 1621.[23] Some almanacs proclaimed on their title page that an astrologer was the author and duly gave predictions for events in the coming year. In Boston with its Puritan population, an almanac explained how "eclipses, conjunctions, prodigious sights, comets etc. are but the oracles of God . . . there are terrible troubles . . . hastening upon the world . . . which may be a means to bring on those happy times promised to the People of God."[24] Almanacs foretold the end of the world for the edification and trepidation of the pious, although English Protestant almanacs, unlike their Dutch counterparts, were willing to make radical pronouncements with a political edge. They reflected the turmoil of the 1640s and 1650s: civil war followed by regicide, a republic proclaimed only to be ended by the restoration of the Stuart king, Charles II, in 1660.[25]

By the mid-seventeenth century, it may be surprising to know—given their dire pronouncements about the end of the world—English almanacs left blank pages where the owner could record his coming appointments. Such mundane spaces also appear in seventeenth-century Dutch almanacs, and in French almanacs by the mid-eighteenth century.[26] The possible end of the world did not mean business could or should be avoided—and dealt with punctually. German speakers in the American colonies also subscribed to the Christian time frame but provided news from other colonies and the value of various currencies.[27] The mundane began to mix effortlessly with prophecy. At century's end, the age of the earth, therefore the time available to humankind, had also been vastly expanded.

all which may be contrary to the narrative of Moses." He told friends that he would rather be humbled than hanged. Privately in his unpublished manuscripts, Buffon came to speculate that the earth was probably 10 million years old. Our current thinking places it at about 4.5 billion.

Also, writing anonymously but earlier, and possibly as a result of his contact with Eastern thought, Benoît de Maillet (d. 1738) looked at fossils and argued for a purely natural origin of the earth, assigning it an extraordinary duration of over 2 billion years.[29] In de Maillet's account all life came from the sea. Multiple copies of his handwritten text circulated in enlightened circles that included Buffon and Voltaire. Less fancifully, after many years of experiments on the cooling time needed by iron, among other substances, Buffon thought the age of the earth to be probably just shy of 75,000 years, and not the roughly 6,000 commonly accepted as biblical time.[30] That was the only figure he too dared put in print.

Britain in the eighteenth century possessed no clerical body with the power of France's Sorbonne theology professors. Fearing little censorship and with his reputation for irreligion recognized by his friends, the medical doctor and would-be poet, Erasmus Darwin, grandfather of Charles, took up the issue of human time in relation to the vastly expanded earthly time. Taking inspiration from the previous generation of French writings on earth's time, Darwin postulated a gradual evolution for all forms of life. As he put it in *The Temple of Nature* (1802), the forms of organic life, "These, as successive generations bloom, new powers acquire and larger limbs assume." Life evolved in the vast expanse of time now allotted to the earth.

By 1800, belief in the end of the world and the millenarian paradise to follow had receded among the educated. Time available to humankind expanded as the result of the study of purely natural, physical transformations visible on the earth's surface. Evolution seemed the next logical step. Scripture had nothing to do with the earth's age or that of human kind. By 1800, French educators began to publish books about improving one's use of time.[31]

The explorers of mountains, collectors of antiquities, and classifiers of fossilized remains, who contributed decisively to the expansion of time, could be found in every walk of life with clergymen exceptionally well represented. Their discoveries forced the conclusion that the world had been around far longer than the biblically inspired account of 6,000 years. Unlike the vast majority of on-the-ground naturalists, the speculative philosophers and fanciful poets who boldly expanded human time had one thing in common: they were materialists. They saw the physical and human universe as governed solely by material forces, by the push and pull of bodies. In effect, matter could move itself.

The Specter of Materialism

Because materialists conceived nature as vitalist, and as a mechanism governed by universal laws, they could postulate that the earth might be eternal. They also conflated body and soul, matter and spirit. In matters religious—from any perspective— they were heretics, and their philosophical assumptions derived from one reading of the new science of the seventeenth century as well as from a medical vitalism, a school of medical thinking found on both sides of the English Channel. In an age filled with deviations from Christian orthodoxy, more than any others, materialism stood out. It left no room for the providential God or the Christian mysteries. Allowing the earth to possess seemingly infinite time then opened the door to the gradual evolution of living beings or species. Both Darwins, grandfather and grandson, were materialists.[32]

The enlightened expansion of time could, however, be divorced from its materialist underpinning. The pious might believe that biblical stories of creation serve not as literal truth but as metaphors for a process that had actually taken many millennia. Yet materialism had enormous implications with staying power, and every believer in the Judeo-Christian tradition would—at some time—have to confront it. Materialist assumptions became the philosophical moorings upon which an entirely secular understanding of life and time rested.

A vast literature developed, attacking materialism wherever it lurked. Especially in Catholic Europe, the clergy took to the barricades to denounce materialism and its attendant atomism. They saw the ancient Greek and pagan roots of the doctrine that "all beings . . . are machines."[33] They claimed that contemporary materialism had taken root in polite society, and certainly in Paris by 1760 such ideas had become commonplace and easily attributed to leading philosophers such as Diderot and Helvétius. There is a defensive tone in some of the attacks, one that recognizes that the religious persecution of Protestants under Louis XIV may have poisoned the well of religion and made heresy more fashionable. Yet in Protestant Europe beginning with the sermons of Newton's followers, Samuel Clarke and Richard Bentley, home-grown materialists like Hobbes and John Toland were mercilessly attacked. Seeing human beings as akin to soulless machines became the caricature used against them.

The Technology of Time

In the period from 1650 to 1800, machines did in fact become more commonplace throughout northern and western Europe. Just as time expanded conceptually, technology in the form of clocks and pocket watches brought it into daily living. The modern way of thinking about time made its most dramatic appearance in the eighteenth century and primarily in England and the Dutch Republic, where the expensive timepieces were most commonplace. Relevant to this story, the price of watches fell markedly in the period from the 1680s to 1810. By late in the century, English watchmakers were producing about 200,000 watches a year. The least expensive could be acquired for as little as one pound. That was still slightly over one week's wage for a day laborer. Throughout the century, watch prices dropped as much as 75 percent as materials and techniques improved. Where once only the wealthy used pocket timepieces, access to them increased decade by decade.[34] Late in the seventeenth century, new clocks came with minute hands and time could be felt, and even heard, as persistent.

When the young Dutch university graduate from a prestigious family, Constantijn Huygens (b. 1596), made his tour of Europe, every arrival and departure had its time recorded, as did the events of an entire day. Occasionally, Huygens, like most people, used the local church clock to tell the time, but as his diary makes clear he and his entourage were traveling with some sort of timepiece.[35] He became a poet, diarist, confidant of the House of Orange, and the father of one of the most important Dutch scientists, Christiaan. The son in turn revolutionized time keeping by inventing a new type of clock that used a pendulum to enhance accuracy; to it, Christiaan added yet another remarkable invention, a spiral spring making minutes and seconds accurate, audible, and portable. Newton's was the first generation to possess pendulum clocks, and rarely—only among elites—pocket watches. The pendulum clock of Huygens's invention was almost immediately recognized as a superior way of ensuring same-interval minutes.

By the mid-eighteenth century, watches were still items worth commenting upon. When stolen, victims often went to court to prosecute the thief, thus suggesting that watches were prized. With them, time could still be external, other, and hence to be watched and observed, not taken casually. Or pocket watches could suggest ways to enjoy one's time. An expensive tortoiseshell watch with wood inlay decorated its face with a brothel scene, and the nudity of the prostitute enticed every time the hour was checked.[36]

At first, the new technology of time flourished in France, where the monarch, Louis XIV, sought to cultivate innovations in time telling for navigation. Both invention and inventor soon traveled. Fatefully, Louis XIV sought to rid his kingdom of Protestants, and with the departure of thousands of them and their watch-making skills, France lost its preeminence in time keeping.[37] Christiaan Huygens left France before the rug was pulled out from under the Huguenots with the revocation of the edict of Nantes in 1685. In London at that time, Christiaan's brother, Constantijn Jr., frequented the shops of watchmakers, where state of the art clocks and watches could be seen. So too did leading natural philosophers of the period. Constantijn Jr. introduced the term for "time management" into the Dutch language.[38] In the course of the eighteenth century in Antwerp, criminal trials demonstrate the slow but real penetration of timepieces in homes both elegant and modest. Yet before 1800, the majority of Europeans got their time from public clocks on churches, city walls, or local shops.[39]

The Huygens family belonged to the Dutch Reformed Church. In France, Christiaan self-identified as a Protestant and was treated accordingly. Despite the experience of religious prejudice, no one in his family seemed vexed on religious matters. When his father contemplated his own death, Constantijn simply begged God to receive him and take away his sins.[40] None of the Huygens family, as far as we know, worried about the end of time or the afterlife. The writings of both father and son evince less anxiety about the fate of their souls than what can be found among English contemporaries with their obsessive watching of how to use their time in Godly ways. At the same time, around 1700, Dutch heretics who endorsed a simple natural religion attacked the Christian concept of earthly time and invented far-away utopias where thousands of years preceded the present (although time was not infinite): "according to the European calculation the world has existed for 5702 years [in 1702] . . . but [in our blissful land it is] 20,038 [years] . . . according to ours . . . here that is Truth; but not in Europe. Just as your Mass, Purgatory . . . are truth in Spain, and are not true here." The Dutch Reformed Church excommunicated the author, a doctor in Zwolle who had read Descartes.[41] The doctor turned heretic relativized earthly time; it was just one of the many issues that could be treated as heresy by one side or another, like the various doctrines that separated Catholics and Protestants.

Obsessing about Time: The Religious Origins of Secular Time

In the absence of consensus about the correct forms of Protestantism, English contemporaries, far more than the Dutch, allow us to see the anxiety over, and the reinvention of time. This process can be illustrated by a brief look at a sampling of English Protestants as new experiences of time informed their consciousness. Lacking any of the sacramental supports open to Catholics such as confession, Protestants had a particular temporal burden: the necessity to self-monitor their use of time, to classify their behavior as useful, or worthy in God's eyes, or impious and in need of correction.

To complicate matters, by late in the seventeenth century, in Newton's lifetime, contradictory perceptions of time, secular and religious, existed simultaneously; different times existed in the human mind "at the same time."[42] In addition, in the previous generation the English had fought civil wars between Puritans and Anglicans. They were meant to settle the nature of English Protestantism and resolve doctrinal issues; they did not. The end of time and what came after it was only one of a series of fraught issues. During the civil wars, radical Protestants generally believed that time would end according to God's will and a millennium—a thousand-year reign of the saints—would soon be instituted. Moderates tended to avoid such doctrines precisely because of their call to action, their revolutionary associations.

The generation active from the 1680s to the 1720s was the first to experience—and contribute to—the illusive phenomenon of the secularization of time. Among them, we see religiously inspired anxiety about time, one gradually replaced by a growing nonchalance, a normalization and domestication that permitted linear time to be valued as a back ground to events. These understandings of time, while fundamentally different, could be found to co-exist, or at the very least, to overlap temporally. The essentially religious understanding of time saw it as separate, and God-given, yet residing in a culture that could, at the same time, also begin to imagine time as internal, possessed by the self even, and especially when demanding obedience to its pace.

Perhaps the tension between religious and secular time within Protestant thought confirms what one theorist predicts, that Christian revelation, while it "supposedly imposes itself on human understanding proves to be something that humans can actually appropriate or renounce, something whose meaning they can penetrate and whose repercussions they can independently experience from within." Christianity, and in particular Protestantism, provided "a religion for departing from religion."[43] The tensions about time and the disputes about the rapidity of its ending forced the believer to treat time as a concrete entity, to seize it and meditate upon it.

The relationship between the self and time was markedly different when experienced by anxiety-ridden religious men and women as opposed to those who effortlessly embraced, and came to live by, secular time. Such an observation about the meanings assigned to time, thus about the historicity of time, does not in any way contradict the notion that concepts of time lie at the bedrock of the mind's architecture.[44] Indeed, that notions of time would possess such a persistent historicity, and occasion such varying responses, should only support the realization that time is more than simply an intellectual construction. It forms part of the scaffolding that undergirds narrativity. The shift among Westerners toward an embrace of worldly time was profound, one of the singular and lasting consequences—or better said, causes—of the Enlightenment. But it occurred gradually and millions of believers in biblical time can be found to this day.

Protestant lives from the 1680s to the 1720s allow us to come closer to understanding this shift in the understanding of time. The moderate Protestant sensibility in that generation displayed two contradictory impulses about time: one moved in the direction of censoring and monitoring the usage of time by one's self and others; the other—encouraged ironically by the devout but heretical Isaac Newton (and his followers)—moved to instantiate time as an absolute, and thus ironically propelling the gradual acceptance and domestication of time as a secular universal. Newtonian time—simply duration—is an absolute entity not relative to the passage of events. It provided the foundation of the modern understanding of temporality; time in the world becomes the only framework wherein experience unfolds and is remembered.

Despite Newton's own belief in the coming millennium and the passage out of human time into Christ's, his principle of absolute time laid the template wherein timepieces could now be read and life's worldly passage noted and remembered. Gradually, in the eighteenth century linear time enabled the secular to grow in importance; eventually, the sacred became private and internalized, made less visible in time and space. Sacred time and space retreated—or so this narrative goes—decade by decade in the course of the century. Throughout the earlier part of the eighteenth century, Christian commentators fretted about the irreligious implications of Newtonian time. They said that time, like space, is an idea in the mind, not a real entity with a separate existence.[45] At century's end, Kant said the same thing but asserted that such ideas were indeed real.

The contested but progressive liberation of the secular assumes a uniform, linear progress in the understanding of time that needs to be modified. A better formulation would note that multiple discourses existed by which religious people from the 1670s onward addressed the realm of time. Gradually in some, if not most, minds, the secular crowded out the religious, but this was a much more complicated process than the linear account permits. In the last decades of the seventeenth century, moderate Protestants, on both sides of the Channel and in the American colonies, moved away from the rigid doctrine of predestination, from believing that salvation had been predetermined, a doctrine that left the pious either hopeful or deeply pessimistic.

Leaving behind a rigid doctrine of predestination meant a new approach to time. This new, post-1660 religiosity had to be crafted in direct rejection of Puritan notions of faith as the key to salvation and of predestination, general or specific. The temporal rigor being sought was meant to rival the zeal and rigor associated with the sectarian groups of an earlier age, only without the strait jacket of predestination. The emphasis now centered on living and practicing a religiosity of pious control over time. It would lead to self-disciplining and self-control imposed by habits, customs, and comings and goings in the service of faith. Every action was to be monitored; the self had to be constrained within the parameters set up by worldly time. This was more than simply a resurrection of the Catholic doctrine of salvation through good works, although it may be said to share certain similarities. The late seventeenth-century sensibility of moderate Protestants assumed a monitoring of self, and interior disciplining so that good works might be undertaken—without the benefit of sacraments or clergy or even the assumption that one had been predestined to live an eternal life among the saved.

One theme emerges at this point that will repeat itself in subsequent chapters. The elements of the early Enlightenment enjoyed more fertile ground in moderate Protestant rather than Catholic Europe. Indeed, it was Protestant Germans who first brought enlightened ideas into Polish territory.[46] This was especially true in England after the Restoration of Church and monarchy in 1660 and the defeat of the Puritan revolutionaries of the 1640s and 1650s. The Christian meaning of time remained, but like predestination, millennial time seemed less and less relevant. Salvation had to be worked out in the here and now.

Living with the Anxiety of Time

The pious household of the diarist John Evelyn (d. 1706) can illustrate the ways by which devout and moderate Protestants of the period understood or experienced time. This famous commentator on his life and times loved the Church of England even more than he loved his creature comforts.[47] And he imparted that love to his children, at least to his adored daughter, Mary (1665–84), who died of small pox before she reached her twentieth year. Evelyn's motto, "redeem the time," became hers.[48] In Evelyn's case, his desire to redeem time led him to become a diarist whose extensive commentary on events would eventually make him one of the most famous English men of letters of the seventeenth century. Mary's achievement was more modest and fatefully cut short before she even reached twenty-one.

Mary Evelyn took her father's written "Directions for the Employment of your Time" deeply to heart. He told her to rise early, to get moderate exercise, possibly in his beloved garden, but even there not to linger. His instructions must have assumed that she had recourse to a timepiece, either a clock or pocket watch. She in turn penned a booklet with a title page that called it "Miscelania . . . Book of several designes and thoughts of mine for the regulating my life upon many occasions. Remember thy Creator in the days of thy youth." She wrote the motto "Redeeme the Tyme 1683" at the bottom of its title page as if it were the publisher and then below it inserted the date.[49] In her "Rules for spending my pretions tymes well," she admonished herself against laziness, in particular against the habit of "Lying late in bed," which she said "causes laziness, stupidity, & dulness of the senses, the limbs are by it made unactive, & the tyme lost by it hinders many holy & seasonable duties all the rest of the day for that I may be in due tyme at family prayers." This was almost identical to what her father advocated in his seventeen "directions for the employment of your time."[50]

Whether at home or in London, Mary Evelyn thought carefully about the hours: "In term tyme I will rise by 6 of ye Clock to go to prayers yet I may not miss both ye morning hours for I will not go at ten of ye Clock Prayers because of Crowding through Westminster Hall among ye Lawyers & other Inconveniences. I must pray longer now than when I was at home." She searched for "a Methodical course of Holy Living . . . the pleasures of piety." She wanted the constancy and perseverance so that "I may be always ready to dye well."[51] She asked the Lord Jesus to "bring me in thy good tyme." She resolved "through God's assistance never to rise later than 7 of ye clock for the future but constantly in summer at 6. . . . I should go to Bed in tyme, that is by Eleven of ye Clock."[52] She resolved never to play.[53]

One particular phrase from Mary Evelyn's account of how to use time stands out: "of ye clock." Other contemporaries used Mary Evelyn's phrase, as witnessed in diaries of the period.[54] Gradually, this became shortened, and a generation later, English writers could note time by the hour of "a clock."[55] Very slowly, "by the clock" became "a clock," and finally, by the 1730s if not earlier, our modern usage "o'clock" became the norm.[56] The abbreviation tells a tale. Only very gradually, among some people but not all, did time as measured by clocks and pocket watches became internalized, and as time was universalized, it became the casual "o'clock" that could be used to measure every mundane gesture, meeting, or experience. There were fewer temporally anxious Mary Evelyns to be found generations later.

Pious Anglicans of the late seventeenth century measured time earnestly and self-monitored their use of it, although their goal was ultimately out of this world and in a heavenly place. Eternity was timeless. Sermons of the period told Mary Evelyn to "set ye affections on things above, not on things of ye earth" and admonished her as to "how unvaluable & worthless all sublunary things really are on one side & on the other . . . the beauty and happyness of a spiritual & Divine treasure which attainable most by taking off an affection to this world."[57] In this world, "tis all vanity & vexation of spirit."[58] A favored biblical text was Ephesians 5.16, "Redeem the time because the days are evil."

The importance of time only grew. Less pious but most assuredly Protestant contemporaries thought ill of public places where no one saw fit to display a clock. Sir Robert Southwell said of Plymouth in 1659, "I never observed a clock to be in any Inn or Tavern forever against the interest of the place to mind the purpose of precious time."[59] The Yorkshire naturalist Ralph Thoresby lay awake "2 if not 3 hours" and fretted about his sins, "in particular of spending so much previous time vainly."[60] He too resolved to "redeem more time" and set about having "an alarm put to the Clock." Likewise, the pious could hope for the ending of time: "I may reflect how I filled [the year] with God's fruitful Service, and rejoice in hope, that at length Time will be ended."[61] Yet significantly few diarists in the period before 1700 paid close attention to the hours, noting most commonly that they did things "in the evenings," or the mornings. A generation later, a growing timeliness can be witnessed at least at the level of diary keeping. By century's end, daily diary entries tell us that it was possible to rise at an appointed hour punctually every day.

Evelyn's contemporary, Mary Rich, titled as Lady Warwick and a younger sister of the natural philosopher Robert Boyle, recorded her finding God in her mature years and a subsequent turning away from a previously vain and idle life. She too then began to reference time, "to redeem my former misspent time," and fretted that she "not to be drawn by company to misspend my time and to neglect the service of God."[62] Suddenly, a life that had been concerned largely with courtships, marriage, and births, and evinced not a scintilla of interest in time as an entity, became rhetorically obsessed with its use, fearful of vanity, and ever "watchful." Lady Warwick had discovered that "thoughts of eternity were so much upon my mind, that I delighted in nothing so much as being alone in the wilderness. . . . I am not I." While before she had sought out only "vain companions," now the house was filled with "holy and strict divines."[63] With her sense of temporality altered by the turn to religion, her lady-ship said that she lost her fear of death.[64] She professed to care not in the slightest for the elevated status and inheritance that befell her family upon the death of their husband's elder brother and their father. When contemplating the possibility of her own death, she professed it, "not at all terrible or affrighting to me, but very pleasant and delightful."[65] The monitoring of time by the pious involved no exclusive commitment to the secular—quite the reverse.

Lady Warwick belonged to the same pious generation of Anglicans who, like the humbler-of-birth Isaac Newton, could imagine time as an absolute, a thing in and of itself, as an entity not simply relative to events or their sequence.[66] Earthly time invited contemplation of eternity. Relative, commonplace time should be made as accurate as possible so as to better reflect duration or absolute time.

Such an understanding led to efforts to reform time, the reading of time, to make it more uniform and universal. Even Newton himself entertained projects for reforming the calendar to make it more regular and uniform.[67] As with everything to do with Newton's religiosity, those efforts are filled with irony. The Newtonian definition of time sprang from his deep religiosity, his desire to use creation to display the boundless power of the creator for whom space—like time—operated as his *sensorium*, his connection to his creation. In Newton's own words found in his *Scholium to the System of the World*, "Since every particle of space is *always*, and every indivisible moment of duration *everywhere*, certainly the Maker and Lord of all things *cannot* be *never* and *nowhere*."[68] Gradually, the universalization of time advocated by Newton's followers, who, like himself, awarded it a real and independent status, contributed to its normalization, and not least pointed toward the secular.

Almanacs by students of physic or astrology, even of astronomy, routinely prognosticated, predicting future events in a time controlled still by the movement of the stars. The early almanacs were Janus-faced: on one hand, they allowed their owners to manage time efficiently; on the other, they gave the traditional Christian age of the earth plus added future predictions that aroused fear among those who still practiced magical thinking. By 1690, almanac makers had to acknowledge that astrology was controversial; then they went right ahead with a prognostication.[69] Astrologers still made a living in London at least up to the 1730s—if not, we suspect, well beyond.[70] For them, as for their true believers, there was nothing casual about time.

The renewed consciousness about time, about how lives were lived in the here and now, fitted quite precisely into the historical situation of the restored Anglican Church. In sermon after learned treatise throughout the 1660s, Anglican clergy laid emphasis upon "the whole duty of man" as they aimed to "reconnect morality and godliness."[71] In deep reaction against the emphasis placed during the 1650s on faith and faith alone, after 1660 and the restoration of Church and king, the Church turned toward good works and sought to rekindle belief in the relationship between faith and a good life. John Evelyn recorded countless sermons that he heard where the preacher attacked abstract notions of faith and urged the congregation to embrace a practical, lived form of piety.[72] Lady Warwick expressed this sensibility when she prayed for her nieces, "O make them not only to be good, but to do good."[73] This emphasis upon practice and good works led to the obsessive observing of oneself in time, such as we see among the Evelyns.

The revered spiritual leader of the period, Jeremy Taylor, preached that the Puritans had all but wrecked Christianity, "those ignorant Preachers, who think all Religion is a Sermon, and all Sermons ought to be Libels against Truth and old Governours."[74] Indeed, he assured the pious that the haters of bishops singlehandedly had destroyed monarchy. To restore the Church and state, he prescribed a careful watching over time: "there being no way left to redeem that time from loss, but by meditation and short mental prayers."[75] He wanted the faithful to watch themselves: "counsel thy self, reprove thy self, censure thy self, judge thy self impartially . . . they that follow their own sensuality stain their consciences, and lost the grace of God."[76] He urged his congregations to pursue their callings and avoid idleness, because for "a busy man temptation is fain to climb up together with his business."[77] Such advice was accompanied by elaborate rules for temperance in food and drink, for living in chastity, humility, contentedness, obedience to superiors, reading and hearing the word of God—in short, rules to govern every waking hour and minute. Every moment required an examination of conscience and a constant self-monitoring if eternity in heaven were even to be imagined as possible.[78] Nothing that Taylor advocated approached an enlightened worldliness.

Our *locus classicus* for the religious person and the understanding of time as found decades after Taylor preached is the Dissenter and Leeds clothier Joseph Ryder. Beginning in the 1730s and writing into the 1760s, Ryder left a remarkable forty-one-volume spiritual diary, a long, extended meditation on whether or not his worldly interests would compromise, indeed undermine, his chance at salvation. Ryder's understanding of time—his usage of the word—commands our brief attention. He gives many hints that he measured time with some device, remarking early in the diary about the trivial nature of conversation after a visit of a quarter of an hour with friends.[79] He noted an exposition of Matthew 8.17 that "if Christ be with his people it will greatly sweeten his peoples passage thro Time."[80]

For Ryder, "my Time was in Gods hand I would not pray that God would Take me out of the world but that he would keep [me] from the evil of it."[81] He noted that when too much conversation revolved around "things of this profound life," time had been spent "unprofitable," and he left remorse when "Things of the Lower world had engrossed our Time." He feared that "the Things of Time" would distract him from his Sabbath obligations.[82] Time brought cares and concerns; "the things of time . . . eat out my concern"; he begged God "to improve sabbath time" and found that "worldly business" stopped him from setting aside time for repentance.[83] Ryder recorded sermons given in his Presbyterian chapel in Leeds that might have been given by the Anglican preachers to whom Mary Evelyn listened so intently seventy or more years earlier. Ryder heard his contemporary preachers proclaim that "time is short . . . he came to show us how to improve time, namely in watching against an inordinate care about ye world."[84] For Ryder (as for Newton) time was a thing in and of itself, it was absolute and separate from him. But this did not lead Ryder to contemplate calendar reforms, even when living through the great reform of 1752 and the loss of eleven late summer days from the British calendar.[85] While so many of his contemporaries blithely accepted that time could be altered for the sake of uniformity and went on with their daily business, Ryder found deeper meaning in the face of time.[86] For him, time only fed his anxiety to have a purchase on it so that he might better worship God.

Such anxieties about time possessed a long lineage in Protestant thought, indeed arguably for the whole of Christian thought. A contemporary of Joseph Ryder who danced, gambled, and drank in excess—whose grasp on piety might seem slim at best—the quite ordinary Thomas Turner, a grocer in Sussex, could nevertheless open his twenty-ninth birthday entry by saying, "may I, as I grow in years, so continue to increase in goodness; for, as my exit must every day draw nearer, so may I every day become more enamoured with the prospect of the happiness of another world, and more entirely dead to the follies and vanities of this transitory world."[87] Even for an Anglican of the mid-eighteenth century who evinces almost entirely secular interests, it was possible to imagine stepping out of time. He exhorted himself "to lay hold of the present minute, that when my exit may be, I may ever more live a life of happiness and bliss."[88]

Punctuality

It would be many decades before recorders of personal time could be both punctual and casual about time spent, finding in it no religious significance other than its usefulness in containing the flow of events. In a jump of some decades, one diarist would illustrate the point, and he records a day like any that we might associate with our own modernity. The soon to be politician William Windham, beginning on July 13, 1783, could note just as matters of fact:

> Sept 27 returned to Oxford around 2; 28th at coffee house
> continued talking until 8; 29th stayed at the Banks' til 8;
> October 11 interrupted by a visit by Mr Burke around 1 . . .
> returned about 8 . . . in the coffee house til near 10; sept 19 . . .

walked out before breakfast; returned about ½ past 9—Price
called for a few minutes—at 12 went with . . . to see Worces-
ter Coll. Returned by the observatory til dinner, about an
hour & half . . . dinner at All Souls . . . woke at about ½ past
7 . . . dipped into books, thought of idle things til it is now
near ten o'clock . . . rose by eight—came down . . . shaved,
about ½ after 8 till 11 employed but with a mixture of other
things . . . drank water & rode before breakfast from 10 to past
12 entered in . . . articles from Forster ½ past 12, went out . . .
after my return only time to dress returned home no more
til bed time ½ past 12.[89]

Windham's attention to the hour, and the flow of his life around
it, may be reasonably described in its precision and tedium as
both secular and modern. All the preaching about minding
one's time, once stripped of its religious moorings, could result
in a Mr. Windham, with his timepiece punctual to the minute
and forever busy.

One way of imagining the complex issue of temporal secularization would be to imagine a lessening of anxiety, of watch-
fulness about time in relation to salvation. For moderate Protestants in early modern England, time presented a paradox and
therefore a source of anxiety. Regardless of how defined, by calendars or seasons, by feasts or fairs, time needed to be watched;
its waste was to be scorned, its fruitful use, valued.[90] The actions
or motions that the pious take in the world had to be monitored
for their virtuousness and made purposeful, and all actions had
temporal consequences.

There is irony in what the pious diaries and sermons of the
late seventeenth century tell us: time, however expansively
measured and loosely recorded—the morning, the evening,
at midday—was ever intruding. It had to be addressed and

meditated upon. And typically the odyssey of the Protestant soul, as witnessed in the autobiography of Lady Warwick or the diary of Joseph Ryder, and in countless Protestant self-narrations, seemed to require a time spent out of grace, in vain pursuits, a period of life simply "altogether sinful and vain," as one early eighteenth-century diarist of Scottish Anglican origins put it.[91] This time of wickedness provided the setting for "an account of the rise, progress, interruptions, revivals and issues of the Lord's striving with me during the ten or eleven ensuing years of my life."[92] The soul's temporal development was what counted, provided the narrative moved in the right direction, from sin and vanity to its redemption in time.

Words and their usages serve to introduce us to the trajectory taken in the understanding of time in the course of the eighteenth century. Until roughly midcentury, one could be "punctual," meaning simply be precise, accurate, attentive to every detail, or make a small point. Someone could understand "good breeding to a Punctuality."[93] But in 1777, the playwright Sheridan, in School for Scandal, could offer unqualified praise of a person's timeliness, and even gender the trait as masculine: "O, madam, punctuality is a species of constancy a very unfashionable custom among ladies." Clearly, being on time, literally landing at the designated spot just as the minute hand of the clock coincided with one's arrival, had evolved into a value. But not for everyone and only gradually, with varying directions taken by religious thinkers trying to come to terms with the anxiety induced by temporality.

Later in the century, time could be seen as a subject of learned scientific disagreement, with journals describing the quarrels among "the metaphysicians" about the issue of absolute versus relative time. Time had largely lost its religious meaning, and in its place time became a backdrop, seemingly endless, the setting wherein human, secular history could unfold. Knowing time came to mean actually recording the moment of birth, "Louisa Harriet Renison Born September 2, 1808 / 20 minutes before 6 o'clock . . . died Thursday, August 31, 1809, 10 minutes before 2 o'clock in the day."[94] Such recording did little to console for the death of a child not yet a year old. It is little wonder that timepieces came to be viewed with rapt curiosity especially by those not yet possessing one.[95]

Living an Entirely Secular Life

Understanding how contemporaries lived in the secular sphere requires different evidence from what an author may have put in print. We need to enter a largely private world. One intriguing example can be found in the remarkable diaries written by Constantijn Huygens Jr., secretary to the stadholder-king, William of Orange. They begin with the Grand Tour that Huygens undertook in 1649, but for our purposes, the entries from the period 1673 to 1683 and 1688 to 1697 are the most captivating and most germane to the transformations at work in a new cultural universe. Unpublished by their authors, Huygens's diaries (by father and son) have been compared to that of Samuel Pepys, and both display an almost limitless worldly engagement, and are explicit about sexual matters, sometimes recounted in code.[96]

Huygens Jr. was by far better connected to the major players in political events in both England and the Dutch Republic. His diary gives an intimate view of the Glorious Revolution and its major participants, both Dutch and English.[97] That alone would secure its value, but for our purposes the student of the period is struck by the complete absence of reverence for religion or religious belief, even during the tense days of November 1688. Religion was never a topic of conversation, despite Huygens's

philosophical and classical sophistication. He was highly educated, having studied law at Leiden, and owned a splendid
library of more than 5,000 volumes with an emphasis on literature, law, philosophy, and science. There is not a scintilla of
evidence that Huygens was moved by any of the sermons he
heard or possibly read, even those he attended with William of
Orange and given by Gilbert Burnet, justifying the providential
nature of the Dutch invasion. Experiencing a powerful earthquake while on military campaign in the Southern Netherlands,
Huygens—although afraid when it was happening—records
only his interest in the natural causes of the event, a subject he
in turn went on to study.[98]

Huygens's remarkable library, catalogued for sale at his death,
is a study in what a highly educated layman with wide-ranging interests did, and did not, care to read. Of course, Huygens owned
Balthazar Bekker, many Bibles, and hermeneutical or philologi-
cal commentaries on them, with the biblical historicist Richard
Simon notably visible.[99] Massive numbers of books propped
up the legal and scientific sections—indeed, all the important
natural philosophers of the seventeenth century were there. Histories, travel accounts, poetry (in several languages), emblem
books, accounts of antiquities, numismatica, guidebooks for Europe, French plays, and many accounts of seventeenth-century
history, particularly in England, complemented the *amours* of
various kings and courts, a significant number of naughty books
without an author and published in Cologne (almost certainly
the imprint of the fictitious Pierre Marteau), and not least, add
prohibited books in folio, quarto, octavo, duodecimo, and some
unidentified manuscripts. In the category of the prohibited, we
find books by all the usual suspects: Hobbes, Faustus Socinus,
Spinoza, still others by Vanini, Beverland, the Socinian Johann
Crell, Thomas Browne, and from a specifically Dutch context,

works by various Remonstrants, others on the life and death of Oldenbarnevelt, various combined Dutch works of a political nature, often anonymous. Most interesting is the nearly total absence of sermon literature except for texts that explicate one or another book from the Old or New Testaments. It would seem that when reading, Huygens preferred to be informed or entertained, but not spiritually exalted.

The people Huygens knew evince worldliness similar to that found in his library. At court, Huygens Jr. could spend "the evening engaged in dirty talk," and gossip, often of a sexual nature, was commonplace. Huygens's diary also provides vivid details about the brothels of Amsterdam sometimes taken from stories told him by friends. Cross-dressing, bastard children, madams and pimps, venereal disease, rape, "deviant" sex that included rumors about William of Orange, gave Huygens plenty to record and comment upon. Like Pepys, Huygens owned and discussed pornography, a novelistic genre new to the age. The salacious mixed effortlessly with the mundane, with the comings and goings of servants, friends, booksellers, and family members.[100]

In the Huygens family, the pea did not fall far from the pod, at least in matters concerning religion. Huygens's son, Tiens, a student at Leiden, led a life that was an endless source of grief, anger, and worry to his parents. Always more drunk than sober, he died a young death, and with him ended that branch of the Huygens family. Nothing in the diaries explains the sources of his dissolute and violent unhappiness. Many among the godly would have seen his fate—dying with the date and place of burial unknown—as just rewards and probably have blamed his worldly father for the son's premature demise. There is no evidence that Huygens would have accepted guilt or turned away from his secular pursuits. By the 1770s, there were many more people like him.

3

Secular Lives

IN THE PRECEDING CHAPTER, we met William Windham, man about town, living in London, possessed of political ambitions and carefully monitoring his time. His crowded use of time was not unlike our own. A century earlier, we also encountered the Dutch courtier, Constantijn Huygens Jr., who lived through the revolution of 1689 and enjoyed secular pursuits—gossip, bawdy talk, military campaigns—seldom with a thought about the religious meaning of his actions. These early modern secular lives tell about living in limitless time and space, in the here and now, and point to new ways of being in the world. We know a great deal about the Enlightenments of Voltaire, or David Hume, or Immanuel Kant, but what about lesser mortals, the ordinary, literate, reasonably educated eighteenth-century people we may legitimately describe as enlightened? They may not have been original thinkers like the great philosophes—who deserve and will receive separate treatment—but they enable us to see the Enlightenment at work in more "ordinary" lives.

Secular and enlightened, they occupied time and space differently from their very religiously inflected contemporaries. We need to know what that might have been like, and we will choose our examples somewhat randomly, delving into lives generally obscure that may nevertheless demonstrate enlightened values. As participants in different activities, such men and women brought a set of interests different from those motivated by religion; we might say that their agendas were worldly and enlightened without being overtly hostile toward the religion into which they had been born. Secularity, like religiosity, entailed more than a set of doctrines, or heresies; it meant being at ease in this world with little thought about any other. Their lives were markedly different from that of the midcentury clothier Joseph Ryder (whom we met in chapter 2).

And they can turn up anywhere. The wife of the literary figure who introduced the French materialist Helvétius into Germany, Luise Gottsched wrote to a good friend that Helvétius's *De l'esprit* (1759) "displayed a great spirit, a declaration of war against prejudices whether very old or very sacred." Her husband, professor of philosophy Johann Gottsched, was far more restrained but not hostile. By contrast, the Dutch-trained German medical doctor Albrecht von Haller spied Spinozism and materialism in the work of Helvétius and attacked him passionately. Someone like the moderate Johann could introduce into Germany works by the French philosophers, beginning with Bayle, while still refusing to embrace the radically secular stance imbedded in the materialism fashionable after 1750. With this cast of literate characters in various Western countries from England, the American colonies, and Europe, we will begin with the enlightened but moderate.[1]

Henry Penruddocke Wyndham (b. 1736, and not related to William Windham) provides insight into how literate men and women could absorb enlightened ideas. A gentleman tourist in the age that invented the pursuit, Wyndham journeyed into deepest Wales in part to show that its beauty had been neglected and its people mischaracterized as rude and backward.

He might have said "unenlightened." He wrote at some length about Welsh antiquities of Roman and Norman origin, the beauty of Welsh churches, and the efforts being made to preserve these antiquities "against the savage and plundering curiosity of the common people."[2]

Wyndham saw an ancient Roman as having been on a civilizing mission; by art and architecture he "gained as much by his art . . . than by his sword." The integrity of Roman art and architecture excited him and, by contrast, "the heterogeneous mixture of architecture [that] prevails within the modern Church . . . I find by no means agreeable to the eye."[3] Back in the 1960s, the late Peter Gay described the Enlightenment as the revival of paganism. This sensibility finds expression in the musings of Wyndham as he traveled throughout Britain and then the Continent, where he saw various Catholic churches. Like other enlightened reformers in Catholic Europe, Wyndham valued primarily the order and regularity of pagan architecture. Given half a chance and faced with a contemporary city destroyed by an earthquake, Wyndham—like the Portuguese mid-eighteenth-century enlightened prime minister—would have rebuilt Lisbon to reflect geometrical order and uniformity of design.[4] Such was the style adopted by the mid-eighteenth century for Turin.

Beginning early in his youthful travels, Wyndham went through the whole of Britain, Ireland, and much of the Continent. He always commented upon the relative beauty of the churches but never once does he tell us that he stopped to worship. He loved the grandeur of castles and mansions, yet in Ireland he saw social injustice: "It is shamefully inhuman that while the Noblemen past in more luxury than Princes, the Poor should live worse than Dogs!"[5] Rousseau could have written the sentence. In Sicily, Wyndham lashed out at the appalling poverty seen on every street, where children could be found naked and coated in dirt.

Such lofty sentiments about the poor cannot conceal what was in general a distain for commoners, for tradesmen who swarmed a visitor's carriage and were "animals in the world."[6]

Politeness and civility remained Wyndham's ideal model of genteel behavior, praised at every opportunity.[7] They stood as rational barriers to credulity and rudeness. Protestant in background, this English traveler found "idolatry" in French religious customs, where in one church he witnessed "its chief Idol ... an old ugly wooden crucifix which *formerly* spoke. The miracle is daily acknowledged by kneeling crowds of credulity."[8] Wyndham is ever mindful of what he regards as backwardness, a lack of progress. In Italy, the custom of opening up the tombs of the deceased even if they had died from smallpox elicits the outcry, "how obvious is the absurdity and danger of this practice!" Elsewhere, a painted depiction of Jesus as the groom of St. Catherine is found to be nothing short of blasphemous.[9] Closer to home, Methodism was seen to have a "baleful influence" whose "mechanical preachers" offered "poisonous tenets."[10] To many who identified with the Enlightenment, Methodism and similarly emotive forms of religion were seen as "enthusiasm." Not as bad as the French prophets or the *convulsionnaires*, but hardly a complimentary label.

As he travels, our enlightened gentleman reveals that his aesthetic prejudice lies with the ancient Romans over the achievements of the Christian moderns. The sensibility on display is more classical than Christian, and Wyndham is never shy to point out the ugliness of a church or cathedral; only the ancient ruins left by the Romans uniformly inspire. That said, his enlightened bias found Protestant church architecture far preferable to Catholic.[11] In general, the term "modern" is used with approval, and cities of geometrical proportions are considered especially pleasing. An interest in science complements the process of traveling, and he comments on thermometers used to measure hot and cold, or the debased reputation of a university singled out for the decay of its science teaching (such is the mention given to Leiden).[12] The creation of lending libraries receives special commendation, as does the early practice of inoculation against smallpox.

Wyndham is best described as a representative of the moderate Enlightenment, and he displays little interest in materialism or atheism. There were many such seekers after an aesthetic that turned away from the harshness of Protestant predestination or the Catholic Inquisition. As we have seen, foreign lands offered the possibility to articulate the previously unimagined; recall the tract that claimed the Australian people were possessed of both male and female attributes. There were many such philosophes, like the well-traveled French author of the *Telliamed*, who wanted to completely revise the age of the world. Sometimes, not knowing their actual identity allows us to postulate these anonymous authors as a kind of enlightened everyman.

Such was an anonymous author who at midcentury attempted to articulate a self-controlled *via media* aimed at a happy life in society. Note in passing that Maillet's *Telliamed* may have inspired *Le Philosophe Indien*; both were supposedly by an Indian philosopher.[13] It was a common enlightened trope. The actual author of *The Oeconomy of Human Life: Translated from an Indian Manuscript, written by an Ancient Bramin*, known in French as *Le Philosophe Indien*, is widely believed to be the British publisher and poet Robert Dodsley. Safely ensconced in London, he claimed to have learned philosophy and religion from the ancient Brahmins and to have traveled to China and Tibet.

On the Continent, the French version of *The Oeconomy* was attributed to the English aristocrat Lord Chesterfield. It takes its place among a raft of clandestine texts, often materialist in inspiration and dating from the 1740s. It advocates an entirely natural religion, albeit a theistic one suitable for living a happy life in society. And it claimed to have been composed by an ancient Brahmin, not by a contemporary Englishman. German heresy hunters tracked its various translations and lumped it with other freethinking texts.[14]

There are Spinozist elements in the Indian philosopher's theism; he praises the wisdom of God by noting, "The marvels of his mechanism are the work of his hands. Listen to his voice."[15] Thus anthropomorphized, "the Lord is just; he judges the world with equity and truth. . . . The Great and the Small, the Wise and the Ignorant . . . are received equally in accordance with their merit."[16] This is not the God of the materialists, nor is he particularly identifiable with any of the three monotheistic religions. No text we can associate with the Enlightenment went through more editions and translations, printed and manuscript, with copies in German, Hungarian, Welsh, and so on. In the eighteenth century, 200 editions appeared and again half as many were produced after 1800.[17] We might describe the sentiments in *The Oeconomy of Human Life* as enlightened religiosity "light," close to physico-theology but nowhere near as theistic. It was intended to guide a worldly life well lived.

The bulk of the prescriptions coming from our Brahmin philosophe concern the dangers of laziness, envy, grandiose speech, raillery, and not least, the necessity of being intrepid in the face of "the malice of fortune."[18] The ethics at the root of the text are neo-stoical with republican implications: a condemnation of luxury and extravagance, anger, and sexual excess. The same virtues hold for women, although they are seen as primarily the keepers of the household and the solace of their husbands. The creed being advocated by this anonymous author anchors itself in the secular, in temporal pursuits that discipline the individual. He or she has religion without the need for priests, churches, sermons, or the Testaments. Someone like Wyndham could have read it with pleasure, without taking offence.

Dodsley, the presumed author of this new natural religion, began his career as a publisher with an anonymous imprint from the pen of one Paul Whitehead. *The Manners, A Satire,* is blatantly anti-court, full of republican sentiments, and invokes "Thrice happy Patriot, whom no courts embrace, No Titles lessen, and no Stars disgrace." The text landed Dodsley in prison, from which only the solicitude of an influential friend got him released. He went on to publish just about any author of distinction from Samuel Johnson to Edmund Burke, not least becoming the English publisher of Voltaire. While his personal religious views are hard to establish, Dodsley seems most easily identifiable as a deist.[19] When writing to a friend about a baptism to be attended, Dodsley described it as "the solemn foolery of a christening."[20] As we have seen in the study of Dutch publishers and authors like Picart and Bernard, a commitment to making a good living did not exclude an ideological predilection for enlightened causes.[21]

Openness to the new and exotic was not confined to armchair philosophers like Dodsley. Where we can find testimonies from travelers, even sailors in the service of empire, by midcentury they could perceive a common humanity—for example, with Africans encountered on the small West African isle of Goree, one of earliest sites of the slave trade. Samuel Dickenson, a chaplain on an English ship, the Dunkirk, wrote of the Africans: "with respect to their manners & behavior [they] seem to me a most quiet, inoffensive, good-tempered people. I experienced a great sense of gratitude in some of them & am of the opinion there are few of them where affections might not be conciliated by an obliging & prudent behavior in Europeans; &

consequently that it is the fault of the latter if they do not live with them in peace friendship & harmony." Dickenson knew that standard prejudices applied to "the Negroes," and sought naturalistic explanations: "They are said to have like other Negroes much indolence in their disposition, but this may proceed from the fewness of their wants; & the facility with which a family is here supplied with all the necessities of life; which exempts them from the obligation of great exertions of industry, and is itself a peculiar blessing in so sultry a climate."[22]

Although a committed Christian, the enlightened chaplain could contrast the labor of both men and women on the island to the drudgery found particularly among European women. The Africans lack only two attributes: "an increase of Christian knowledge to banish superstition, refine the morals & exalt the hopes of this people with the bright prospect of future bliss and glory," and a good system of government "to limit the sovereign regal power & thus free them from the arbitrary impositions & tyranny of their kings."[23] Despite the prevalence of polygamy, Dickenson describes the women of the island as being of "excellent character" and faithful to their husbands.

The survey of mores, occupations, food supply, types of grain and liquors, trees, plants, and animals allows Dickenson to contrast the relative prosperity he sees in Goree to the extreme poverty witnessed in Ireland.[24] The English habit of visiting other parts of their kingdom in search for progress continued unabated throughout the century. Scotland always beckoned, and in town after town, county after county, English travelers looked for commerce and manufacturing. These invariably signaled vitality and progress.[25]

One of the most perplexing dilemmas faced by Europeans of the eighteenth century concerned how to explain relative prosperity or poverty as seen within Europe or outside of it.

Such wide disparities required careful study, and all who tried to make sense of them—from our ship's chaplain to Adam Smith and the Scottish philosophers—spent time in science-inspired observations. Dickenson described in detail every animal and plant he saw in Africa—"Coracias Senegala, a curious bird of passage ... visits this country at a particular season; it is a species of jay"—and cited published accounts of travelers like William Dampier and Michel Adanson. He applied the same observational skills when visiting France—"plants observed at Lyons," and so on. And like Wyndham, this traveling chaplain disdained the practices of Roman Catholicism and rejoiced in the Roman ruins encountered in Nîmes, in the south of France. He waxes, "glorious remains of ancient splendor have sustained much less injury by time ... the simplicity, the grandeur & harmony of the design cannot fail of impressing every spectator with pleasing awe and admiration."[26] The joy inspired by ancient ruins complemented a dedication to science and an education that was strong not just in theology but also in natural history, botany, and mechanics.

Faced with the foreign and strange, enlightened travelers could easily have assumed the inferiority of their subjects. Like the Scottish philosophers who came to see human change and development in terms of different stages, this ship's chaplain observed and classified with a generous eye. As in his defense of the Africans, Dickenson praises the French for their humanity and generosity from "a people whose national character too often suffers from misrepresentation and prejudice."[27] In coming to terms with strangers, our enlightened travelers depict a cosmopolitan impulse, a willingness to accept and appreciate difference, and in the case of Dickenson, to regard the south of France as offering "the blessings of the delightful land of Promise." He even praised the Turks he encountered as being "very neat and cleanly in their persons . . . to be indolent, but brave and honest."[28]

The willingness to engage in intellectual exploration could overtake any young person in a household committed to enlightenment learning and open to scientific pursuits. Such was the education offered to Richard Lovell Edgeworth (1744–1817), whose daughter Maria would become a famous novelist in the first half of the nineteenth century. In a memoir (which Maria completed for him), he describes the commitment to learning found in his youthful home under the tutelage of his mother. Edgeworth belongs to the first generation of British industrialists, although his landed wealth left him without the necessity of making a living in industry. What he shared with them was a passion for science, in particular for mechanics and invention, encouraged by his mother.[29]

The Edgeworths prided themselves on their liberal attitudes toward the Irish—without for a second feeling any discomfort at their privileged status as rich Protestant landlords. They sought improvements that would be profitable for themselves and their class. Aside from various scientific publications, Richard Edgeworth left an invaluable set of lecture notes taken when he was a student at Edinburgh in the 1790s. It was the university of choice for aspiring industrial families, and the notes make clear the advanced state of the art in scientific lecturing, complete with demonstrations of the steam engine.[30] They give us a window into the Enlightenment in Edinburgh.

Indeed, the ambiance in Edinburgh and Glasgow universities during the turbulent 1790s betrayed enlightened sentiments at almost every turn. The treatment of the mid-seventeenth-century English revolution made clear that the king, not Parliament or the Puritans, caused the upheaval. Governments rested on social contracts that were made by the people and clearly capable of being unmade by the same or future generations. Student circles indulged in the pornographic and when not being naughty, displayed passionate support for the French Revolution. The children of some of the leading industrial families like the Watts were front and center in such clubs. After Edinburgh, they made common cause with young poets like Wordsworth, Coleridge, and Southey—soon to be famous as the English Romantics—who shared their commitment to enlightened French politics.

In their radical phase, these aspiring poets and politicians rivaled the midcentury French materialist philosophes in their hatred of slavery, their penchant for republics, even democracies, and their complete disdain for organized religion. They embodied—they lived and breathed—secular impulses. They followed the lead of their professors. On the Glasgow faculty from the 1750s to the 1790s, John Anderson (d. 1796) evolved into an ardent supporter of the French Revolution.[31] Among the subversive ideas he taught in his class on natural jurisprudence (attended by Gregory Watt), he proclaimed that primogeniture is "an institution fraught with absurdity and evil . . . it should be a man's duty to provide equally for all his children."[32] None of these attacks on the established social order should be seen as simply bombast; Anderson, like the Enlightenment itself, also promised ever-increasing progress.

Anderson's moral philosophy begins almost lyrically: "Man is chiefly distinguished by his power of intellectual improvement. . . . The measure of his intellectual improvement is unlimited. It only ceases with his life. He can communicate the knowledge he himself acquires to his descendants so that mankind continually becomes more learned. . . . The supreme being was pleased to endow certain men with preternatural powers in order that they might instruct others." The improvements in learning have been everywhere but especially in physics and

chymistry.[33] Even the lower classes are the beneficiaries of progress: "Labor can be greatly abridged by the proper application
of machines. More accuracy can likewise be attained than man
could otherwise arrive at. Man by the aid of mechanics can
overcome obstacles otherwise insurmountable . . . can achieve
things otherwise impossible."[34] The paean to modernity continues: "No praise could be spared for mechanics [which] have
been carried to a degree of perfection of which at first sight we
should suppose them totally incapable . . . the assistance which
mechanics offered to mankind is incredible."[35] At Glasgow
in the 1790s and before, young men like Gregory Watt could
find enlightenment mixed with political radicalism, as well as a
heady embrace of progress, both economic and political.

The presentation of history, in keeping with the precepts associated with the Scottish Enlightenment, was stadial, ending with
the final stage of modern commercial societies.[36] But Anderson's
lecturers offered a twist on the standard account: "The progress
of commerce and manufacturing became very rapid at this period." Wherever possible, the lectures on the stages of history
added manufacturing to commerce as a crucial part of modern
political development: "The consequence of arts and manufactures being improved is a great accession of wealth. . . . Hence
Manufactures occasion great towns. In rude countries there is
no such thing."[37] Manufacturing creates luxury that in turn stim-
ulates industry. Coming from industrial families, students could
hold their heads high. They had become acquainted with what
one historian has called the "Industrial Enlightenment."[38]

Continental Lives

Britain differed from the Continent in the advances of its industrial base, which by the time of the Watts and the Edgeworths

exceeded what could be found anywhere in Western Europe. In terms of social and political practices, the story is more complicated. Authoritarian and monarchical governments prevailed in France, the Iberian Peninsula, the Austrian empire, and the German-speaking lands. The big exception lay in the Dutch Republic. Its prosperity matched what could be seen in England, and its institutions of local government dominated throughout most of the century, stopped only by the French invasion in 1795. While even more oligarchic than Britain, Dutch society, particularly in the period before 1750, displayed a surprising and radical secularity. We saw evidence of it in the diary of Constantijn Huygens Jr., but given his elevated social status we might be tempted to dismiss his worldliness as a privilege of high birth.

It would be hard to mistake the Dutch freethinker Isabella de Moerloose for high born. Isabella's date of birth, probably 1661, cannot be firmly established, but we do know that she was born a Catholic in Ghent and eventually married a Protestant minister in Zeeland. She was a contemporary of Huygens Jr. She was also highly literate and could write letters in French. That would have distinguished her from her plebian neighbors, as did her marriage to a clergyman. What would have debased her social standing totally was her eventual imprisonment for heresy and then madness.

Before going mad, Isabella published an autobiography of over six hundred pages that makes clear her disillusionment with the Catholic clergy, indeed her general disdain for the strictures of organized religion, and her willingness to discuss sexual matters explicitly—everything from menstruation to coitus interruptus and fellatio.[39] This rare work got her into considerable trouble with the authorities, although it was hardly her first encounter with the watchdogs of piety. Dutch freethinkers of the next generation (she may have died in 1712) counted her as one of their own and put her in the same league as Vanini, various Spinozists, and John Toland.[40]

We do not know the route she took to qualify for such a dubious honor. We know nothing about what she read or with whom she discussed her ideas. But her clergyman husband, before his death in 1692, would have known the religious disputes of the day and the efforts made by reformers such as Balthazar Bekker to banish belief in devils and witches. Certainly Isabella knew of such beliefs, even accepted them, and her mother believed that her daughter might have been bewitched. In the 1690s, Isabella ran a small school near Amsterdam, where the local clergy found that she taught "very godless and abominable things." She was placed in irons and hauled off to the local prison, *het Spinhuis*, for heresy, and there she remained until transferred to a prison for the mentally ill. In 1712, when she was fifty years old, she disappeared from the surviving records.[41]

Few Dutch autobiographies survive from the period, and none is as revelatory about private beliefs or sexual practices as Isabella's. If we use our knowledge of other heretical "unknowns," we can surmise that Isabella arrived at such beliefs partly from what could be heard or read in the Republic at the time, and partly from folk traditions in which pagan beliefs collided with what the clergy wanted the faithful to believe. What made her different was the audacity with which she propagated her views and her lack of respect for the authorities in church and state. In that posture, she resembled many other heretics in the Republic, most commonly associated with the ideas of Spinoza.

Curiously, Isabella might best be described as a religious thinker, however heretical. She had toyed with becoming a nun, then fell away from the Catholic Church. In every town in which she lived, she drew the wrath of the clergy, disputing Scripture with them and generally making her disdain clear.

Her odyssey would be replicated in the lives of major and minor philosophes about whom generally more is known. She described her autobiography as an effort to get to know herself and as a guide for other women, particularly in matters sexual. She was a seeker who had the misfortune to fall into the hands of the religious authorities.

There is reason to believe that the state of religious contestation was greater in the Republic than in England in the same period. When the London periodical *The Spectator* began circulation in 1711, its tone was breezy and gossipy. One of its first Continental imitators, *La Bagatelle*, appeared less than a decade later in 1718, written in French by a Dutch journalist, Justus van Effen. Its opening text promised to be truthful and to be careful not to label ideas either orthodox or heretical. Such labeling is the work of "the ministers of the Gospel" who are duped by their "indiscrete zeal." The journal launched its preface with a lengthy meditation on the nature of religious truth that in passing reveals what a vexed subject it had become.

Justus van Effen gradually transformed into a conservative thinker who by the 1730s came to see moral decay everywhere. Indeed, the decade revealed the depth to which suspicion had sunk. In the period, men were accused of homosexuality, and it was also the decade in which worms ate at the wooden dikes, threatening the possibility of inundation by the sea. To make matters worse, signs hinted at Dutch economic decline. A pessimism about worldly progress set in, nurtured in part by the religious authorities.

Throughout the first half of the century, the Dutch Reformed Church saw itself surrounded by various heresies, anti-Trinitarianism to be sure, and also by followers of Spinoza. It even believed pietistic forms of Protestantism owed a debt to Spinozism.[42] Certainly, one way to read Spinoza—that he was seeking to be one with God—can be found in enlightened circles throughout the century. We might be surprised by the relative absence of Dutch contributions to the European Enlightenment, but this was truer in the second half of the century than in the first.

In the first half of the century, the Republic was one of the first places outside Britain to accept and teach Newton's science. The Dutch Newtonians, with Willem Jacob s'Gravesande as the most famous, did not replicate themselves at home. During the second half of the century, Dutch science remained largely derivative, but it was accommodating in matters of gender. As far as we can tell, the first European scientific society for women was established in Zeeland in the 1780s. It remained active for nearly a hundred years.[43]

In 1747–48, the Republic experienced revolution, and one of its leaders was a minor philosophe, self-described pantheist, and freemason, Jean Rousset de Missy. He and his followers sought a British-style government with much greater authority vested in a central government and not in local oligarchs. For his trouble, Rousset was forced into exile. Calls for reform and the end of oligarchy failed. Another generation passed before the endemic problems of a Republic in decline were addressed. In the 1780s, both the southern and northern Netherlands led Europe in ushering in an age of democratic revolutions. Before there was revolution in Paris in 1789, both Brussels and Amsterdam erupted. A reactionary Prussian invasion stopped revolutionary change in Amsterdam, but by 1795 the revolutionary French army, first in Brussels and then Amsterdam, brought democracy to the Low Countries both north and south.

Yet amid expansion, then decline, the Dutch continued their global outreach, particularly in areas with British and French competition. All moved east toward the Ottoman Empire and

India, while retaining colonies in North America.[44] There, the Dutch gradually retreated, while the British and French, entrenched in their northern colonies, largely left South America to the Spanish.

The Spanish experience of spectacular conquest in Latin America also put them into the business of foreign exploration and global mapping. The published diaries of Spanish travelers give some insight into the penetration of enlightened values, or the lack thereof, in the approach to the native peoples they encountered. Quite obviously, scientific values had penetrated the Spanish imperial mission; everything was to be measured, mapped, observed, and explained.[45] No frontier seemed impenetrable. Spanish travelers reported back to their government about California and Louisiana—and the need for modernization. Peru and Chile, as well as most parts of Europe, were carefully examined.[46] On the whole, the Spanish travel literature demonstrates little contact with the vast literature generated in other languages, but all shared a global curiosity without which the Enlightenment cannot be understood.

A similar curiosity can be found among Russian travelers, for whom foreign fiction supplied a framework for the expression of emotions. Novels provided a template for such expression, and everything from Rousseau's *La Nouvelle Héloïse* to Goethe's *Sorrows of Young Werther* made Russian readers feel that they were in contact with a universal Western form of sensibility.[47] Traveling freemasons may also have brought the new ideas from West to East.

The same spirit of curiosity gripped a young, virtually unknown Lutheran theologian, a German speaker who took a job as a schoolteacher and librarian in the Latvian port city of Riga. Placing the great Johann Herder (b. 1744) in the same company with largely unknown travelers or heretics seems outlandish,

but when we encounter him in his travel journal of 1769 (unpublished in his lifetime), there is little hint of the towering
intellectual he would become. What we do find is a young man
already familiar with the major writers we now associate with
the Enlightenment, and eager to find a place in its reforming
momentum. Having studied at university with the philosopher
Kant, Herder already knew the importance of natural philosophy and mathematics. He set sail for France with insufficient
French and an immense excitement at the prospect of finding
something new and foreign.

Once again, like so many other European travelers we met
in this chapter, Herder displays a fascination with the ancient
Greeks and Romans and their civilizations. His meditation on
travel reveals a catholicity of taste for any and all of the ancient
civilizations—sentiments without bias. When faced with the
poverty seen in the Duchy of Courland—a "moral and literary
desert" not far from Riga—Herder embraces wholesale reform.
The place needs a library; the aristocracy needs masonic lodges;
and the entire territory could use his services as an educator.
Scientific instruments need to be purchased. Once enlightened,
the culture of Courland will spread into Hungary, Poland, and
Russia; "the Ukraine will become a new Greece." Herder believed that the century of Montesquieu, Rousseau, Hume, and
Mably could bring reform even to Russia. No other people except the Russians could do this for them; "this is the moment
to act in Russia."[48]

More than any of the other travelers and seekers we have so
far encountered, Herder allows us to see the intellectual struggle
set off by the provocative thinkers of the period. His familiarity
with them is obvious, his commitment to free inquiry genuine, and his fear of religious fanaticism deeply rooted. It fuels a
spirit, he observes, that burns libraries and printing presses.[49]

But the philosophes do not get a free pass from Herder. He says at times that they lower themselves by making encyclopedias and dictionaries, and that the best days of French letters are over. Even Montesquieu, whom Herder otherwise praises greatly, can venture into pseudo-philosophy, piling up example after example that seem ultimately to contradict one another. In the end, Herder wants to see German philosophy and letters reach the standard—however imperfect—set by the French.[50]

Herder's meditations on civilizations ancient and contemporary display no commitment to European superiority, but rather a willingness to see all peoples as capable of intellectual creativity. In embryo among the enlightened travelers, even more so with Herder, there is an openness and a curiosity that will lead gradually to the birth of anthropology. This open-mindedness complemented a growing commitment to reform visible in many places in Germany and the Dutch Republic in the last quarter of the century.[51]

The late-century reform movements eventually yielded to the fury unleashed by the French Revolution. In the 1790s, no one on either side of the English Channel could avoid its implications. Herder's life span stretched well into the nineteenth century and thus permits us to see continuity between his youthful dedication to enlightened values and practices and his commitment to the principles of the Revolution. In its wake, Herder offered his own meditation on freemasonry and the state, and he returns to the theme briefly mentioned in the travel journal of 1769 when he wanted to see the aristocracy of Courland civilized by masonic membership.

In 1778, Herder's contemporary, the freemason Gotthold Lessing, had published a dialogue on freemasonry that in effect constituted a call to action. *Ernst und Falk* urges a commitment to worldly reform to be undertaken by the lodges, many

of which he believed had fallen into frivolity. In 1793, Herder
begins his meditation on freemasonry by also emphasizing secular action, "all the good that has been done . . . in the world."
Herder, himself a freemason, reiterates "in the world." He starts
with Falk's question: are men created for the state, or the state
for men? He then, like Falk, notes all the divisions that states
impose upon men, and he ends by invoking his desire for a society composed of all the thinking men in the entire world.[52]

Herder's embrace of a cosmopolitan and utopian order is another example of masonic language being employed to promote
the ideal of a vibrant form of civil society. This order, too, is perfectly in keeping with the logic of the secular impulse visible by
1700, and it fosters attention to civil society and the state. In the
wake of the Revolution—an event that the far right blamed on
the philosophes and freemasons—Herder sees in freemasonry
a secular way toward progressive reform. He was not alone in
looking to the German lodges as places where the new democratic ideals could be realized.[53]

While Continental men could bond with one another in the
fashionable lodges, women could visit and they could read. For
those who turned to the new and progressive ideas of the age,
an affection for English texts—provided they had the education to read in a second language—opened up another world,
rather as travel had done for Herder.

The Spectator, a daily journal that appeared first in London in
June 1711 and lasted only eighteen months, offered commentary
and moralizing, as well as gossip and wit on the politics of the
day. It expressly courted a female readership, which extended
to educated French women who knew English. Louise-Suzanne
Curchod (b. 1737), the wife of the famous finance minister Jacques Necker and mother of the equally famous Madame de
Staël (b. 1766), read a later version of it avidly. It prodded her

to begin her own journal, which she said would have various themes and include literary criticism, in the first instance on the published correspondence of Voltaire.

Suzanne Necker wanted to create the "interior spectator," an interior mirror of the exterior world, a register of "all sorts of useful things... [and it will be] a chronicle of our affections, our gratitude, fortune, health and happiness." Except for the Bible, such a journal would render all other moral guides superfluous; it would provide a way of thinking for one's self. Mme. Necker was a Protestant who would enlighten herself through the interiority of the self and the study of the world. She was a theist, however, and never dabbled in the materialism fashionable in the salons of her day.[54]

Herder traveled; Mme Necker read in English and French. Both found ways to relate to the intellectual innovations of the age. Necker worshiped Voltaire and originated the proposal for a statue of him by Houdon. Done in 1778, the bust became world famous and now resides in the Metropolitan Museum in New York.[55] Herder, as we know, was engaged in an interior conversation with Montesquieu. Both used enlightened principles to sort out the meaning of the French Revolution, but at a safe distance from Paris.

Some of the women and men on the fringes of Parisian *salon* life, or freemasonry, found themselves in the midst of the revolution, and they stepped up to the challenge and opportunities that it offered. The Creole poet Évariste Parny, born in 1753 on the French Caribbean Island of Bourbon but educated in Paris, developed a radically secular and anti-clerical voice that Voltaire admired, and it made him famous among his contemporaries.

Parny's erotic poetry appeared in 1778 and became an instant success.[56] It revealed a tender and passionate love for a woman back on the Island of Bourbon, where paternal opposition forbade their marriage. Perhaps it was experiences like the one with the tyrannical father that drew Parny to support openly the American revolutionaries. Or perhaps it was his meeting with Benjamin Franklin, also a member of the Lodge of the Nine Sisters in Paris, that made him sympathetic. Parny had joined the lodge in 1776 or 1777, and Franklin was made its "Venerable Master" in 1779. To Parny, the Americans were "heroes of Albion," who were ushering in the birth of liberty. They did so in the face of "the inexorable tyranny" of the European monarchs. Parny also became a lifelong opponent of slavery, which he had witnessed firsthand on his father's Caribbean estate.[57]

Clearly inspired by revolutions against tyranny, Parny nevertheless kept a low political profile during the French Revolution. He was nowhere as reluctant when it came to his views on religion. His *War of the Gods* (*La Guerre des Dieux*), a deeply anti-Christian poem published in 1799, could not have been published safely in the old regime. Despite some official hostility from Napoleon, who was trying to negotiate a concordat with the pope, Parny prevailed and was elected a member of the prestigious Institute of France. His reputation was sealed for much of the nineteenth century. By the twentieth, he had become *un illustre inconnu* and so he remains to this day—a trajectory exactly the opposite of Herder's.

The Catholic Church put *La Guerre* on the Index of Forbidden Books in 1817 and largely kept it there into the 1840s. The Index was abolished only in the 1960s. In Russia, Parny had much greater influence, and as late as 1970 a translation of *La Guerre* appeared in Leningrad. Some of his poetry was also translated by Herder, and in the twentieth century a few of his poems were set to music by Ravel. In the last century, its anti-clericalism and disdain for religion survived in the Soviet Union and in European circles on the Communist Left.

The war about which the poet sings is between the pagan and Christian deities. Introducing Jesus, the poet describes him as "this poor devil, son of a pigeon" (keeping in mind that the Holy Spirit is most commonly and symbolically represented as a dove), and he is joined by Mercury, chief among the pagan deities.[58] The Virgin Mary makes her appearance along with "Jeune Panther," "the object of my tenderness" and a figure who in Talmudic tradition is said to be the natural father of Jesus.[59] All sing and dance, eat heartily, and converse, with Mary assuming a voice equal to that of God the Father, Christ, and the Holy Spirit. This is pagan naturalism with a vengeance, and contemporaries recognized it as such.

Many of these small voices from the eighteenth century remain relatively unknown to our day. In some cases, we rely on unpublished manuscripts to form an acquaintance with them. They speak without assuming that they are in the vanguard of a movement of ideas that will transform Western thinking on a wide variety of topics. They are therefore all the more valuable because they allow us to see the "seepage" of ideas in an age that was coming to terms with the discovery of the world's peoples, with religious conflict, and with vast differences in the wealth of regions close to home or far away. These ordinary voices also display a willingness to inspect and embrace the new and the foreign, even to endorse revolutionary reform.

4

Paris and the Materialist Alternative

THE WIDOW STOCKDORFF

WITHIN BOUNDLESS SPACE AND TIME, enlightened lives unfolded, and they did so more commonly in cities rather than the countryside. The most densely urban area in Western Europe existed in the space between Amsterdam and Paris. Therein, various European languages could be found—Dutch, French, and German in Maastricht, for example—but the bulk of the population was French speaking. While not being French, the whole of the southern Netherlands—first owned by Spain and then Austria—was francophone. This was territory overseen by the Catholic Church and as a result heavily censored. By comparison, until the 1760s Brussels was a harder place to promote heretical literature than Paris.

Yet France was one of the most heavily censored states in Western Europe. The French monarchy would not permit the Roman Catholic Inquisition to operate within its borders, but nothing stopped its own censors from achieving a similar effect. Works that concerned religion were especially inspected, but the censoring gaze extended also to almanacs, racy accounts of life and love, and even to general histories of countries or military heroes. The French edition of John Locke's *Essay Concerning Human Understanding*, published in Amsterdam, was forbidden to cross the border into France. This repressive system was the handiwork of the regime of Louis XIV (d. 1715), and it was relaxed only in the mid-eighteenth century.[1] In 1685, the same king stopped religious toleration for Protestants and promulgated the repressive *Code Noir* in the French slave colonies. The vast majority of the censors were drawn from elite circles of the literary establishment. And by century's end, their numbers had expanded from "four in 1658, . . . 41 in 1727, 73 in 1745, 82 in 1751, 119 in 1760, 128 in 1763, and 178 in 1789." There were lucrative gains for the highly literate, for university professors or journalists.[2] The censorship could be for content or style, and its application, deeply arbitrary.[3]

All these forms of repression were intended to support royal absolutism, and they complicate any effort to find the origins of the Enlightenment in France. By far the best place to look for it must be Paris, the largest French city with a population of over 600,000 in 1700. Spy reports offer one tangible way into the *demi-monde* of Paris and its sites for subversive ideas. In the reign of Louis XIV, the police and spy reports reveal officials of church and state most preoccupied with religious heretics— that is, Protestants, Jansenists, Quietists, and so on. In his youth, Jean-Jacques Rousseau fell afoul of the censors when a trunk he was forwarding to himself was confiscated at the French border. He lost everything because a Jansenist flysheet had been found in his shirt pocket. The Jansenists were austere critics of church luxury and clerical corruption, and uniformly interpreted by the authorities as enemies of the monarchy.[4]

Despite the audacity of the Jansenists, they were not the harbingers of secular thought, regardless of the amount of grief they caused. They were deeply pious and not particularly interested in the new science. To look for the early stirring of enlightened ideas appearing in French, we must leave Paris and journey north to the French Protestants in the Dutch Republic. En route, we may pass through Liège, controlled by an absentee bishop, French speaking, and a place where naughty books could be published.[5] The freer presses in parts of the Low Countries, combined with French-language exiles, brought enlightened ideas into the French linguistic orbit. The best judgment a recent historian can make about the first two decades of the century in Paris notes the existence of an underground "counter culture in the French capital."[6]

We can identify a dozen French-speaking men and at least one woman who took maximum advantage of the freedom accorded Dutch publishers. Exiles such as Pierre Bayle, Anne-Marguerite Dunoyer, Jacques Bernard, Jean Frederic Bernard (who fled as a child), Prosper Marchand, Bernard Picart, Nicolas Gueudeville, and Jean Rousset de Missy took the political battle against French absolutism into an international arena. They were primarily, but not exclusively, journalists who wanted to disseminate news about, and throughout the Republic of Letters.[7] And not least, having been forced into exile (sometimes—like Marchand and Picart—they went voluntarily), they were deeply angry.

Written from the safety of Rotterdam, Bayle's *Dictionnaire historique et critique* (1697) used skepticism, satire, irony, and great erudition to mock Louis XIV, to give a lengthy explication of the thought of Spinoza, to suggest that even atheists could be good people. In the process, the refugee Bayle invented the encyclopedic format imitated so brilliantly two generations later by Diderot and d'Alembert in their *Encyclopèdie* (1751). Bayle gloried in the new science, believed in the English system of government, and took a dim view of orthodoxy, whether

Catholic or Protestant. Other refugees revered him as their "Patriarch."[8] The dictionary went through multiple editions throughout the eighteenth century and appears in English in 1710. It was translated and protected by French refugees like Prosper Marchand, editor of the 1720 edition.

Bayle died in 1704, and a younger generation of refugees grew into prominence. Marchand, one of the editors of Bayle, also had ties with the English freethinkers John Toland and Anthony Collins, from whom he learned about the nature of English government. Manuscripts found in Toland's papers reveal that Marchand belonged to a club or masonic lodge in embryo—we will never know its exact nature. Complete with "brothers," a "Grand Master," and meeting under the statutes of its "constitutions," the society included Charles Levier and probably Rousset de Missy. In 1710, when the record was written, these two can be associated with bringing into the world the most outrageous text of the entire century, *Le Traité des trois imposteurs*. It labeled Jesus, Moses, and Mohammed as the impostors and equated God with nature. Working within the same Francophone circle, Levier brought out the first printed edition in 1719.[9]

Le Traité caused such scandal that the Dutch authorities, who never bothered much with French-language books, confiscated every copy they could find. Only about two survive at this time. Nevertheless, its manuscript circulation throughout Europe became widespread, and only later in the century was *Le Traité* again published—predictably by Marc Michel Rey operating out of Amsterdam. His wife was the daughter of Jean Frederic Bernard, from whom she learned about the book trade, and she conducted a lively relationship with one of Rey's other authors, the soon to become famous Jean-Jacques Rousseau.

The diaspora of Huguenots brought their publishers, journalists, and writers into prominence. Having fled France in 1701,

Anne-Marguerite Dunoyer (d. 1719) lived by the fruits of her pen. Her first contribution, *Lettres historiques et galantes* (1707), claimed to be published by the phony imprint "Pierre Marteau," and it helped introduce the spectatorial genre into the French language. Following *Lettres*, Dunoyer published *Quintessence des nouvelles historiques, politiques, morales et galantes* from 1711 to 1719, and it combined literary news with overt support for the allies' war against Louis XIV. She laid down an ideological template that fitted the political interests of the refugees who crowded into the Republic and whose admiration for Louis XIV's enemies, particularly Britain, only grew under the impact of war. In France, the great political theorist Montesquieu avidly read the journals produced by the Huguenot refugees writing from the safety of the Dutch Republic.

Without exception, the refugees cast a cold eye on the injustices of Louis XIV and his successor as regent to his grandson, the duc d'Orleans.[10] The remaining French Protestant families got out as quickly as they could, and in 1714–15 the Benezet family made their way to Rotterdam, then London, and finally Philadelphia. Sometime after 1731, young Anthony Benezet embraced Quakerism and married a Quaker minister. He began an odyssey that made him one of the first and most fierce opponents of slavery. He collected first-person accounts by traders who could speak directly to the horrors of their trade. He preached and published against the injustice of slavery and its violation of the rights of man. Benezet translated the Huguenot experience of persecution and exile into a universal moral voice against all human injustice.[11]

The trick was to translate rage against monarchy and church into creative energy. Born in the previous generation of refugees, none had greater grievances against the French church and king than Jean Frederic Bernard. His father, pregnant mother, grandmother, and younger brother made their way out of France on foot through the Alps in late 1685. Both the grand-mother and brother would die as a result, and the family was displaced from the area in the south of France where they had resided for decades. The men in the family had been pastors, lawyers, professors—in short, part of French intellectual life. Their contacts extended throughout Protestant Europe, and eventually Bernard's family settled in Amsterdam.

Jean Frederic showed no inclination to join the ministry, and his business interests took him in the direction of publishing. In 1704, he went to Geneva, not as a student of theology but to make a living in the book trade. He was then apprenticed to a Huguenot dynasty of publishers in Amsterdam, family relations of his future friend, Pierre Humbert. In Geneva, with the help of his Swiss relations, his Amsterdam contacts, and their interna-tional network, he set up a brokerage business. Books formed an important part of the business, but soon Bernard became active in other markets as well. An ideal profession for those who had little capital but an extensive set of connections, brokerage meant long-distance trade. Such trade was a matter of trust, and only well-connected brokers could supply that trust. Before long, Jean Frederic established an important clientele in books and other commodities. Even Pierre Bayle made use of his services. In 1707, Bernard returned to Amsterdam to continue the brokerage busi-ness. He lived in lodgings, renting a separate warehouse from which he ran his firm. In 1711, he decided that he had enough cap-ital to become a full-scale member of the booksellers' guild and a publisher.[12] Note that by 1700 about half the books published in Continental Europe came from the Dutch Republic.

Bernard's first published work, *Réflexions morales, satiriques et comiques sur les moeurs de notre siècle*, appeared anonymously in 1711, and it too was supposedly published by Pierre Marteau. In a later edition, Bernard listed himself as the publisher. With wit and sarcasm, Bernard examined human habits and follies aided by a Persian philosopher who, spending time in Europe, wrote about "our *moeurs*." The visitor found that riches offer a cover to conceal vices, and the treatment he meted out to God errs on the side of anthropomorphizing.[13]

Throughout, the focus is on kings and noblemen—the setting is not Dutch but French—and the Persian visitor casts a cold eye on "the Infidels," which is what he called the Europeans. "The wolves . . . have an exterior *politesse* that admirably hides their natural savagery."[14] They cannot be trusted. Their systems of government, whether monarchy or republic, are also capable of being abused. One characteristic seems to dominate the human condition: *l'amour propre*, which is a proud self-regard and accompanies self-interest. Both suit ruthless competition and arrogant self-promotion, but not amicable social experiences.

Only a few European cities offer an experience that shapes the man of affairs; they can be schools to shape an honorable man. Bernard reserves special praise for Amsterdam, for "the beauty of its streets and the proportions of its houses. Its inhabitants enjoy a simple liberty and live with abundance." In the Republic, Bernard found an economically vibrant place that could be celebrated.[15]

Throughout the reflections, Bernard, in the person of the Persian observer, makes reference to the mores, customs, rituals, religious differences, and *amour propre* of the strange people he has been called upon to assess. Listening carefully to what the text tells us would prepare the reader for Bernard, in conjunction with the soon-to-be-famous and also exiled engraver Bernard Picart, becoming a major chronicler of all the world's religions (see figure 4).

Together, they created a seven-volume, folio-size work that would remain in print for several centuries, *Cérémonies et coutumes religieuses de tous les peuples du monde* [*Religious ceremonies and customs of all the people of the World,* 1723–].[16] In both the

Reflections and then *Religious ceremonies*, Bernard displays his overarching interest in religion and his willingness to relativize and criticize its tenets.

Particularly in the matter of religion, the French refugees in the Dutch Republic blazed an intellectual trail that in turn flourished in the French Enlightenment. They quickly had their imitators. Yet nothing in Bernard's text quite prepared the audience for the immense success of Montesquieu's *Persian Letters* (1721). Born in a chateau in 1689 and to the nobility, Montesquieu received his education from the clerical Oratorians, studied law, and finally at the death of his father in 1713, inherited his title and estate, then married a noblewoman who also happened to be a Protestant. The death of an uncle brought yet another title and the right to take over as the head of the regional *parlement*, a judicial body. There, Montesquieu learned the intricacies of French governmental institutions and their many deficiencies.

Montesquieu had a variety of travel accounts upon which to base the opinions of his fictional Persian travelers, but his greatness lay in his distinctive style and wit. His writing is much more fluid than Bernard's but no less biting. For example, of the French king and the pope, Montesquieu writes,

> there is another magician even more powerful . . . , one who has just as much power over the king's mind as the king, does over his subjects. This magician is called the Pope: he can make people believe that three are but one [the doctrine of the Trinity], that the bread one eats is not bread, and that the wine one drinks is not wine [the sacrament of the Eucharist].[17]

In short, according to Montesquieu, the mysteries of Catholicism are a form of magic.

What other interpretation would one expect from him who, writing a few years after Bernard, has his Persian imagine that the

Jesuits are dervishes? Montesquieu never misses the chance to mock the clergy and puts in the mouth of Usbek, his Persian visitor, sentences such as, "The libertines here [in Paris] support an immense number of prostitutes, while the religiously devout support an immense number of dervishes." The main occupation of the priests is casuistry, and our Persian visitor makes his contempt for their pastime abundantly clear. Montesquieu echoes Bernard in seeing deceit and duplicity as commonplace in Europe, but of course gives his account a Persian inflection: "Anyone who would try to number all the clerics here trying to get their hands on the revenues from a given mosque might as well try to number the grains of sand on the beach, or the slaves of our monarch."[18] In case the reader doubted the relativism that the author brought to the subject of religion, Montesquieu explains that all people project their own image onto that of their god: blacks see him as black, and the devil as a brilliant white color. "It has been well said that if triangles had a god, they would imagine him as having three sides."[19]

Montesquieu's secular relativism is complex. This is nowhere clearer than in his analysis of the similarities and differences between men and women. Montesquieu was clever enough to know that universalist statements not anchored in actual social experience would never be sufficient. He was fascinated by the extreme differences between the status of women in the West as distinct from the Islamic East. His Persian traveler reports in horror on the "impudence" of European women in contrast to their harem-bound Persian women who exercise an "attractive modesty."[20] A great deal of commentary is spent on European sexual mores, a subject that clearly vexed and fascinated him.

Montesquieu knew that the new science of Descartes and Newton postulated uniform laws at work in matter and its motion. Montesquieu wanted to understand those laws as they are tempered and refined by social experience, by history. He saw the enormous differences in the behavior and status of women and men. Nothing in his social experience allowed that men and women might be equal, yet some commentators have argued that he moved in the direction of a proto-feminism. He was clearly disturbed by the inequities he saw in Europe, or about which he had read in the literature about Islamic cultures. He knew that education was a big part of the disparity between the opportunities, privileges, and status of men over women. He also knew that the uniformity of matter in motion meant that such socially constructed differences had to be explained and relativized.

Montesquieu's approach to the problem and reality of gender inequality was more anthropological than philosophical. He was among the first to postulate that climate had a profound effect on all peoples and, not least, on men and women. In all of his writings, this is a theme to which he will return time and time again. The cold allows the blood to circulate better, and in such places people can be stronger than those consigned to hot climates. In them, "the number of dervishes or monks seems to increase together with the warmth of the climate."[21] Liberty would arise among the stronger, first and foremost. Yet sometimes, the weaker can prevail by virtue of their character.

Montesquieu had no illusions about the brutality of human nature. He has the dying wife of Usbek, Roxane, writing from her Persian harem, say in her final words to him, "How could you ever have thought that I was credulous enough to believe I was put in this world to adore you and your whims? That while you permitted everything for yourself, you had the right to thwart all my desires? No: I was able to live in that servitude, but I was always free."[22] Sometimes a moral imperative can triumph over physical impediments.[23]

Montesquieu possessed a veritable obsession about human freedom, its nature, the forms it takes in monarchies, aristocracies, and democracies, and the many ways it could be abused. Political liberty, so central to his concerns, was to be found "only in moderate governments . . . it is there only when there is no abuse of power . . . in societies directed by laws . . . liberty is a right of doing whatever the laws permit."[24] In search for the spirit of liberty and the ways to protect it, Montesquieu prescribed a three-part division of governing authority: executive, legislative, and judicial. The results of his prescription are well known from the American Constitution, written late in the century. Montesquieu sought a system of moderate government institutionalized by checks and balances. In such a system, privileged elites would naturally rule.[25] Some of the American founders began as deeply respectful of Montesquieu only later in life to see his shortcomings.[26] Perhaps they came to understand that Montesquieu had given his support to the French monarchy as the only guarantor of stability and the rule of law.[27]

He also spent much ink discussing the nature of punishments: there can be no arbitrary decisions, no capricious legislators, only punishments "founded on reason." Montesquieu cast a cold eye on punishments that derive from "public hatred." His vision included the treatment meted out to "criminals" born out of religious hatred and superstition:

> It is very odd that these three crimes, witchcraft, heresy, and that against nature [homosexuality], of which the first might easily be proved not to exist; the second to be susceptible of an infinite number of distinctions, interpretations, and limitations; the third to be obscure and uncertain—it is very odd, I say, that this three crimes should amongst us be punished with fire.[28]

Montesquieu was far more interested in the nature of good government than he was in punishing people for their private beliefs or intimate actions. As a result, religiously motivated critics saw his approach to religion as defective, if not heretical.

The emphasis on climate also provoked a critical response. We might see it as a formula that would lead to racism or as a justification for African slavery, and we might expect that critics would repudiate such conclusions. Indeed, the subject of human equality, or inferiority, vexed all the philosophes—nowhere more so than in Scotland. However, one of the leading lights of its Enlightenment, David Hume, concluded that "there never was a civilized nation of any other complexion than white."[29] His racism has troubled all admirers of eighteenth-century enlightened intellectual life. By the lifetimes of Hume and Montesquieu, the Western empires had wreaked considerable damage, the consequences of which we still experience. Hume wrote in ways that ignored the damage.

By contrast, Montesquieu focused largely on the means by which Europeans might liberate themselves. Moral causes, and not physical ones as Montesquieu would have it, shaped the peoples of the world. Only late in the century did the leaders of enlightened thought finally find a way out of the dark tunnel vision of racism. Led by the Quakers, the Anglophone world produced a phalanx of abolitionists whose arguments against slavery stretched across the Atlantic to the American colonies and beyond. Various French philosophes—Diderot and Raynal, for example—joined in the attack.

First, theorists needed to find the best forms of government. After examining ancient and modern texts about politics and government, particularly from the seventeenth-century English revolution, Montesquieu believed that England possessed the form of government he could endorse. This conviction put him front and center into one of the preoccupations of Enlightenment thinkers: Anglo-philia. Bayle and the Huguenot refugees first fed the flames of devotion to post-1688 Britain, and by the time Montesquieu waxed eloquently, Voltaire had already told the best stories about the England he had come to love. He paved the way for Montesquieu's reading of English history and mores.

Between 1726 and 1729, when in London and after, Voltaire penned an amazing set of letters concerning the English nation.[30] He billed them as necessarily private at first, reluctantly released to an eager public. In fact, it was his target all along. The *Letters* appeared first in English in 1733 and the following year in French as *Lettres philosophiques*. They were an instant success.

Voltaire's passion to know all things English began with the variety of its religions, followed by government, trade, Newtonian science, *belles lettres*, and not least, the honor the English accorded to their writers and intellectuals. Like the volumes by Bernard and Picart—Voltaire had met him during a trip to Holland—Voltaire's letters give favorable coverage to the most cerebral forms of Christianity, even to the Quakers. In an enlightened taxonomy of sects, they were normally seen as "enthusiasts," but in Voltaire's account they are presented as reasonable, having no clergy nor sacraments, and spurning the trappings of wealth and self-regard. The pluralism of sectarian life met his approval, "An Englishman, as one to whom liberty is natural, may go to heaven his own way."[31]

Voltaire regarded the Church of England as too close to Catholicism for his taste; intensely disliked the Presbyterians, but true to his penchant for the cerebral, he thought that the Socinians or Unitarians had got religion about right:

the principles of Arius [anti-Trinitarianism] begin to revive, not only in England, but in Holland and Poland. The celebrated Sir Isaac Newton honored this opinion so far as to countenance it. This philosopher thought that the Unitarians

argued more mathematically than we do. But the most san-
guine stickler for Arianism is the illustrious Dr. Clarke. This
man is rigidly virtuous, and of a mild disposition, is fonder of
his tenets than desirous of propagating them, and absorbed
so entirely in problems and calculations that he is a mere
reasoning machine.[32]

Indeed, everything about Newton's science pleased Voltaire
and his partner, Madame du Châtelet. Her French translation
of Newton's *Principia* is still considered definitive. There were
many British Newtonians, aided by Dutch converts, who spread
Newton's science in classrooms and journals, or in private experimental demonstrations in Scotland, France, as well as the
Low Countries. However, no one quite equaled Voltaire's witty
propaganda that was backed up by his own understanding of
Newton's science.[33] Châtelet's understanding of physics and
her debt to the German natural philosophy of Leibniz made a
serious but unattributed contribution to Diderot's *Encyclopédie*.
It has required modern computers to find her text anonymously
copied into various of its essays on "the pendulum," "space,"
"gravity," and so on.[34]

Being a Newtonian became one of the defining characteristics of the philosophe. Even in France, being conversant with
Newtonian mechanics and optics signaled a truly educated person who had turned his or her back on what was taught in the
schools and universities. There the clergy controlled the philosophy curriculum, and it was either Aristotelian—as interpreted
by the medieval St. Thomas Aquinas—or by the 1730s, Cartesian in a few places. The Jesuits who controlled the plurality
of French *colleges* continued to reject Newtonian science until
their expulsion from France in 1762. As one historian has put it,
"If Newton finally triumphed in France, it was over the corpse

of the Jesuit order."[35] In 1762–63, Adam Smith in Glasgow and Edinburgh regularly taught his students: "the Newtonian method is undoubtedly the most philosophical, and in every science, whether of Morals or Natural Philosophy, etc. is vastly more ingenious ... more engaging, than [the Aristotelian]."[36]

Newtonian natural philosophy, despite the best efforts of some of Newton's followers, offered no real antidote against irreligion and materialism. In no other part of Western Europe did clandestine literature play as big a role as it did in the French Enlightenment. To be sure, such literature could be found throughout Europe, in various languages. But French was the foreign language known by Continental and British elites more than any other. Through that linguistic avenue Newtonianism also entered, albeit frequently dressed in heretical garments.

Toland's *Letters to Serena* (London, 1704) appeared in clandestine French translations, and it linked Newton's theory of universal gravitation to the subversive idea that motion is inherent in matter. Such materialism, or pantheism as Toland named it, had a clear debt to Spinoza's notion of God as Nature, but also to the pagan naturalism of the late Renaissance most easily found in the writings of Giordano Bruno. These were texts that Toland knew well.[37] Thus in French, as it appeared in the clandestine literature, and also in journals coming from the French exiles in the Dutch Republic, Newtonian science entered European thought tied—in a manner that horrified Newton, Clarke, and their many followers—to a deeply threatening materialism.

By 1750, French texts promoting the new science and reform in general never shed the identification with religious subversion. The so-called High Enlightenment, with its home in Paris, gave pride of place to materialists like Diderot, D'Holbach, Helvétius, and a host of other materialists, some of them anonymous. Voltaire was horrified—his deism never admitted atheism, implicit or explicit, nor materialism. So too Montesquieu never partook in such impiety. But the leading French Newtonian of the 1740s, Pierre-Louis Moreau de Maupertuis, wrote a scandalously pornographic and materialist tract, *Venus physique*, that owed many philosophical debts—to Leibniz, Spinoza, as well as Newton—and succeeded in linking the new science and natural philosophy of the seventeenth century to the most extreme forms of irreligion found in the eighteenth.[38]

Precisely at midcentury, the French presses were flooded with materialist books. Some anonymous, like *Thérèse philosophe* (1748), combined the pornographic with materialist philosophy—all as described by the prostitute who never took money, Therese. It included raunchy and explicit engravings, and the commentary introduced the sex lives of father-confessors, nuns, noblemen, and of course, Therese herself. As she explains the mechanics of sex, "It is the arrangement of the organs, the dispositions of the fibers, a certain movement, the liquids, which make up the genre of the passions . . . nature is uniform."[39]

Little was left to the imagination, and the Paris authorities arrested everyone they could find connected with the book, even the women who sewed together the pages and distributed the book.[40] They constituted just a few of the many practitioners of the mechanical arts, looked down upon by elites, but vital to what has been called the "artisanal Enlightenment." To this day, we do not know their names, but then neither are we entirely sure who wrote *Thérèse*, although the Marquis d'Argens has his name attached to it. Across the Channel and in the same year, another pornographic work, *Fanny Hill* by John Cleland, was found to be equally shocking in matters sexual and philosophical. There, no one went to prison for it.[41]

French materialism had many sources: Spinoza writing in the Dutch Republic, other seventeenth-century philosophers like

Hobbes, exiled Huguenots and English freethinkers, a perverse reading of Newtonian science, and not least a bitter anti-clericalism that believed the only way to rob the clergy of their power was to deny the very existence of a spiritual realm. Early in the century in the Dutch Republic, the creators of *The Treatise on the Three Impostors* summed up the materialist take on God and religion:

> this chimerical fear of invisible powers is the source of the Religions which each form after his own fashion. Those to whom it mattered that the people be contained & arrested by such dreamings have fostered this seed of religion, have made a law of it, & have finally reduced the peoples by the terrors of the future, to obeying blindly.[42]

There were roots also in the naturalism that surfaced in the Renaissance and can be associated with Boccaccio, Rabelais, Aretino, Machiavelli, and Bruno. Gradually, this form of materialism was replaced by one derived from the mechanical philosophy of the new science, and on occasion the clandestine texts even made reference to Descartes or Hobbes.[43] By 1800, materialist metaphysics of the natural and social sciences had been laid out, and following that achievement came Comte, Marx, and Darwin. Without a specific philosophical commitment to materialism, nevertheless all the natural and social sciences from that time onward excluded any appeal to divine intervention to explain the subject of their inquiries.

Enter the Widow Stockdorff, Book Merchant from Strasbourg

As we saw, secular lives, however obscure, have much to tell us about the nature of the Enlightenment. So too do booksellers, especially if they specialized in the materialist and pornographic and had the misfortune to be imprisoned in the Bastille for their illegal trade. Such was the widow Stockdorff from Strasbourg, who journeyed to Paris in 1771 in the company of two abbés. She was on the trail after only heretical, irreligious, and scandalous books. Her book bag, as well as her shopping list, when confiscated by the authorities, offer a rare window into the universe of forbidden books.

The widow knew what she was doing, and she assembled just about every forbidden book known at the time. They reward careful examination and offer superb insight into the subversive power of the materialist tradition. Out of it came the metaphysical foundations of the human and natural sciences. The widow's central role in the traffic earned her two years in the Bastille, where she left behind a dossier of letters—some in her native German—that pry open a world that was trying very hard not to be seen into by the police.

The genre of materialist works must be broadly defined to include the rabidly anticlerical and anti-Catholic. Into that category came works out of the English republican tradition—by the 1720s sometimes identified as the "country" opposition—and found on the Continent written by the exiled Henry St. John, Viscount Bolingbroke. His British political life need not be recounted here—suffice it to say "complex" would be an understatement. What the widow and her buying public, who knew little about Bolingbroke's domestic politics, found in *L'examen important de Milord Bolingbroke* was an attack on religious fanaticism, priests, and Catholicism. Indeed, so central was religion that the discerning reader might have suspected the real author to have been none other than Bolingbroke's good friend, Voltaire. The book claimed to date from 1736, but in fact it was published in 1771, the year the widow and her traveling abbés landed in the Paris book market. In the same year, the Roman Catholic Inquisition put *L'examen* on the Index of Forbidden Books, noting that "it judges, attacks, condemns and lacerates one after the other book in the Old and New Testament, the dogmas that are essential to the Christian faith, the doctrine of the Fathers of the Church."[44]

It is doubtful that the widow knew about the condemnation, but had she, the book would only have been more eagerly sought. The widow's list and inventory are among the best evidence we have that contemporaries recognized the *genre* of the forbidden and knew exactly what belonged in it. In short, historians have not invented the category; it was there at least by the 1770s and we suspect before.

To begin with the most famous examples, we need only consult the list of what she owned and for what she was shopping. Of course, she wanted to buy *Thérèse philosophe*, and under it she listed *La fille de joie*, the French title of Cleland's *Fanny Hill*. The only problem with that title is, as far as the French national library can ascertain, the first published edition of the French translation was around 1776. Either there is an earlier edition missed by bibliographers, or the widow had in mind a manuscript about which she had heard and knew she wanted to buy. Either way, her shopping list shows expertise and a keen eye for what would sell.

The widow was not put off by the scandalous reputation of an author. She sought out *La Chandelle d'Arras* by the defrocked priest Henri DuLaurens, which approached sex and religion with the same comic and satirical *esprit*.[45] She would also traffic in "old" books that were hard to come by. Into that category we must put the first work ever to describe the new style of philosophizing, called *Le Philosophe*. It appeared anonymously, probably with a phony imprint on its title page, "Amsterdam, 1743." From that title came the habit of describing the leading thinkers of the Enlightenment as *philosophes*.

In the 1740s, *le philosophe* became *engagé*. Dedicated to the memory of the English freethinker and republican Anthony

Collins, *Le Philosophe* [*The Philosopher*] was probably written in Paris. The tract proclaimed *le philosophe* as one of those special people who saw through popular errors. One in particular required eradication. *Le philosophe* had figured out that God does not exist, and in his place, one should put "civil society . . . the only deity he will recognize on earth."[46]

By being dedicated to a notorious English republican, *Le Philosophe* signaled an international cosmopolitanism, as well as an active engagement with change in the political order. Its anonymity confirmed that its atheism still lay on the fringe, at the margin of acceptable opinion—even among the self-fashioned who imagined themselves as enlightened. The linkage between *Le Philosophe* and English freethinking only added to the bona fide credentials of the tract. It was a taste of what was coming in the world of clandestine publishing.

In the 1770s and subsequently, the most famous materialist work was (and is) the Baron d'Holbach's *The System of Nature*, first published in 1770. It sought to discover the moral and physical laws of nature that governed humankind: "The source of man's unhappiness is his ignorance of Nature." It worked on the premise that just as there are laws of motion that govern matter, so too human beings are also governed—however ignorant they may be of the laws at work in their fate.[47] The highest human duty is to dispel the ignorance that clouds the mind. There are plenty of forces arrayed to stop the search for truth: "the insupportable chains which tyrants, which priests have forged for most nations. To error must be equally attributed that abject slavery into which the people of almost every country have fallen. Nature designed they should pursue their happiness by the most perfect freedom." And the Baron d'Holbach has come to their rescue; the widow Stockdorff happy to assist.

D'Holbach sets out the basic principles that govern the human condition:

> Man is a being purely physical: the moral man is nothing more than this physical being considered under certain point of view; that is to say, with relation to some of his modes of action, arising out of his individual organization. But is not this organization itself the work of Nature?

Once human beings realize their entirely material condition, they will pursue pleasure and avoid pain:

> The *civilized man*, is he whom experience and sociality have enabled to draw from nature the means of his own happiness. . . . The *enlightened man* is man in his maturity, in his perfection; who is capable of advancing his own felicity, because he has learned to examine, to think for himself, and not to take that for truth upon the authority of others.[48]

To seal the truth of these materialist maxims, d'Holbach assures his readers—as did Toland from whom he was lightly plagiarizing—that all these principles come from the great Newton. They work as follows:

> SELF-GRAVITATION: NEWTON calls it INERT FORCE: moralists denominate it in man, SELF-LOVE which is nothing more than the tendency he has to preserve himself—a desire of happiness—a love of his own welfare—a wish for pleasure—a promptitude in seizing on everything that appears favorable to his conservation—a marked aversion to all that either disturbs his happiness, or menaces his existence—primitive sentiments, that are common to all beings of the human species; all their faculties are continually striving to satisfy them; all their passions, their wills,

their actions, have them eternally for their object and their end. This self-gravitation, then, is clearly a necessary disposition in man, and in all other beings; which, by a variety means, contribute to the preservation of the existence they have received, as long as nothing deranges the order of their machine, or its primitive tendency.[49]

D'Holbach produced a veritable science-based bible for materialists, and those who followed him laid out a philosophy that licensed living in this world because there is no other. Notice how the *amour propre* that so offended Bernard, writing at the beginning of the century, has been transformed into a love of pleasure. Materialism offered liberation from the strictures that religion imposed on human nature. At the time and subsequently, the materialist impulse has been equated with ruthless self-promotion, with an amoral will to power. Bernard came from good Protestant stock; few of the French philosophes had any familiarity with religion other than the Catholic Church and its legally protected clergy. This was the context that pushed the Enlightenment's French leaders into a virulent campaign against the Church, its leaders, and its doctrines.

The intellectual climate in France changed at midcentury. Censorship relaxed, and texts that had been written earlier managed now to find a publisher. We saw that with the publication date of Voltaire's *Examen* supposedly by Bolingbroke. Increasingly, nothing was sacred. Nicolas Fréret wrote his *Lettre de Thrasybule à Leucippe* in the 1720s, when it became a clandestine manuscript of atheistic materialism and critical-historical biblical scholarship, first published in the 1760s. Cleverly, he turns the tables on the traditional claim that divine revelation was authenticated by prophecies and miracles: he remarks that the Jews were more obedient to God after the return from the Babylonian captivity, despite the lack of miracles, whereas their worst disobedience to God had come in earlier times, when miracles were (allegedly) in plentiful supply. His conclusion is that the miracles had never happened. The significantly new factor occurred after captivity; the Jewish people had, for the first time, come under the spell of a Scripture claiming that they had so succumbed: "Those miracles . . . were inserted after the event into a history which, as they admit, was compiled by the person—Ezra—who led them back from Babylon, who established their new government, rebuilt their city with the temple of their God, and determined the form of their religion, which had been entirely abolished."[50]

Voltaire almost certainly knew *Lettre de Thrasybule à Leucippe*, and it inspired his own *Sermon des cinquante*.[51] It contained a violent attack on the veracity of the Scriptures, and advocated a purely deistic natural religion to supplant Christianity. Although not materialist as such, it made its way onto Madam Stockdorff's list. Various of Voltaire's philosophe colleagues laid the book at his doorstep, but he always denied his paternity. It also had circulated as a manuscript for many years before its publication after 1760.

The same year as *The Sermon of the Fifty*, another text by Voltaire—again one that he denied was his—appeared, *La pucelle d'Orleans*. The maid of Orleans was the common name for Joan of Arc, the patron saint of France. This mock-heroic poem had circulated in manuscript form and as such it was an instant success. Voltaire's irony treated Joan as courageous to be sure, but also as sexually desirable. She was always depicted as a virgin; in Voltaire's hands the story became, "But greatest of these rare exploits you'll hear. Was, that she kept virginity—a year." We can imagine that the widow sold many copies of *La pucelle*, assuming that she was able to procure and send them back to Strasbourg before she was arrested. Her list lumped it with the pornographic.

We know from her Bastille dossier that she was also trading in the Dutch Republic. It possessed a significant Jewish population, as well as being Protestant, and we can only wonder how some of these poems and tracts would have been received. One element in the forbidden literature centered on the Jews and the accusation that they, more than any other ancient people, had infected the Western world with superstitious stories, then summarized in the Old and New Testaments.[52]

The slur never escaped its anti-Semitic associations and left the French philosophes open to the charge that they had failed to escape the common prejudices of the clergy. Voltaire in particular has been seen to have a prejudice against Jews, but given that Voltaire had so many prejudices—against the clergy, various Christian doctrines like the Trinity, the authorities that persecuted Protestants—it is hard to know what emotions lay behind his comments. The *Sermon* was his most dangerous blasphemy, and could Voltaire have been proven to be its author, prison would probably have been his fate. Certainly, in 1762 it was the most sustained attack on the Scriptures and Christian doctrine that had ever appeared in print.[53]

Perhaps inevitably, the multiple criticisms of French life and society fostered a new way of writing and thinking, what came to be classified as utopian literature. *Discours sur l'apocalipse l'an 2440* (1771) made its way to the widow's list of the principal books for which she searched in Paris. It was a well-told tale written by Louis-Sebastien Mercier that moved "utopian" thinking from a perfect society frozen in time to one created by human beings in historical secular time and capable of even further perfectibility. Mercier's novel, set in the year 2440, imagined Paris with an enlightened populace, without clergy or aristocracy, that read only the philosophes. So too, Mercier portrays a global order where European technology and values have become universal. The novel became perhaps most famous for its repudiation of slavery and the endorsement of abolition. In fact, Mercier changed his views many times subsequently, yet what captured the popular imagination concerned his vision of human liberation and endless progress.

So confident was Mercier that in 1789, he claimed that his novel had foreseen the French Revolution. One of the few philosophes to live through the Revolution and escape the slaughter of the Terror, Mercier became an apologist for French colonialism. But in 1771, the widow could hardly have foreseen his imperialist evolution, and we can imagine that she made a tidy profit from an immensely popular book that the Church put on its Index of Forbidden Books two years after it was first published.[54]

In 1791, Mercier embraced the principles of the French Revolution and enlisted Rousseau (d. 1778) to the cause. Rousseau, he said, had seen through the indomitable pride of the old aristocracy, its impertinent prejudices, and unlike Voltaire, he had seen the wisdom to be found in a purely natural religion, one entirely compatible with Scripture and "christianity." At the same time, Rousseau attacked superstition as an "anti-social barbarity." According to Mercier, he respected women and the elderly and saw both as essential for the well-being of the state. Last, Rousseau's *Social Contract* laid out the fundamental ideas upon which the nation can be now constituted. This was not the Rousseau that everyone would have recognized, then or now.[55] Interestingly, Rousseau was not on the widow's shopping list.

Jean-Jacques Rousseau: The Forceful Combination of Natural Religion and Politics

Few literary genres escaped the brilliance of Rousseau's pen (figure 8). He wrote one of the most widely read treatises on politics, *The Social Contract* (1762); so too his novels were sensations

FIGURE 8. Rousseau, whose writings on society and government
are among the most influential of the age. Maurice Quentin de la
Tour (1704–88) (ID# 70897). Courtesy of Bridgeman Images.

in their day, with *Emile, or Education* (also 1762) perhaps the most famous. He took autobiographical writing to a level of self-consciousness and candor never seen before—and seldom since—with his *Confessions*, published after his death. In all, he searched for the conditions that enhance human virtue, for the universality of human nature and human rights. He said that *Emile* was his greatest book.

It is a good place to begin. Within its most famous section on the beliefs of the Savoyard Vicar, Rousseau laid out his understanding of human nature and virtue. After his death, what had appeared in part IV of *Emile* became a separate book. It was what in the original had garnered him his greatest condemnation, and it offended both Catholic and Protestant censors. Mercier had glossed over its incompatibility with Church teachings, and its repudiation of doctrines beyond reason.

As a denizen of Parisian enlightened circles, Rousseau knew well the fashionable materialism of his day. He broke with it, believing it to be the work of metaphysicians, whom he condemned as sophists. He also knew that materialism would always be a minority report and he wanted to set forth a natural religion that could spread widely, that could speak to people regardless of their education. Furthermore, he spied not a little hypocrisy in the fashionable atheism of his day, "Among believers he is an atheist, and among atheists he affects to be a believer."[56] Perhaps we can better see why Rousseau was not on the widow's shopping list.

Rousseau knew the materialist (and anti-materialist) literature well. He begins his own search for the truth with the Cartesian assertion of his own existence, his existence as a thinking being who can ascertain through his senses the matter around him, whether at rest or in motion. As he perceives both, Rousseau deduces that motion cannot be essential to matter. In addressing the claim first made by one of the main sources of

eighteenth-century materialism—Toland's extrapolation from
Newtonian science—Rousseau takes up the anti-materialist
cause, even invoking Samuel Clarke, one of Toland's first clerical combatants.[57]

Rousseau aimed to demonstrate that "a *Will* gives motion
to the universe, and animates all nature." This first active cause
is God. Rousseau's assertion proclaims him as being a deist,
even a theist, who unlike Voltaire, can imagine God as active
in all life, natural and human, "a beneficent deity."[58] It follows
that man is a free agent, free to do good or evil. We are placed
on earth endowed with liberty, and in the creed of the Savoyard Vicar we can hear the stirring proclamation of *The Social
Contract*: "Man was born free and everywhere he is in chains."
Rousseau's natural religion cannot be separated from his political vision, his "dreaming of democracy."[59]

He wanted for a free people a natural religion that would ed-
ify and could be embraced without the prodding of the clergy.
They describe a divinity "who is a vindictive, partial, jealous,
angry Being."[60] By contrast to their vision, Rousseau proclaims
that "all religions are good and agreeable to God" and they can
be known only through "the dictates of reason."[61] And true
to the vision of all the philosophes, Rousseau proclaims that
"the supreme Being is best displayed by the fixed and unalter-
able order of nature." That far, Newton would have agreed. But
Rousseau would have humankind learn this religion "among
the people." And knowing the travel literature, he is mindful
that one must think carefully, "two-thirds of mankind are neither Jews, Christians, nor Mahometans." Rousseau professes
great reverence for Jesus as God, but he also has great affection
for Socrates. He admonishes his readers, "the love God above
all things, and thy neighbor as thyself, is the substance and summary of the law."[62]

The Savoyard Vicar was a product of Rousseau's mature thinking, and Rousseau claimed that in his youth he met his real-life prototype, the abbé Jean-Claude Gaime. The meeting was in the period when Rousseau was clearly searching for a personal religion, having converted from the Protestantism of his Genevan birth to Catholicism. The need for food and shelter may have facilitated the conversion when he was penniless in Turin. Whatever the cause, Rousseau's frankness about religion, his account in the *Confessions*—like so much in this autobiography—was unprecedented. The Savoyard Vicar also laid out the foundations of the civic religion Rousseau identified as essential if the social contract is to be properly lived and obeyed.[63]

As part of his conversion to Catholicism, Rousseau had to go before the Inquisition to receive absolution for the crime of heresy. He described being seized by "secret terror" but "indignant" when the Inquisitor asked him if his dead mother, being a Protestant, had been damned. He was too frightened to show how the question angered him. By the end of that day, he was dismissed from the seminary for men where he had been converted and had hoped to find a paying job in Turin. He was exhorted to live a good life, given some pocket money, and sent on his way.

Few of the philosophes had such experiences, or if they did, chose not to write about them publicly. If Rousseau's admission of his early conversion was shocking, so too was his description of his sexuality, his sexual awakening, his homoerotic attachment to other young men, his repulsion at homosexual seduction, and last his many passionate encounters with young as well as mature women. He boldly describes his desire for "ladies," not servants like himself. He feels "shame" when passionately aroused; he was "obtuse" to sexual advances, and when faced with his first real sexual experience, he "felt something little short of repugnance and fear."[64]

This emotionally confused young man, given to fits of pique or despair, deeply distrustful of the world, even of his friends, became the most powerful critic of French society, of what came after the French Revolution of 1789 to be called the *ancien régime*. So powerful was his influence that during the Revolution, his bones were disinterred (he died in 1778) and placed in the Pantheon; he became a secular saint forever more. What had Rousseau seen that rendered him such a powerful critic?

All his writings betray a deep disaffection from social hierarchy, from the powerful, the titled, the refined—in short, from his betters. At the same time, he was caught in the trap set by the old order: he wanted the company of the refined and educated: "seamstresses, maids, and little shop girls did not interest me. What I wanted were young ladies. . . . It is not the vanity of condition or rank that attracts me, however, but rather the better-preserved complexion, more beautiful hands, a more graceful appearance, an air of delicacy and neatness about the whole person. . . . Even I find this preference quite absurd; but my heart makes it in spite of myself."[65] Rousseau knew he was in the clutches of his own socially enforced snobbery. He knew that he was attracted to an elite that was capable of being the oppressors of "the wretched populace."[66] In being masters, they actually make themselves "greater slaves."[67] Perhaps Rousseau could see more clearly than most, the contradictions and absurdities of the social order because he had to confront daily the same emotions and confusions in his personal and sexual life.

The conflicting emotions that gripped this young philosophe can partially explain his deep love and attachment to nature. "The wandering life is the one for me," Rousseau confesses, and best experienced amid "rushing streams, rocks, pine trees, dark woods, mountains, rugged tracks to scramble up and down, precipices on either side to fill me with fear."[68] The turn to nature permitted the expression of deep emotions, a way for the self to find authentic and pacific feelings. Rousseau's understanding of nature shaped his political philosophy and enabled him to embrace the Hobbesian contract without the dark vision of the "war of all against all" at its heart. Without nature being beneficent, Rousseau cannot get out of the trap set by Hobbes, nor could he depart from all previous contract theorists by assigning sovereignty to the people and not to the state.

Seldom has a theorist of government put as much faith in the social. In the state of nature, instinct prevails; the individual thinks only of himself. There are gains and losses that occur as we move from the state of nature to that of society:

> What man loses by the social contract is his natural liberty and the absolute right to anything that tempts him and that he can take; what he gains by the social contract is civil liberty and the legal right of property in what he possesses.[69]

We might think that Rousseau has issued a blank and absolute check to anyone who possesses property in a society. But very much unlike Hobbes or Locke, Rousseau had grave reservations about the privileges brought about by property: "the right of any individual over his own estate is always subordinate to the right of the community over everything."[70] In a few sentences, Rousseau bequeathed to the modern world the possibility of communal property being universal and opened the door to the socialists and communists of the nineteenth century. Rousseau left little doubt that he regarded money as inherently corrupting.[71]

In the democracy that Rousseau would have established, the people possessed sovereignty, which is "nothing other than

the general will, [it] can never be alienated."[72] The general will
guarantees the equality of all. It is not the will of the majority;
rather it is the common interest that unites all the people. That
is the truth, however much the authorities and their theorists
like Grotius want us to think the government possesses sovereignty. While factions may still exist, the more the better; thus,
not one of them can get the upper hand. With such precau-
tions in place, the general will "is always enlightened."[73] It is
protected by institutions such as the law and by an education
appropriate for the republican citizen.

Hostile critics spotted in Rousseau's articulation of the "general will" a license for tyranny. That is both a perverse reading of his theory and an incorrect one. This is not to say that
Rousseau's account of the general will can be easily grasped.
It is not one size fits all. Rather, the general will differs from
country to country, and the republican theorist must be clear
about the local institutions that need to be accommodated.
When asked by the Polish state to discuss the best form that
its constitution should take, Rousseau carefully noted that
given the size and power of its aristocracy, their needs must be
accommodated as part of the common interest. Like so many
eighteenth-century theorists of political economy, Rousseau
looked with favor more on the landed than the moneyed, and
on those who worked with their hands. Last, Rousseau insisted
on the need for a common religion, a faith that would bind all
believers. Again, it could vary from state to state, but in most
cases, it would resemble the principles articulated by the Savoyard Vicar, and they would be required. Only religious intolerance would be prohibited.[74] Critics have argued that Rousseau
had in mind a political entity more like the city-state and his
birthplace, Geneva, than a large and multicultural state such
as France. More to the point, he believed that every commu-

nity had to find its own consensus embedded in its history and customs.

French Freemasonry

Given his search for a universal natural religion, it is interesting to note that Rousseau showed no interest in freemasonry. There were lodges in the 1760s that gave orations to the assembled brothers wherein Rousseauian sentiments could be found. Later, others regretted that he had not come to know the fraternity: "If only the unfortunate Rousseau could have known our august assemblies; if only you had enjoyed the sweetness of the union that reigns among us."[75] What could Rousseau possibly have found in these assemblies?

Freemasonry began in Britain during the first two decades of the century. By the 1720s, if not before, it had made its way onto Continental Europe and shortly thereafter to the American colonies. Nowhere more so than in France, the masonic lodges grew in importance and provided an outlet for progressive thought and an alternative to organized religion. At the French Revolution—by the autumn of 1789—the lodges and the philosophes were accused of having formed a conspiracy to bring down the monarchy and the Catholic Church. In effect, the secularism of the Enlightenment, they argued, had caused the French Revolution.[76]

The conspiracy charge stuck, and it became a steady element in far right-wing thinking well into the twentieth century. It had no basis in fact, but conspiracy theorists are seldom bothered by facts. And it is true that after 1815 and the reign of Napoleon, the lodges were spied upon by agents of the restored monarchy.[77] All far right governments in Europe up to 1945, and in Spain until the death of Franco in 1975, cast a cold eye on lodge activity and carried out a propaganda campaign against the freemasons.

In 1738, and again in 1751, the papacy condemned the lodges and forbade Catholics from joining them.[78] The edict proclaimed "the great harm which is often caused by such societies or conventicles not only to the peace of the temporal state but also the well-being of souls." The effect of the condemnation on membership was very limited. In the fifty-plus years after 1750, the number of French lodges had doubled, some had admitted women, and the content of lectures given at lodge meetings could often offer a political message. In that period, some lodges circulated and believed the myth that Cromwell had founded the first lodges.[79] However untrue, the myth enabled them to embrace a revolutionary tradition of English origin.

Quite a few of the famous philosophes, such as Voltaire, Montesquieu, Helvétius, and Benjamin Franklin, became freemasons, while, like Rousseau, Thomas Jefferson saw little of value in the lodge experience. Lodges could be deeply aristocratic and even use religious symbolism—putting a copy of their *Constitutions* on an altar in Strasbourg, for example. Also, displayed in the "sanctuary" of the lodge were silver candelabra, images of the sun and moon, and not least "an altar of antique gold . . . covered by a cloth of red serge . . . enriched by braids and fringes of gold."[80] In this setting with its invocation of the Grand Architect of the Universe, if a brother wanted to find a natural religion, there was little to stop him.

The lodges were liminal spaces where men and some women— although their membership was always controversial—could learn to deliver orations, vote, contribute to charitable causes, and meet relative strangers in an atmosphere that was solemn and at least before dinner, dignified. The lodges could instill reformist values; they could also reward aristocratic patronage and sponsorship. They could be schools of government, even places of worship for those disaffected from traditional religion. Perhaps just as important, on either side of the Channel and in the American colonies, men of different religions could live, if only a few hours a week, in harmony and toleration. While reading the philosophes, they could also live the new, enlightened culture, or at least a version of it.

The Enlightenment in France depended partially on foreign influences, generally coming from England and the Dutch Republic. That does not detract from the brilliance of its leading lights nor the courage of the denizens of its clandestine markets. All were eager to make a profit, to be sure, but they also wanted a different social and political order, a secular order with fewer churchmen, less censorship, more tolerance, and justice for the poor and oppressed. Similar sentiments motivated Thomas Jefferson to separate the clergy from the process of governing. He said that their *esprit de corps* "has been severely felt by mankind, and has filled the history of ten or twelve centuries with too many atrocities not to merit a proscription from meddling with government."[81] The philosophes on either side of the Atlantic encourage us to seek similar goals.

5

The Scottish Enlightenment
in Edinburgh

SEARCHING FOR MATERIALIST or forbidden books amid
the shops of publishers and printers in Scotland is, by and large,
to search in vain. If there was a widow Stockdorff, we have not
found her. Indeed, in the 1690s the authorities did search for
forbidden literature but came up empty-handed. That said, the
eighteenth century in Scotland witnessed a secular Enlightenment as vibrant as what could be found in Paris or London.
Yet it was different.[1]

For one thing, size mattered. The largest city in Scotland
in 1700, Edinburgh, contained probably 40,000 people, and
50,000 to 60,000 by midcentury. Glasgow and Aberdeen, also
associated with the Scottish Enlightenment, were smaller still,
although Glasgow grew rapidly after 1750. Only seven other
towns had populations of more than 5,000. It is much harder
to police thought and behavior in cities with hundreds of
thousands of inhabitants, such as London, Amsterdam, and
Paris. Scotland was also far more rural than either England or
the Dutch Republic, and at the turn of the century possessed
a subsistence economy capable of descending into famine. Its

great landed barons and their clans embodied the remnants of a feudal system, established in Europe after the fall of the Roman Empire. Yet Scotland possessed five universities of medieval origin amid a population in 1700 of barely 1 million. In a city like Edinburgh, the educated elite, among whom we might reasonably expect new ideas to germinate and take hold, can best be described as led by presbyterian clergy and university professors marked by "an extraordinarily high degree of inbreeding and clannishness."[2] The social cohesiveness of the urban elite with its strong ties to the landed gave Scotland a distinctiveness all its own.

The political and intellectual ascendancy of this elite derived from the Revolution of 1688–89. Before it, episcopalians (in England known as Anglicans) legally ruled both church and universities. In Scotland, their loyalism to the Stuart crown—hence to James II (in Scotland known as James VI)—seemed boundless, matched only by their devotion to bishops and hierarchy. In both kingdoms, the Whig party supported the revolution, and hence William of Orange, and there were few enough Scottish episcopalian Whigs. In England, the church had split, and the majority of Anglican clergy supported the revolution, with the low-church faction providing its justification. High-churchmen were jealous of their prerogatives, devoted to monarchy, and could on occasion turn into Jacobites (the dedicated followers of the Stuarts in exile). In Scotland, the presbyterian majority within the Kirk made the revolution its own.

After 1690, the Whig presbyterian (or Calvinist) form of Protestantism held sway legally for the ensuing century. It in turn ruptured gradually into factions—one orthodox and rigidly Calvinist, the other moderate and given to an embrace of natural religion and an abandonment of predestination and original sin. Already one characteristic of the Enlightenment

in Scotland has become clear: Whig presbyterian moderates—
not materialists, radicals, or Jacobites—dominated enlightened
culture and turned increasingly to secular concerns.

Their ascendancy as moderates took decades, well into the
1740s. One example should suffice: Adam Smith, born in 1723
in the small town of Kirkcaldy, came from minor presbyterian
gentry who often enjoyed positions in government, thus making them firm supporters after 1689 of the Whig ascendency and
anti-Jacobites. His academic career took him to the universities
of Glasgow and Edinburgh; both ultimately flourished under
moderate Whig and presbyterian leadership. After the publication in 1776 of the book that made him famous, *The Wealth of
Nations*, Smith moved to Edinburgh (having spent some time
on the faculty of Glasgow), and took up a lucrative position
as commissioner of customs. Smith's connections, both social
and political, left him without the deep alienation from church
and government that can be seen among some of the French
philosophes. His private religious beliefs will probably never be
known; he had his papers destroyed at the end of his life in
1790. Smith's identification with his social setting made him less
alienated, but just as critical of the status quo as many Continental reformers.

A century before Smith's death, Scotland had been a deeply
troubled place. From the 1630s into the 1720s, it possessed two
warring religious camps. Their fortunes rose and fell, first with
the Stuarts, generally supported by episcopalians, and then as a
result of the Revolution of 1688–89, the presbyterians came to
power in church and university. The religious polemics between
them made English religious life before 1689, despite its violent
past, seem almost pacific. Indeed, so virulent had the conflict
become that the Scots clergy feared irreligion would enter
through a backdoor carelessly left open by sectarian feuding

between episcopalians and presbyterians.[3] Late seventeenth-century Scotland offered the Stuart crown and its episcopalian clergy an almost constant brew of dissent and upheaval: the assassination of an archbishop in 1679, the burning of Glasgow by a presbyterian army in the same year, the torture of suspected plotters, and the burning of seditious books. Last, in 1692 came revenge in the slaughter unleashed by William III's royal troops against the supposedly Jacobite members of the MacDonald clan. Things only got worse by the reappearance of famine brought on in the mid-1690s by bad harvests, exacerbated by war with France and fear of a French invasion.

While the Revolution of 1688–89 in England resulted in religious toleration for all orthodox Protestants, the Scots marched to a different tune. Neither Scot presbyterians nor episcopalians wanted toleration; in 1690, there were few, if any moderate clergy in either camp who were prepared to argue for accommodation in matters religious.[4] Not least, the last person to be executed for blasphemy in the British Isles—in what after 1707 and the union of England and Scotland became Great Britain—was a Scottish student, Thomas Aikenhead. He was a mere twenty years old at the time of his hanging in 1697.

Aikenhead had spoken of Christ as a magician and an impostor, denied the Trinity and the authenticity of the Scriptures, and claimed that "God, the world, and nature, are but one thing."[5] The charges against him give us an idea of what could be discussed or believed in Scotland during the 1690s. None of these ideas were unknown in either England or the Dutch Republic. Indeed, in the papers of John Toland, who was in Edinburgh in 1690, there is a manuscript about Jesus as a magician.[6] There were over twenty-five witnesses called against Aikenhead: fellow students, merchants, a bookseller, and the university's librarian. We do not know their religious affiliations, but we may assume the vast majority were presbyterians. They also took a dim view of the loyalty of the episcopalians who had dominated the university before the revolution. If the Enlightenment in Scotland began in the 1690s, it was a hesitant beginning.

One of Aikenhead's accusers laid out the stakes raised by heresy as many Scots would have understood them: "Will Scotland nourish such *Apostasy? A Covenanted People!*"[7] Since the Protestant Reformation, generations of Scots presbyterians believed they enjoyed a covenanted relationship with God, one that in the 1640s justified civil war. They believed that episcopalians were not truly God's people. The myth of the covenant held well into the eighteenth century and made all forms of open heresy liable to prosecution or worse. After Aikenhead, however, no one was executed again for blasphemy, and freethinking—never mind materialism—kept a low public profile. Decades later, even the most irreligious of Scots philosophes, David Hume, whose French translator was none other than the materialist Baron d'Holbach, published his views cautiously, while his friend Adam Smith kept his religious beliefs very private.

Disaffection from the episcopal church and monarchical state ran deep in Scotland. Before 1685, a radical presbyterian, Janet Hamilton, confided that she "disowned the king," Charles II, "he having unkinged himself by the breach of covenants, and by making our land a land of graven images."[8] While most Scots fell in behind the Revolution of 1688–89 and William III, they were uninspired by the notion of religious toleration, and a significant number of them would retain a love for the house of Stuart, hence for Jacobitism, which, unlike Whig presbyterianism, never became a force for a general, secularizing ethos.[9]

In the 1690s, if we listen to the clergy, Scottish religious beliefs seemed threatened as never before by the twin specters of atheism and deism. In early 1696, the General Assembly of the Kirk, now controlled by presbyterians, passed an act against the "gangrene through this land"—namely, atheism, deism, and skepticism. Contemporaries said these imports came from London and the Continent, particularly the Dutch Republic.[10] There were, however, home-grown philosophes who took up the new science of Boyle and Newton and whose views were labeled heretical and dangerous. Poor Aikenhead might have succumbed to their ideas as well as to his own reading, about which we know very little.

Once again, as in France in the time of Maupertuis, Newtonianism entered learned discourse associated with irreligion. Unlike French universities, however, as early as the 1680s, Newton's science enjoyed a place within the University of Edinburgh's faculty. While no one in the "historical know" now would classify the main Scottish Newtonians, David Gregory, Colin Maclaurin, and John Keill, as irreligious, contemporaries were deeply suspicious.[11] Unlike much of the rest of Europe, the Scottish universities were intellectually innovative and not held in the thrall of a clerically enforced Aristotelianism. Hence, Newtonian science made significant inroads.

When in 1740 the young Adam Smith ventured to Oxford, he was appalled to discover that there Aristotle still reigned, not Descartes, and certainly not Newton. Nothing, however, stopped his philosophical interests. When back in Edinburgh, and as a professor at Glasgow, Smith played a central role in the leading private philosophical society in the capital, the Select Society, with over fifty members. In the 1750s, two principles dominated the proceedings of the Society: No religious doctrines were to be discussed, and no Jacobitism.[12] The society became a place where intellectual curiosity and debating skills could develop and mature. Decades later, members like Smith and David Hume, along with Adam Ferguson, John Monro, and others, would be well known outside Scotland and eventually in all of Europe.[13]

In 1690, the first of these principles banishing religious doctrines would have struck contemporaries as deeply suspect. Indeed, in that year a Whig and presbyterian commission was established to test the loyalty and orthodoxy of the academic leaders of the university. By that time, the well-known Scottish doctor and Newtonian Archibald Pitcairne had earned a reputation for irreligion and drunkenness, and not least, he was a Jacobite.[14] He had both presbyterian and episcopal clerical enemies, or as Pitcairne called them, "these curate rogues, A company of greedy dogs."[15]

From its very arrival in Scotland, Newtonian science had fallen suspect to the clergy, so much so that in 1690 one of the most talented of Newton's followers, David Gregory, being accused of atheism, decamped and fled to a chair at Oxford. It was said that, when subjecting a pigeon to the ever-diminishing air in the vacuum of Boyle's air pump, he told the students that God had nothing to do with the bird's demise. The accusation against the new science claimed that it reduced everything to mathematical symbols—in essence, matter in motion.[16] Indeed, Pitcairne had used mechanical metaphors: "Who doubts but the body of Man, in some sense, may be called a Machine?" He condemned atheism and deism but saw no harm in medicine having a relationship to natural philosophy: "Is not our lot fallen in happy times, in which we shall see this Conjectural Art erected into a science?"[17] In what in hindsight looks like a witch hunt, Gregory, Pitcairne and several others were removed from their positions of leadership within the university.

It is questionable how many of the Whig commissioners knew of the young English dissenter and presbyterian John Toland, who at the University of Edinburgh learned Newtonianism as early as 1690, the year in which he got his master's degree.[18] By 1696 and his publication of *Christianity not Mysterious*, Toland achieved notoriety. The claim that nothing believable in religion should be beyond reason struck most readers as leaving very little left in which to believe. Toland's known association with the university could have done nothing to improve young Aikenhead's situation, indeed ideas about God as nature, and Jesus as magician, can be directly related to Toland's writings.

In 1704, Toland used Newton's science to argue that motion is inherent in matter—in other words, that nature can govern itself, that motion, life, and change have entirely naturalist explanations. Toland described himself as a pantheist; his contemporaries preferred atheist. Newton's great friend and explicator Samuel Clarke answered Toland to condemn him, and this quarrel lived on in Scottish circles, fueled by a Scot Andrew Baxter, a follower of Clarke. David Hume belonged in circles that partook in such polemics, and he cut his philosophical teeth on issues raised by these conflicting understandings of Newtonian science.[19]

From the context of the 1690s, the Enlightenment in Scotland appears on the fringes of polite society, far removed from the intellectual concerns of the clerically dominated universities, far from the heresies of Toland or Akinhead. There is a very long way from the execution of Aikenhead to the gentile philosophizing of the Select Society in 1751, when the leading moderate clergy, and eventually David Hume and Adam Smith, joined the debates on largely secular topics that included the status of women, the role of militias in the well-governed state, divorce by mutual consent, the corn laws, the usefulness of dueling, and not least, the desirability of removing "the repenting stool" from its central place in presbyterian church meetings.

These were places reserved for the particularly wayward—a public shaming—that the moderate members of the Select had come to see as insulting and unnecessary.

One of the earliest tracts published by the moderates and credited to William Robertson, among others, permits us to see an increasingly secular approach to the issues of the day as it grew out of an essentially religious sensibility. Long regarded as a manifesto for the moderates, and hence the leading clerical element within the Scottish Enlightenment, *Reasons of Dissent* (1752) reasoned from "the maxims of government" that are "consistent with the common interests and liberties of mankind." These maxims abhor "tyranny" in church and state but also insist upon order and the rule of law. Individual conscience is to be protected but not to the point of allowing it an absolute right to disobey or to follow solely one's inner light. The principles of this moderate version of the Enlightenment repudiated "enthusiasm" because it permitted equal time, as it were, for any doctrine. The Constitution of the Kirk had to prevail, and that assertion allied these Whig moderates with British constitutionalism more generally.[20] Political democracy never occupied a place on the intellectual agenda of the university or debating societies, and in Scotland the voting franchise was more restricted than in any other part of the kingdom. Moderation in both religion and politics was not always rewarded.

Predictably, the enemies of the moderates struck back and accused them of having a "fellow-feeling with heresy. . . . I never knew a moderate man in my life, that did not honour and love the heretic." Those of moderate religiosity concern themselves solely with social duties, never religious enthusiasm and never grace. Such duties must arise from rational considerations and will prove decisive against the "vulgar, ignorant, hot-headed country elders, or silly women." Enemy critics charged the moderates with distaining the lower orders, so much so that the critic claims moderate men snobbishly insist, "the apostle Paul had a university education, and was instructed in Logic." The heathen philosophers guide the moderates, and in their hands, religion becomes solely "virtue." Above all, the moderate clergyman is polite, skilled not at preaching the word of God, but in the arts of conversation and sociability.[21] Hume set the terms of the moderates' dispute with their enemies, whom he labeled enthusiasts:

> The violence of this species of religion, when excited by novelty, and animated by opposition, appears from numberless instances; of the *anabaptists* in Germany, the *camisars* in France, the *levellers* and other fanatics in England, and the *covenanters* in Scotland. Enthusiasm being founded on strong spirits, and a presumptuous boldness of character, it naturally begets the most extreme resolutions; especially after it rises to that height as to inspire the deluded fanatic with the opinion of divine illuminations, and with a contempt for the common rules of reason, morality, and prudence.[22]

Leaving aside the over-the-top rhetoric of both sides—foes of the Enlightenment always accused its followers of courting religious heresy—the moderate clergy and their lay associates like Hume and Smith did indeed value politeness, conversation, and congeniality. They enhanced and comfortably occupied the secular version of civil society—indeed, they made it their own. Historians have argued that the union of England and Scotland in 1707 encouraged, even launched, the Enlightenment in Scotland. The evidence from the 1690s points to the possibility of an earlier origin, but it seems reasonable to argue that absent a Parliament and privy council, educated Scots after 1707 put their energy into culture and social life. The turn to civil society was not without contestation and could have failed, leaving

Scotland solely with an emboldened presbyterian clergy hostile to the universities and moderacy in all its forms. The success of a vibrant civil society gave the Enlightenment a Scottish home.

The 1750s was the crucial decade: the opponents of moderacy, of theater attendance, of Hume's skepticism failed to gain majorities in the Assembly of the Kirk and the court of public opinion.[23] In 1757, one of the leading moderates, Adam Ferguson, argued for *The Morality of Stage Plays*, and as a consequence there developed a furious pamphlet war between the orthodox presbyterians who abhorred the theater and its champions, the moderates. The former gradually won and the entire affair achieved "international recognition among *philosophes*" as a marker for the triumph of the "light" over "darkness."[24] So pleased with themselves were the moderates that Hume smugly exclaimed,

> Really it is admirable how many Men of Genius this Country Produces at present. Is it not strange that, at a time when we have lost our Princes, our Parliaments, our independent Government...that in these Circumstances we should really be the People most distinguished for Literature in Europe?[25]

Hume was more right than wrong. The moderates of Edinburgh had pursued a strategy that in hindsight we can see as similar to what made the Enlightenment's success in various parts of Europe. By and large, philosophes stuck together, and despite disagreements, they held firm to basic principles: religious toleration, a disinterest in seeking others out to label them heretics, a brilliance with the written word, and a deep interest in reforming the institutions of church and state. Some ventured into irreligion and heresy with materialism, or extreme skepticism, at the forefront, and generally published clandestinely.

The firmness of Scottish camaraderie owed much to the weekly social gatherings that could be found in cities of any size. Here, our focus will be on the capital, Edinburgh, but a similar story could be told for Glasgow or Aberdeen. Certain questions consumed the debates of its Select Society: Are taxes on exports of corn advantageous to trade and manufacturing as well as to agriculture? Should the laws against bribery and corruption be repealed? Should the poor be given money in their own houses or in workhouses and hospitals? Should the amount of land under tillage be increased? Can the intemperance of the vulgar, upon an increase of wealth, be retarded by the care of superiors? Is it advantageous to a nation that the law of private property "be reduced to an art?" Should the repenting stool be taken away? This last question was at the forefront of moderate reforms sought for the Kirk.

By far, secular issues dominated the meetings of the Select Society. Are the provisions in the late Marriage Act advantageous to the nation? Should whiskey be put under restrictions so as to render its use less frequent? Has printing been advantageous to society? Should we prefer ancient or modern manners with regard to the condition and treatment of women? In a gesture toward Montesquieu, the assembled asked: Is the difference of national character chiefly owing to the nature of different climates or to moral and political causes? Is the policy of France inconsistent with the liberties of Britain? Should land be held in perpetuity or be capable of alienation? Are universities better placed in a metropolis or a remote town? Do we exceed the ancients in knowledge and arts, or they us? Should the stage be permitted in a well-regulated government? Does the landed or the commercial interest contribute to the tranquility and stability of the state; which is most favorable to public liberty? Can the strict principles of virtue and morality be made consistent with commerce? Do modern improvements in mechanics, or the multiplying of mechanical machines tend to depopulating the world? Will greater national evils be produced by the tyranny of a prince or the factions in a republic? Should women be prevented from painting their faces? Should rich men be permitted to have more than one wife and thus increase the population? And not least, is slavery advantageous?

Most of these questions occupied less than a full year of meetings.[26] Many were repeated in a two- or three-year period. The well-being of the state and its economy were high on the list, and so too were issues concerning women. Some of the questions about women may have been partly intended to amuse—polygamy had long been banished in Europe—and others—about whether or not women should hold places of "trust and profit in the state"—may have elicited more thoughtful responses.[27] So too might have the questions on whether or not divorce should be by mutual consent, or can a marriage be happy when the woman is of "superior understanding" to that of the man?

Few records exist for what was said at the debates. The question about ancient versus modern mores in the treatment of women may have spurred Hume to take up his pen to produce "An Historical Essay on Chivalry and Modern Honour." And if so, it is one of the few texts that can be imagined as spoken at the Select Society meetings. Hume argued that the barbarian peoples who conquered ancient Rome existed in a "twilight of Reason" and turned to chimeras and whimsies and "thus that monster of Romantick Chivalry or Knight Errantry . . . was brought into the world" and "ran like wildfire over all the Nations of Europe." Out of this errant sensibility, Hume lamented, came the Gothic that heaped "Ornament upon Ornament" and advanced "a new scheme of manners." It was inferior to "the

great men of the first ancient History" and these first moderns displayed "the chimerical and affected politeness" that
attempted to imitate the ancients and invented their "extreme
civility." Like our traveler in chapter 3, Henry Wyndham (who
had probably never heard of Hume's ideas), Hume cast a cold
eye on the Gothic sensibility.

By contrast to the chivalric, Hume asserted that while friendship is "a solid and serious thing," too refined for "common use,"
love is another matter: "Love to which almost everyone has a
great propensity, & which 'tis impossible to see a beautiful
woman, without feeling some touches of." But it is capricious to
be sure, and worse, when mixed with chivalry. Such love reverses
the order of nature and makes women superior. The knight's affection is designed "to relieve distressed Damsels from the captivity & violence of Giants." In the love invented by medieval men,
women became cold and haughty; seeking to impress them,
knights murder in tournaments and go without punishment.[28]
With a few notable exceptions, it was only in the last quarter of
the eighteenth century that the issue of women's equality received extended treatment and then largely in radical circles.

It is hard to know if Hume hated the ideals that dominated
Christian Europe more than he hated the notion of female
equality. Certainly, he was perfectly capable of satirizing it, and
of course there was no woman present. This entirely male society was linked to two others of the same makeup, the freemasons (whose meeting place it shared), and the overlapping
Edinburgh Society to which Select members also contributed.[29]
Perhaps predictably, given this segregation, issues concerning
women recur over and over: were ancient or modern practices
in their treatment better? Would women holding places of trust
and profit in the state be advantageous? And not least, should

divorce by mutual consent be allowed.[30] The "woman question" became central to Scottish social theory, and the treatment of women became a fundamental index by which any society could be assigned a stage from primitive or rude to polished and commercial.[31] Some of this attention to gender may have arisen from a close reading of Montesquieu, whose writings were well known in Scottish circles as was their author, in some cases personally.

A similar set of questions were addressed by the Society for Belles Lettres, another Edinburgh group founded in 1759, contemporaneous with the Select and composed mainly of students.[32] The clergy were more visible in its proceedings. More attention was given to religion than was the case in the Select Society, but once again secular issues dominated. Should women be taught the sciences?[33] Are men of strong or weak passions, the happier? Can slavery be reconciled with human and Christian values? And a question perhaps inspired by Rousseau's *Discourse on the Sciences and the Arts* (1750): Did the invention of the arts make mankind happier? Last, the society asked if physical or moral causes account for the character of nations. And so too the question, with its republican connotations, of whether trade and commerce lead to luxury vexed the assembled. The questions of decay and the direction of political change, and the conditions promoting human happiness, were never far from debating issues explored by Belles Lettres.

In all these Scottish clubs, the search for social and political improvement predominated. Hume put the issue succinctly: "nothing is so improving to the temper as the study of the beauties, either of poetry, eloquence, music, or painting."[34] Montesquieu's theory on the effect of climate on progress lurked behind the question: "What is the reason, why no people, living between the tropics, could ever yet attain to any art or civility, or reach even any police in their government, and any military discipline; while few nations in the temperate climates have been altogether deprived of these advantages?" Hume, among others, set the stage for racist theories to explain the progress of some people over others. Predictably, Hume thought that England was the most advanced country in the world.[35] When the Scots looked south, they saw greater prosperity, but when they looked north to the Highlands, the opposite was true. Postulating that the peoples of Scotland and England were inherently superior or inferior seemed hardly applicable. There must be structural reasons, historically contingent.

Given the prevailing concern with these differences, it is hardly surprising that the Enlightenment in Scotland bequeathed to the modern world a search for the stages of human development, for stadial histories. The Scots were poorer by and large than their English contemporaries and that status perplexed their intellectuals. Hume contributed one critical factor for determining what made progress possible, freedom:

> It had been observed by the ancients, that all the arts and sciences arose among free nations; and, that the Persians and Egyptians, notwithstanding their ease, opulence, and luxury, made but faint efforts towards a relish in those finer pleasures, which were carried to such perfection by the Greeks.[36]

Freedom, while essential, was only part of the progressive story. Commerce and manufacturing also needed to be seen as essential. Hume proclaimed, "When a nation abounds in manufactures and mechanic arts, the proprietors of land, as well as the farmers, study agriculture as a science, and redouble their industry and attention." Bountiful industry in turn enhanced the power of the state and led to the flourishing of the liberal arts. And Hume's notion of the industrial looked to textiles, what by 1800 would drive the First Industrial Revolution: "Can we expect, that a government will be well modelled by a people, who know not how to make a spinning-wheel, or to employ a loom to advantage?"[37] He left religion largely out of the story of progress, but noted that superstition holds back all who seek to be "in the pursuit of their interest and happiness."

Hume on religion could only give offense to all believers. He turned to natural science to argue for the rule of evidence and enquiry, and he wanted to subject religious belief to the same standard used by natural philosophers: "This is their practice in all natural, mathematical, moral, and political science. And why not the same, I ask, in the theological and religious?"[38] Hume asserted the truth to be found in the science of mechanics and in the principles of Copernicus. But there is no certainty to be found in trying to understand the nature of God.

Similarly, the sources of life and motion in the universe must remain essentially unknowable: "matter may contain the source or spring of order originally, within itself, as well as mind does."[39] We cannot know for certain in part because, Hume argued, the substance or essence of a thing cannot exist apart from human perceptions of it. All ideas are the function of the imagination. The French materialists, while not embracing the extreme skepticism to which Hume's philosophy led, would have approved of his observations about mind and matter. Indeed, Hume knew some of them as he spent a good many years living in France.[40]

Hume withheld his most alarming skepticism about religion. After he died in 1776, the daring *Dialogues concerning Natural Religion* appeared only three years later. Written in the form of dialogues between and among three characters, the skeptic among them, Philo, has been seen as embodying most closely the voice of Hume. The fashionable argument from design is presented to him by a believer: "Consider, anatomize the eye: Survey its structure and contrivance; and tell me, from your own feeling, if the idea of a contriver does not immediately flow in upon you with a force like that of sensation. The most obvious conclusion surely is in favour of design."

Hume makes it clear that there is no provable connection between the order and design seen in animals—or even the world—and its cause: "Nature, we find, even from our limited experience, possesses an infinite number of springs and principles, which incessantly discover themselves on every change of her position."[41] Surely God must be the cause of this design, would say the believer. For Hume, the only reasonable conclusion, given the sheer complexity of the world, is, however, skepticism: "His ways are not our ways. His attributes are perfect, but incomprehensible. . . . Nature contains a great and inexplicable riddle, more than any intelligible discourse or reasoning."[42] Philo urges that human beings confine their inquiries to this world, the only one that is knowable. Calvin's harsh and formidable God had come to be unknowable.

Hume leaves his readers in an entirely secular universe where some things, like history or the stages of societal progress, might be knowable. Both American and European thinkers saw irreligion in Hume's repudiation of design in nature. Scottish-trained medical doctors, like the Philadelphia-based Benjamin Rush, saw Hume's philosophy as denying the goodness of the Supreme Being.[43] Closer to home, and even before Hume's posthumous publication on natural religion, the Hutchinsonian bishop, George Horne accused Hume of wanting "to banish out of the world every idea of truth and comfort, salvation and immorality, a future state, and the providence, and even existence of God."[44]

In Edinburgh, the Select Society members, as far as we can tell, avoided such confrontations about religion. Confining their enquiries to knowable topics—the nature of democracy, commercial empire, political stability, and military rule—they must have enjoyed quite remarkable debates. Hume's colleague in the society, Adam Ferguson, told his students at the university that the general expression of a principle "is a law in physics and morality."[45] He thought that human development followed certain stages, the savage, the barbaric, and the polished, and that it would be possible to uncover the principles or laws that governed each stage. The savage or rude condition preceded the acquisition of property.[46] To that point, Hume might have agreed, but his skepticism would have made him allergic to Ferguson's relentless and Christian search for absolute moral laws.

Ferguson devoured the Greek and Roman classics as well as the writings of the French philosophes, especially Montesquieu. He also had available the rich travel literature about the Americas, Africa, and China. With those sources, he reinforced his notions of the rude and the savage, just as he found in the classics accounts of what made the Romans or Greeks great and the issues that led to their decline. There was never any doubt in Ferguson's mind that modern Europe stood as the most advanced and polished place in human history. For it, Ferguson understood decline as the result of vice, as something linked to the moral fiber of a people. Thus, even Great Britain needed to fear the corrosive effects of social inequality and luxury.

When a society is in the throes of its "final corruption," the revolutions or transformations that destroy are whatever removes or withholds "the objects of every ingenious study or liberal pursuit; that deprive the citizen of occasions to act as the member of a public; that crush his spirit; that debase his sentiments, and disqualify his mind for affairs."[47] Ultimately, the rise and fall of nations depend upon the vitality or corruptions of the human spirit. Drawing his model from the natural sciences and the mechanical arts, Ferguson saw discoveries and improvements in every domain of knowledge as limitless— but so too were human virtues and vices. Unlike Hume and Adam Smith, Ferguson regarded commercial society as a mixed blessing. Its propensity to foster divisions of labor, its embrace of luxury and thus social inequality, boded ill for civic mindedness and a willingness to defend the nation.[48] Every Scottish philosophe—more so than their contemporary French counterparts—wrestled with the reality of prosperity, poverty and the seemingly endless search for wealth—with the ethos of an ever-expanding capitalist impulse.

Widely regarded as the founder of capitalist theory, Adam Smith is a curious concatenation of contradictions. His first intellectual commitment revolved around moral philosophy and he sought wherever possible to find the sources of human goodness. Yet he had no illusions about the evil to be found in the world. He was also the product of one of the finest academic educations to be found at the time. Glasgow, which he attended in the late 1730s, had been shaped by Whig principles, by advocacy of moderation in religion and natural philosophy. Its shining intellectual light came from a Northern Irish family of presbyterian divines, and Francis Hutcheson can be placed in the tradition of radical Whiggery—passionate about the Revolution of 1688–89, the right of resistance, and human freedom as endorsed by his Christian faith. Hutcheson should not be confused with John Hutchinson, an Anglican high-churchman and an enemy of anything he assessed as unorthodox. George Horne was one of his followers.

Although Hutcheson's pupil, Smith ended up sounding like a deist—and may even have been an atheist—he came out of liberal presbyterianism.[49] Within it and early in the century, a turn was made away from the harsh religiosity of traditional Calvinism, away from predestination, and from the Hobbesian vision of the "war of all against all." The university in Glasgow and Hutcheson, Smith's beloved teacher, were in the forefront of this intellectual and emotional sea change. Hutcheson, like Anthony Benezet, the French Huguenot reformer we met in chapter 4, thundered against African slavery and laid blame for it on white Europeans.[50] Neither had any illusions about the evil that men could get themselves into without the guidance of God. Hutcheson developed his ideas about human virtue, the passions and the interests, in books and lectures that made a lasting impact on the young Smith and also on David Hume.

Hutcheson also introduced both of them to Newtonian science and believed that universal laws, as in the physical world, could be discovered about the affections.[51] Attraction in the mental world has the same push and pull as it does in the natural. Smith would call it sympathy. Medical doctors like his friend William Cullen used the term to describe the interaction of the nervous system with the body and hence all pervasive in the human condition. He also systematically applied Newtonian concepts to the study of chemistry.[52]

Hutcheson wanted to anchor the passions and interests at the core of human nature to an interaction with the external world. He sought to banish the dark vision of an innate nature associated with Hobbes. Human desires do not all reduce to self-love. This benign vision of human nature allowed Hutcheson to argue that "nothing can be more distinct that the general calm desire of private good, and hence this impulse produces a universal calm benevolence."[53] It in turn allows human beings to temper their passions and—by analogy to the laws of motion—be inexorably drawn toward the absolute good. The desire for particular good that gives pleasure can direct us away from the absolute good, but the impulse for its search is, as it were, hard-wired into the human passions. Whether in agreement with Hutcheson or not, Smith and his generation of Scottish thinkers received from him a template for thinking about benevolence and the common good, modeled on the Newtonian understanding of physical nature, that could be taken in a variety of innovative directions.

Early in his post-Glasgow years, probably in the 1740s, Smith took up the study of astronomy and proclaimed that Newton's system was "the greatest discovery that ever was made by man." If those among Smith's contemporaries, like Hume, who endeavor "to represent all philosophical systems as mere inventions of the imagination . . . [even they] make use of language expressing the connecting principles of this one [the Newtonian], as if they were the real chains which nature makes use of to bind together her several operations."[54] Smith idealized natural philosophers and mathematicians, "they are almost always men of the most amiable simplicity of manners, who live in good harmony . . . are the friends of one another's reputation . . . without either much vexed or very angry when they are neglected." And unlike poets or fine writers, they also do not form cabals or factions. Smith may be forgiven his naïveté.[55]

Indebted to Hutcheson, enamored of natural science, philosophically engaged with David Hume, Smith was nevertheless his own man. He articulated his own stadial understanding of human societies. "Among the savage nations of hunters and fishers," everyone who can works, and yet the people are miserably poor and often forced to abandon the ill, or the too young or too old, who then perish from hunger or are devoured by wild animals.[56] By contrast, "among the civilized and thriving nations," even when large numbers of people do not work, and live off the proceeds of the labor of others, the productivity is such that even the meanest of the laboring poor lives far better than the savage. The amount of "capital stock" used in employment is the key to this expanding prosperity, and ever since the fall of the Roman Empire, Europe has put its capital and energy into the arts, commerce, and manufacturing of the towns and not primarily into agriculture, the labor of the countryside.

There are so many assumptions built into Smith's approach with which we can disagree. He had never seen the "savages" he so blithely consigns to poverty; his vision of the wealth of towns as the source of the nation's wealth would have been derided by French theorists who privileged agriculture, and the economic history of Europe from 500 CE to 1600 CE, as we now know it, would not fulfill Smith's caricature. Our disagreements do not detract from the fact that Smith produced a brilliant work on political economy, unifying all the elements that make up economic and political life and its progress. Writing in the lifetime of Thomas Malthus (1766–1834), Smith, without having read him, saw a way out of the trap Malthus believed characterized improving economic change. Prosperity led to an increase of population and it in turn put unsustainable pressure on the food supply; the inevitable result would be famine and the collapse of advances previously made. Smith saw that the productivity of labor could be enhanced as could the supply of capital—conceivably ad infinitum.

One key to the productivity of labor lay in the practice of dividing tasks in manufacturing. More so in manufacturing than in agriculture, the division of labor, in Smith's example, finds one man being replaced by ten or more, each with an assigned task. Famously, Smith illustrated his point by describing how one man making a pin might produce one a day, ten men with their labor divided into discrete tasks can produce thousands in the same time. It has been argued that Smith got his account of pin-making from Diderot's great *Encyclopèdie*, and that indeed maybe the case. By the 1770s, however, we believe that the practice of dividing labor in British factories was more widespread than was the case on the Continent. Kirkcaldy (also where most of *The Wealth of Nations* was drafted) had become a center for nail production and Glasgow had a significant manufacturing base.[57] Thus, close to home Smith could have seen economic activity especially in manufacturing that fit into his understanding of human progress. He would have noticed that many advances in machinery came out of the ingenuity of the workmen who used the device, but others were the effect of "philosophers" who applied themselves to the study of the whole machine.[58] In 1776, Smith saw what by 1790—and the advent of Watt's steam engine—became visible in British cotton factories and coal mines. The philosopher's improvement of the engine increased both productivity and profit.

Smith postulates that at the root of economic activity lies the universal human impulse to trade, barter, and exchange. In advanced economic settings, everyone, however poor and humble, has capitalist impulses. Given human wants and needs, one man's talent produces objects of use to another. With the surplus earned by his labor, the trader can purchase the commodities produced by the labor of his neighbor. In the best accommodated commercial settings, trade can occur far and wide: the larger the market, the larger the town, the better the transportation, particularly by water, and then exchange will expand and many more actors will join in making and consuming. Smith's analysis draws extensively on travel accounts of markets in China, Bengal, Africa, and of course Europe. He also understood that any commodity can work in the exchange market: cows, dried cod, shells, raw metals before there were coins. However, the invention—and state supervision—of coinage advanced the possibilities for exchange, and it was one important step toward the creation of commercial society. He cautions his readers that while money may appear the arbiter and measure of value, only the value of labor remains "the ultimate and real standard by which the value of all commodities can at all times and places be estimated and compared. It is their real price; money is their nominal price only."[59] The cost of any commodity includes the price of the labor to make it; the "rent," namely the cost of the place where the labor occurs (whether rented or owned); and the profit necessary to sustain the purchasing power of the entrepreneur or seller.

In a market perfectly free, every man would seek the most advantageous reward for his labor. Yet Smith argues, everywhere in Europe obstacles are placed in the way of a perfect liberty to follow one's self-interest. Some of these obstacles are in the nature of the job, how agreeable or disagreeable might its practice be. Smith notes that the common executioner works far less hard than almost any laborer but is paid so much better because of the disagreeable nature of the job. Other obstacles are imposed by law or custom—for example, the necessity of being an apprentice before certain trades can be practiced. Reading *The Wealth of Nations* makes clear that Smith had studied the wages and nature of the craft in almost every form of labor seen in his day. He knew the wage differentials in London as opposed to Edinburgh, in the small towns versus the big ones, in the liberal professions that required years of preparation, in the laboring practices of curates, apothecaries, or grocers. Smith brought the empiricism of the physical sciences into the study of humankind, and in the process, he became one of the founders of the social sciences.

Smith saved his critical edge for what he saw as the state's interference in the perfect liberty of the market. The "corporations" were the greatest culprits and they limited the number who could be apprentices, the required length of their apprenticeship, even the number of apprentices (generally two) allowed to any master. The effect was to keep wages high, and still worse to curtail the freedom of the individual to deploy his labor. Apprenticeships led to habits of idleness and thus were self-defeating. Towns regulated the corporate entities within their borders and thus kept wages and profits high for employers and employees to the detriment of the consumer. Smith's arguments were used for decades by employers to block the formation of trade unions.

The worst effects of this system of corporate control fall on the countryside. Smith's sympathies often went to the farmer, day laborer, and the landed gentry. Indeed, Smith believed that the skills required of the farmer exceed those used in the mechanical arts found in manufacturing.[60] Yet his coldest eye was cast equally on all the practices used by corporations, towns, manufacturers, and craftsmen to keep costs high and thus working for their benefit. His special scorn went to feudal practices such as primogeniture (the eldest male alone inherited) and the notion that the great landed estates constitute the wealth of a nation. Smith saw true wealth as lying in the reciprocal relationship between agriculture and manufacturing. Neither by itself held the key to opulence; rather a healthy interchange between the profits derived from the land, as consumed in the town, and the profits from manufacturing, led to economic growth. The origin of wealth lay not in money, nor foreign commerce per se, and certainly not in capital accumulated and wasted by the state, but in profits derived from labor and the careful management of rent. Smith believed that the contemporary competition for foreign commerce—fostered by imperial rivalries between the European states—threatened the peace and prosperity of all. Smith was as scornful of feudal wealth and the rush into international competition in trade as Voltaire (whom Smith greatly admired) was about superstition and the privileges of clergy and churches.

Unlike many Continental representatives of the Enlightenment, Smith was fascinated by the world of business and trade. As Glasgow University's librarian, he bought and sold while keeping meticulous accounts. The city's Political Economy Club also enabled Smith to hear merchant discussions and to observe their penchant for seeking monopolistic hegemony. He understood the impulse as essential to the zeal for profit. He also understood its destructive tendencies and cautioned his readers against monopolies in *The Wealth of Nations*.

Among Smith's close friends, Joseph Black, the famous chemist, came from a Northern Irish merchant family, helped it out in hard times, and became quite comfortable financially. William Cullen, a professorial colleague of Black and Smith at Edinburgh, sought to make agriculture more scientific, and from these colleagues Smith would have learned a great deal about contemporary science and industry. The links between the university's science faculty and early industrial development were intense, and arguably there was no economic thinker, either European or American, in a better place to observe cutting-edge development. Add to Black and Cullen the geologist and close friend James Hutton, and Smith could learn as much about contemporary science as anyone in Great Britain at the time. At his request, Black and Hutton oversaw the destruction of Smith's private papers and were the executors of his estate.[61] Bachelors one and all, they constituted the primary ties in the lives of each. After 1770 in Edinburgh, a student or professor could learn about the concept of latent heat, the latest medical techniques, and even the working of Watt's steam engine.[62] Black claimed to have developed this concept and the experimentation that supported it in the late 1750s and early 1760s while teaching at Glasgow. In that period, Black developed a working relationship and friendship with James Watt, eventually of steam engine fame. Much ink has been spilled over whether or not Watt needed to understand and apply Black's concept of latent heat in order to make his modifications on the steam engine.[63] Clearly, he did not, but the point here is that Black, Watt, Smith, Cullen, and others knew about the engine, its promise, the science that could be brought to bear in improving it, and its actual application.

In a set of notes taken on the lectures of Black (and his colleague and assistant, Dr. Hope), we know what an undergraduate of the 1790s could learn at Edinburgh.[64] Black (d. 1799) urged the students to put hard work before amusements and to use existing knowledge to build upon by further experimentation. Students needed to understand that in less than a century chemistry had moved away from alchemy, from being "disgustful . . . cultivated in ages of barbarism and superstition . . . void of the ornaments of polite learning tainted with all the folly and credulity of the times." It has been reformed and now uses plain language and is perhaps the most experimental of all the sciences; it is the source of improvements, in medicine and in any form of industry. Textbooks were recommended; most were from Continental sources such as Chaptal and Lavoisier.

In the history of chemistry, as these Scottish lecturers explained, alchemy had deteriorated into the search for wealth, and only the English giants of seventeenth-century science, Bacon, Boyle, and Newton, sent chemistry in the right direction. The history of science reinforced the stadial understanding of human progress. Chemistry reached another stage in its progress thanks to the French school led by Lavoisier. The point is made that anyone who is truly inventive, whether the porcelain maker Wedgwood or a physician who cures the once incurable, should be deemed a philosopher. Smith clearly agreed. Smith, writing on the history of astronomy, and Black, on the history of chemistry, employed the construct of stages, which in turn could be applied to the developmental history of humankind.

At any point in Black's lectures, an industrial application of a chemical experiment was discussed. He labored to explain his theory of latent heat—that is, the heat retained by any body such that ice does not melt all at an instant, but gradually, due to the latent heat at work among its particles. For those who deny its existence, Black responds, "this might be the case if water always froze at the 32 degrees of the thermometer, but this is 0 degree for it will remain fluid at two or three degrees below 32."[65] From this general discussion, he moves on to vapor and more precisely steam. Its force compels Black to discuss how it can be used, how every effort must be made in iron foundries not to let water "fall on the melted iron as the force of the steam drive it into a thousand pieces." According to Desaguliers, a Newtonian of the previous generation, vapor or steam takes up 14,000 times the space of water "but this appeared to Mr. Watt and me impossible."[66] Black then carefully explains to the students how steam is used in the engine. Indeed, the principle of latent heat means that water turns only gradually into vapor. Black then recounts experiments done by Watt with water "in Pepin's digester" and put on the fire for half an hour. Clearly, Watt was trying to figure out how much heat he can apply, how far he can push the expansive power of steam. Black claims that Watt's knowledge of latent heat led him "to consider the improvements which might be made in the steam engine ... he considered the enormous waste of heat." This loss was expensive. In nearly 500 pages of written notes by an earnest student, Black allied philosophy with manufacturing and costs.

To learn the latest science, Smith did not need to be sitting in on Black's lectures; they were weekly dining companions for several decades. As one of Black and Cullen's pupils, John Robison put it, theirs was "a friendship that became more and more intimate and confidential through the whole of their lives."[67]

While in any account of the Enlightenment in Scotland, the universities are central, particularly those in Edinburgh and Glasgow, nevertheless its reach far exceeded its urban base. Professors, theorists, and practical experimenters knew that agriculture lay at the heart of Scottish economic life. Smith made that point repeatedly. So too did his friend, the medical doctor and chemist William Cullen, who lectured on agriculture in his Glasgow lecture hall in the 1740s and early 1750s. He also farmed a country estate that was widely regarded as one of the finest in the kingdom. Again, the thicket of debating and learned societies gave Cullen, and intellectuals like him, a place to expound their ideas and to show the profound relevance of chemistry to a scientifically informed agriculture.[68]

Cullen, like Black and Smith, never failed to cite other European writers on any scientific topic, from the Dutch Republic to Italy. He also carried out an extensive correspondence on agricultural matters, much of it still unpublished. Like so many of the leaders of the Scottish Enlightenment, Cullen developed a friendship with Henry Home, Lord Kames, a largely self-educated polymath who became a lord (hence his title as a judge) of the Scottish Court of Session. Another believer in the progress of society, Kames saw the improvement of agriculture as part of the stadial process. It too should be made scientific, and he believed that the cultivation of the land had been a vital step en route to the last and best stage, commercial society. Cullen and Kames discussed everything concerning the land, from the best manure to flax and grain growing. His writings were well known in Germany and much admired by Thomas Jefferson.[69]

Examining the earth in order to improve its cultivation led perhaps inexorably to geology and a desire to understand its original formation. As was the case in the French Enlightenment, such studies ran into the orthodoxy that limited the earth's age to about 6,000 years. Very little in the geological record could explain the vast changes and contrasts occurring in such a limited time frame. Another one of Smith and Cullen's close friends, James Hutton, took up the task of examining "the appearances of the earth" using the "principles of natural philosophy" to arrive "at some knowledge of order and system in the economy of this globe." Only by these scientific methods, "not in human record, but in natural history" will give us "a rational opinion with regard to the course of nature, or to events which are in time to happen."[70] Like the French theorists before him, Hutton assumed that the power of nature "consolidated the bottom of the sea" and gradually, by extreme heat coming from the center of the earth, it had been transformed into land. In short, Hutton moved from being a farmer and chemist to becoming one of the founders of modern geology. His assumption that the evolution of the earth might have taken millions of years led contemporaries to condemn him as an atheist. Other geologists postulated the earth's formation to have been as the result of various catastrophes, not through a slow evolution. In time, Hutton's theory gained ascendancy and is now universally applied.

Hutton died in 1797, Black in 1799, and Smith and Cullen both passed away in 1790, while David Hume, much to Smith's sorrow, died in 1776. The next generation became quite different in its outlook and values. The decade of the 1790s in Scotland, as in the much of the rest of Europe and the new American republic, was consumed with coming to terms with the French Revolution.

Indeed, Scottish thinkers were at first taken aback by the events of 1789 and only slowly joined in the debate about its merits.[71]

One life illustrates these changes: John Robison (b. 1739) came out of the same circle, had been educated at Glasgow, succeeded Black, and worked closely with Watt on applications of steam power. After spending many years in Russia teaching, he was lured back to a professorship at Edinburgh, where the vicarious experience of the French Revolution made an indelible, and warped, imprint on his thinking. To the consternation of Watt's circle, Robison attacked Priestley and his supposed irreligion viciously.[72] Following on the thinking of an extreme French opponent of the Revolution, the abbé Barruel, Robison took up conspiracy theory ardently and like him, blamed the whole event on a conspiracy of freemasons and philosophes.[73] In *Proofs of a Conspiracy* (1797), Robison claimed to have first-hand knowledge of the subversion of freemasonry by the radical illuminati of German origin. The book became a publishing phenomenon with multiple editions, even into this century. But Robison paid an emotional price:

> The abuse, and ridicule, and reproach which my book has brought on me are inconceivable—the wretches here know how ill I am, and delight in tormenting me. They have even tried to alarm my family by threats of democratic vengeance.[74]

By his own account, Robison experienced a great deal of physical pain in the 1790s, and he explained to Watt, "Long may you enjoy the pleasures of health and exertion. They have bid me farewell. . . . *Never ceasing* torture has now incapacitated me from all mental occupation."[75] The account of his final days in 1805, written by his widow, assured Watt that Robison died in full possession of his mental faculties. Yet we well might ask, what became of the enlightened effort to understand the wealth of nations, or the epistemology of religious knowledge, or the effects of sympathy?

So many Scottish thinkers had analyzed French progress in economics but contrasted it with the repressive force of its political system. Even Smith and Hume, who tended to play down the differences between England and France, knew they existed. Almost to a man, the Scottish philosophes in 1789 could define themselves as Whigs, and in that year, they welcomed the changes being reported from France. But the Revolution moved gradually from reform, complete with social leveling, to violence. In 1793, the king was executed, and what came to be known as the Terror seized large parts of the country, both in Paris and the provinces. At the same time, international warfare against France and also by it put bellicosity on the minds of all Scots. So much of Scottish thought had focused on the sources of progress, and even its inevitability. Where could progress be found amid the tensions of war and warmongering, amid a hyper-patriotism found increasingly on both sides of the Channel? Not least, radical clubs and associations had sprung up in many Scottish towns, fueled by class resentments and the desire for parliamentary reform.[76]

The Enlightenment in Scotland had built an intellectual and emotional wall against enthusiasm, primarily in religion, and used it effectively to beat back extremes of both radical presbyterians and Jacobites. In the 1790s, enthusiasm returned in the anti-revolutionary rhetoric of Edmund Burke, among radical British sympathizers of the French Jacobins, and not least amid the French revolutionaries themselves.[77]

6

Berlin and Vienna
ᔑ𝑡𝑜ᑭ

THE LANGUAGES OF ENLIGHTENED texts encountered up
to now have been largely English, French, and Dutch. But philosophes wrote in every vernacular language found in Europe
and the American colonies; not all of them can be discussed
in this volume. Choices had to be made, and here we want to
examine what was said in German; in the next chapter, Italian. With the exception of the Dutch Republic (Dutch being a
separate, but Germanic language), we do not think of the Germanic lands—with Berlin and Vienna as the largest urban settings—or, for that matter, the Italian ones—with Naples having
around 200,000 inhabitants—as the places where we first look
for the Enlightenment. While not as heavily populated as the
urban corridor from Amsterdam to Paris, the German and Italian cities were substantial. Early in the eighteenth century, both
Milan and Naples fell under the control of the Spanish, then the
Austrian Habsburgs; in the case of Naples, their power lasted
only into the 1730s, and in Milan up to the end of the century.

None of these German territories, or those owned by the
Habsburgs, had formed into nation-states. Before Napoleon
consolidated them in 1806, there were over 300 separate German jurisdictions. Whether as duchies, princely kingdoms,

or cities, all were ruled over by absolute monarchs or princes assisted by an entrenched aristocracy and clergy. Free imperial cities like Hamburg were controlled by oligarchies. Each in its way practiced censorship, and what got prohibited differed enormously depending upon the concerns of the clergy and their princely benefactors. In the German-speaking lands, generally in the north, the religion was Protestant, either Lutheran or Calvinist. Even within the Lutheran fold, there were disagreements. Orthodox Lutheranism relied upon theology and doctrines to impose piety on the faithful; Pietism sought to create a more emotional, personal form of Protestantism. Southern Germany and Austria were Catholic territories where papal authority mattered when it came to censorship. True or not, Bavaria had a reputation for being a place where superstition flourished. These were not the only differences from the rest of Western Europe.

By the eighteenth century, the Germanic territories, bound in a loose federation, belonged to the Holy Roman Empire, with an Austrian Habsburg emperor whose court resided in Vienna. The central German territories had experienced unprecedented turmoil during the seventeenth century. Religious warfare, known as the Thirty Years War (1618–48), drew every major power into the life or death struggle to restore Catholicism or to defend Protestants. France, Sweden, the Dutch Republic, and Spain sent armies into the empire to fight on one side or the other. The Catholic League was led by the Habsburg king, and by the early eighteenth century the dynasty had passed from its Spanish to its Austrian branch. It is estimated that over eight million people perished or were displaced in the course of the thirty-year conflict. Several generations had to pass before the German-speaking lands recovered from the carnage. Peace was restored by the Treaty of Westphalia (1648), but religious and structural problems remained acute—not least, competition between the kings of Prussia in Berlin and the emperors in Vienna was endemic.

The German Enlightenment, and indeed the Enlightenment in general, cannot be understood outside the conditions created by a generation of religious warfare in central Europe. Theorists and ministers of state in the period after Westphalia looked for a political solution that would prevent another Thirty Years War. In the search, German universities played a prominent role, and therein emerged the first stirrings of ideas we can later associate with enlightened thinking. German university culture, like that seen in Scotland, nurtured liberal, even radical approaches to the problem of religious authority and political instability. At their root lay the new science, from Descartes to Newton and Leibniz. All elevated mathematics as one key to the acquisition of all knowledge, as a way forward in both philosophy and empirical studies. Leibniz's impact was greatest in Germany and his difficult doctrine of God having created "the best of all possible worlds" remained important into the 1770s. In France, Madame du Châtelet was attracted to his ideas.

The universities displayed the tension between orthodox Lutheranism and the more emotive, evangelical—even millenarian—Pietism. For centuries, they had been dominated by the teaching of Greek and Latin and by rote memorization. Change began early in the eighteenth century partly under the impact of Locke's ideas on education. In general, the leaders of the Enlightenment in the German-speaking lands paid greater attention to theology and religion than did their French or Scottish counterparts. German-speaking rural populations saw the execution of witches as late as 1775 in Germany and 1782 in Switzerland. In the Catholic south, exorcism of demons occurred into the 1770s.[1] Yet everywhere the universities were dominated by the secular authorities, who cast a cold eye on controversies that spilled into the public arena and, of course, heresy.

One of the leading intellectuals who laid the tentative foundation for enlightened values, Christian Thomasius (b. 1655) was a jurist and moral philosopher from a Lutheran family in Leipzig, Saxony. Taught by his father, another university professor, Thomasius spent much of his career trying to find a secular foundation for ethics and politics. He rebelled against the merger of theology and scholastic philosophy taught at the Lutheran University of Leipzig; then he made his way to the university in Calvinist Brandenburg. Its prince endorsed a moderate form of Calvinism, one suitable to promoting social order while avoiding doctrinal quarrels. Thomasius also sought out the general reader and created the first German-language journal, *Monatsgespräche* (1688–90), founded in Leipzig.

Returning there, and commencing his career as a university lecturer, Thomasius took to heart the lessons he had learned in Brandenburg. He became a contentious critic of doctrinal absolutism and then had the temerity to intervene in the political storm raised by the marriage of a Saxon royal nephew, a Lutheran, to the sister of the Brandenburg elector, a Calvinist. Thomasius argued that confessional differences mean nothing in the eyes of God, and that under the Treaty of Westphalia, both religions were of equal standing. Within months, he was prohibited by the Saxon court from lecturing, and he had little alternative but to move back to Brandenburg, where he was instrumental in founding a new university at Halle. It became a center for liberal and anti-Scholastic teaching for much of the eighteenth century. Note that scholastic ways of thinking had become the hallmark of orthodox Lutherans in contrast with other forms of Protestantism, where the scholastic followers of Aristotle aroused suspicion because of his use in Catholic theology. The reformers, in the spirit of Locke, sought to make education fitting for virtuous and practical men.[2]

Because of his commitment to a firm separation of church and state, and his desire to confine doctrinal quarreling to the private realm of individual conscience, Thomasius earns a place in the early German Enlightenment. Yet there were major differences between his views and those of his more radical contemporaries and students, and certainly the next generation of liberal German thinkers. One constant theme in enlightened thought started with a repudiation of the doctrine of original sin.[3] With its dismissal, theorists found it much easier to lay emphasis on human goodness. That was not a notion found in Thomasius. He argued that

> All men by nature are in the same miserable shape. All demand to live long and happily, that is, cheerfully, well-off, and honored. In spite of this, every thought and desire they have had since their youth leads them to do things that make their lives unhappy, wretched, or both. Thus, the natural end of life is cut short. Man becomes the agent of his own misfortune.[4]

A grim vision, but one that allowed Thomasius to dismiss the smug certainty of the absolutist clergy. He sought to separate theology from philosophy and to ground political life on free rational judgment, however imperfect. The light of reason must be distinguished from divine revelation, and reason shows men "the means and whys by which [they] can get out of this misery using . . . natural powers and without special supernatural grace."[5] In Thomasius, there is a direct link between Christian teaching about human reason and a more secular understanding of what reason can accomplish. Yet while giving reason its due, he never admits the possibility that the light of revelation will contradict reason.[6] He blames the ancient pagan philosophers for having introduced metaphysics into religion thus making it harder for humans to use their reason in religious matters: "in the teachings of Christ nor in those of the apostles does one find much in the way of theological formulas. These arose a few hundred years later, when the passion and honesty of the first love had become rather lukewarm and dull."[7] Thomasius looked for a way to downgrade theology, and thus provide a space for the secular. His anti-Scholasticism also opened a path away from dogma, from the constant accusations of heresy and the arrogance of the monks who taught in the universities. He labeled them "ignoramuses."

Thomasius was undoubtedly a pious man with little desire to displace church teaching root and branch. Some of his students at Halle were altogether differently motivated. They pushed his ideas in a radical direction, in some cases with disastrous effects on their careers. They branched out in search of new sources for anti-orthodox positions and found them in clandestine Jewish texts written against Christianity as well as the writings of Socinians, anti-Trinitarians whose ideas originated in the borderlands of Christianity and Islam.[8] All this churning for new approaches to the problem of religion and authority occurred within academic circles, somewhat closed, with participants fearful of being exposed. They were however internationally connected, remarkably well read, and could engage in learned conversations about Thomas Hobbes, John Locke, Spinoza—in short, about the foundational ideas at the heart of the early Enlightenment. However, we must keep in mind that university teachers were salaried by the local prince and any hint of irreligion would have been disastrous to a career.

There were many texts produced by former pupils of Thomasius, but only one of them, *The Book of the Three Impostors*, achieved a notoriety that followed it into our own time. The

impostors were Jesus, Moses, and Mohammed, and it was supposedly written by Peter Friedrich Arpe, a jurist in Kiel.[9] In fact,
the Latin text originated from the mind of another Thomasius
student, Johann Müller, writing before 1700.[10] It was shared with
close friends in both Germany and Denmark, and Arpe was a
confidant in those circles who, after Müller's death, identified him
as the author. From there, the text gradually spread. It may have
been written as an elaborate and naughty joke, but the humor
vanished as more atheists and freethinkers got their hands on it.

Much confusion has surrounded the "three impostors" and
the attribution of an author. Its existence had been rumored for
decades but no one was sure if it had ever been written. The
German context is critically important. In the search for a way
out of doctrinal certainty, heresy hunting, the destruction of
careers, and the ongoing bickering between Lutherans and Pietists, one way lay in ridicule and satire. Why not mock all the
religious leaders and do so anonymously? And once the existence of such a manuscript could be established, what would
another scholar pay for such an outrageous text? This Latin text
could command serious attention only from those who could
read Latin, but most well-educated men of the period could read
it, however imperfectly. Clandestine circulation only enhanced
the mystery and outrageousness of any manuscript. And scholarship in our own day has managed to get to the bottom—at least
partially—of who wrote it, when, and less clear, why.

Since the 1980s, we have known that the manuscript and
book that got most of the attention in the eighteenth century
was not the Müller text in Latin but one of very different origin,
written in French and in circulation in the Dutch Republic by
1710.[11] As recounted in chapter 4, a manuscript in the possession of English freethinker John Toland revealed the existence
of a coterie active in The Hague in 1710 and using discernably

Religions, sensing clearly that the basis of their impostures was the ignorance of the Peoples, resolved to keep them in it . . . as the number of fools is infinite, Jesus Christ found Subjects everywhere.[13]

When one of the "brothers" published the *Traité* in 1719 (as *La vie et l'esprit de Spinoza*), the effect was immediate and the Dutch authorities moved to confiscate every copy they could find. Slowly but surely, nonetheless, the manuscript spread throughout Europe, and anyone who was someone in enlightened circles had by 1750 seen or read it.

Probably so too had Pieter Friedrich Arpe. True to the international character of the secular Enlightenment, he knew Marchand and Picart—indeed, two of their "brothers" became his publishers. Arpe probably had a reading, but not a good writing knowledge of French, so when he wrote to Marchand he did so in Latin. He and the Marchand circle shared an interest in Lucilio Vanini, an Italian heretic burned at the stake in 1619 in Toulouse. Arpe wrote a laudatory appreciation of him, as did an associate of the "brothers," David Durand.[14] Another German pastor, Christopher Balber from Hessen, also corresponded with Marchand, telling him that he found Christian theology—but not the religion—an embarrassment.[15] He urged the Marchand circle to continue their publishing activities that began with an enigmatic text by Bonaventure Des Périers, *Cymbalum Mundi* (1711, originally 1537). Widely regarded as heretical, the book of sixteenth-century origin aimed to subject all religion to ridicule, or so Marchand claimed in a published opening letter to Picart describing its content.

Vanini and Des Périers, separated by nearly a century, had been classified as atheists, naturalists who paid no attention to established supernatural, Christian doctrines. Decades after

Durand and Arpe sought to praise Vanini, and in the context of rehabilitating Spinoza, Johann Herder briefly tried to vindicate him. Vanini, we are told, wrote sincerely and from the heart. A theist with pantheist leanings, he deploys all his rhetorical eloquence "in order to represent to us the One without whom we are nothing, but through whom we are all that we are, and can, and do." One of the characteristics of the philosophes had been to liberate heretics while always reminding their readers of the cruel persecutions inflicted upon them by the church.[16] Long before Herder, Vanini had earlier champions, Dutch radicals who can also be associated with heresy. Possibly through them, a portion of a text by Vanini made its way into the *Traité des trois imposteurs*.[17]

The quest to undermine religious dogmatism took decades and crossed national and linguistic borders; it brought men into contact because they shared a similar goal. They wanted a way out from under the doctrinal quarrels that had left large parts of German territory in ruins, forced French Protestants to flee north and seek refuge in the Dutch Republic as well as Prussia, and made an entire century from the 1620s to the 1720s perilous for anyone out of step with the prevailing orthodoxy of a state or region. The Enlightenment in the Germanic lands was fed by, and fed into, the search for a secular freedom. At times, we can only marvel at the linkages formed between disparate seekers whether in The Hague or Hessen. Somehow, they found one another.

There were a number of German scholars and intellectuals—largely forgotten today—who played a part in the move away from the theology of Christian orthodoxy. Perhaps the most extreme of these seekers will never be identified. He left behind a manuscript, *Symbolum sapientiae* (*Symbol of Wisdom*), which proclaims simply that "there is no difference between religion and superstition." This mysterious freethinker knew the writings of just about every major philosopher of the seventeenth century, and cast a cold eye on "people ... who let themselves be cheated and persuaded by secular and spiritual rulers."[18] Echoing Hobbes, the anonymous text speaks about a state of nature where there is no religion and no fables. There are also many borrowings from Spinoza. The best the historian can do in identifying the author is to assume that it was someone from Halle and probably in the circle of Thomasius students. It could also have been done in Hamburg, Kiel, Wittenberg, or Leipzig. Today, the manuscript sits in the National Library in Vienna, and we are still none the wiser about who wrote it.

Looking at the most radical texts found in the first stirrings of enlightened thought coming from Germany only puts into sharper focus the more moderate minded of the early German philosophes. Being moderate, however, was no guarantee that controversy could be avoided. Such was the fate that awaited Christian Wolff in Halle, a formal philosopher, a professor of mathematics and natural philosophy, who started with the new science of Newton and Leibniz and sought to find the same level of certainty in philosophy. Like the Newtonian medical doctor from Scotland whom we met in the preceding chapter, Archibald Pitcairne, Wolff wanted to bring to every discipline—to politics, medicine, agriculture—the same rigor of theorems and observation found in astronomy.[19] He was influenced by Leibnizian philosophy, by the belief that this is the best of all possible worlds and that one key to knowing it lies in empirical exploration. Wolff also discussed with Leibniz mathematical proofs and the Cartesian philosophy.[20] However, Wolff was no slavish follower of Leibniz; indeed, he was an original philosopher who influenced the great Immanuel Kant. In matters educational, he was also influenced by Locke and believed education should provide usable skills.

Yet Wolff ran afoul of the religious authorities in Halle in 1723. There is irony in that fact. The University of Halle had been founded in 1694, under the patronage of the Elector of Brandenburg, Frederick III (d. 1713), in the hope that it would practice academic freedom in an atmosphere of religious toleration and moderation. Halle could embody a new, enlightened approach to learning and give pride of place to philosophy independent of theology. In practice, this meant that each faculty enjoyed independence from the other and resented any apparent advantage awarded to one and not the other. The result was constant in-fighting (in private) about appointments, salaries, teaching responsibilities, and basically about which faculty would control the university.

By 1710, three Halle professors exemplified three radically different approaches to the search for autonomous, enlightened learning: Christian Thomasius (d. 1728), who would give pride of place to the law faculty and its role in training the next generation of lawyers and court councilors; August Francke, who wanted Enlightenment to be about spiritual renewal and favored the training of the clergy; and after 1709, Wolff (d. 1754), who would give preeminence to philosophy and its independent search, by empirical means, for truth about the world.[21] He saw mathematics as the discipline that should provide the method of learning appropriate to all the other disciplines. Wolff further extended his influence by taking up the teaching of physics and astronomy, both informed by his mathematical method.

All believed that education should be useful in life—but for what? Law, business, court service, or to facilitate eternal salvation? Francke wanted "enlightenment" guided by Christ and the Holy Spirit, while Wolff would follow reason inculcated by the study of mathematics and science. One of his followers of the next generation, Moses Mendelssohn, explained when defending theism, "All propositions of mathematics, therefore, permit themselves with complete confidence to be applied to actually existing things, on the assumption that these things exist . . . in our discourse about God, there is a speculative part that . . . can be treated with the utmost rigor of the exact sciences."[22] As this next generation would discover, anything, even the existence of divine Providence, could be rigorously disputed.

Disputation, complemented by the search for patronage and prestige, had long prevailed as a way of life in European universities. In Germany for many decades, the contestation between Lutherans and Pietists had only intensified and naturally spilled over into the universities.[23] By the 1720s, the stakes had, however, risen: the new king of Prussia, Frederick William 1 (d. 1740) sought to consolidate his power and the hegemony of orthodox Protestantism. His major preoccupations focused on building the military, frugality, and various objects of his obsessive anger; his son became its prime target. Frederick William's temper may have been a factor in creating the first crisis of the German Enlightenment.

Christian Wolff had long been a thorn in the side of Halle's theology faculty; they vied for students and their fees, for prominence in the university, and for the mantle of religious orthodoxy. Both sides were happy to try to enlist the court, even the king, in their struggle. Wolff taught a version of Leibniz's optimistic philosophy—that this is the best of all possible worlds—a position easily open to misinterpretation. If the world is set as it is, where is human free will and where is God's power to alter it at will? The specter that haunted the discussion came from the influence of Spinoza's claim that human actions are determined; the passions are involuntary. In that direction lay atheism. The theology faculty's confrontation with Wolff turned Spinoza into the ogre of choice among the orthodox who became obsessed with freethinking and pantheism right into the 1780s.[24]

With the issue of free will, the theology faculty had its smoking gun; it claimed that students were visibly upset by Wolff's teachings: his metaphysics led to atheism. Events turned ominous when Francke, assisted by Joachim Lange, managed to get the personal ear of the king. The theology faculty took its disputes right to the source of all power, and just to make the point clear to Frederick William, Francke asserted that the application of Wolff's teachings would undermine military discipline. Deserters could be seen as only following their predetermined purpose.[25]

The importance of the military for Prussian government had long offended participants in university life. There were frequent disturbances between students and soldiers. Yet this tension did not inhibit the faculties from trying to exercise their influence at court and play upon its militaristic obsessions. Francke and Wolff vied for influence, but the theologian got the better of the philosopher.

The gambit of direct appeal worked, and in November 1723 the king condemned Wolff, ordered him to stop teaching, leave Halle in forty-eight hours, or face death by hanging. Wolff left the next morning, crossing the river that separated Halle from neighboring territory. Within a month, he had offers from other German universities that included a 300 percent increase in salary. In time, Frederick William relented and sought to bring Wolff back. His much put-upon son Frederick, who took the throne in 1740, further righted the wrong.

Wolff's treatment at the hands of an absolutist monarch carried a lesson that would stay in place for the rest of the century.[26] German and Austrian professors, and indeed all intellectuals, needed to take note of the power of the state and grapple with its meaning. Right into the 1780s, dissenters from the absolut-

ism of the German and Austrian states sought refuge in anonymity and utopian thinking.[27] Predictably, the 1790s turned
grim, as princes all over Europe reacted with fear and alarm to
the forces unleashed by the French Revolution.

Few dared challenge absolutism, and even Kant argued for
the obedience of the civil servant, for the necessity of public order. In another respect, the preponderance of Leibniz and then
Wolff in German intellectual life meant that well into the 1740s,
little attention was paid to Newtonian physico-theology or to
the search for knowable laws in the human sciences. Newton
was treated as a great mathematician, not a metaphysician. It
was only in the second half of the century that Leibnizian and
Wolffian optimism about a preexisting harmony and the best
of all possible worlds fell out of favor and Newtonian natural
philosophy became paradigmatic.[28]

Yet Wolff retained many followers. Johann Melchior Goeze
(1717–86), a Lutheran pastor and Wolffian theologian in Hamburg, took umbrage at the religious views of Gotthold Ephraim
Lessing, among other representatives of the Enlightenment.
Their quarrel turned nasty and eventually led to Lessing being
prohibited from publishing his ideas on religion. In the confrontation with Lessing, Goeze, who was the spiritual head of
the state church, put Lutheranism into conflict with possibly
the greatest philosophe of the German Enlightenment. Both
Goeze and Lessing wrote for a wider audience; keeping religious controversies in Latin had ceased. With these battle lines
drawn, the public hunt commenced for the heretical within the
new enlightened culture.

As in the rest of Western Europe, the public sphere in the
German-speaking lands expanded in the course of the century.
It was in the court of public opinion that we can pinpoint the
moment in the 1740s when the Leibnizian system fell out of

favor at least with the Berlin Royal Academy of Sciences.[29] An essay that argued against the existence of Leibniz's monads—minuscule particles of sensate matter—won its prize for being the best in 1747. Without dwelling on the tortured metaphysics of the monad—and its eventual demise—what is important about the controversy is the entry of new journals and periodicals into the fray. What in decades past would have remained a matter for university faculties and their many rivalries became a subject for the public. That ever-illusive entity, filling secular space and signaling an opening—the realm of opinion, educated, combative, and curious—the public belonged to a new modernity with which we still live.

From the 1720s onward, German-speaking Europe took up the fashion of spectatorial literature, first English, then Dutch, and now European. Educational goals informed this growing periodical literature, sometimes called the "moral weeklies." They sought to lessen the gap between the learned and the unlearned, and the first approaches to the public were open imitations of the immensely popular British periodicals like *The Spectator*. In this decade, weeklies appeared in Zurich, Hamburg, Halle, and Leipzig. By midcentury, there were over one hundred being published, and they singled out superstition for special ridicule. Their purpose became the cultivation of virtue, and it rested on a belief in the progressive nature of Enlightenment philosophy. No social change was advocated, although the weeklies did break with custom and address women directly. By the last third of the century, journals appeared that were intended for women, and even edited by women. Perhaps the most important journal of the period, *Briefe, die neueste Literatur betreffend* (Letters concerning the most recent Literature, 1759–65) originated among some of the leading German philosophes, Lessing (1729–81), Moses Mendelssohn (b. 1729), and the publisher, Friedrich Nicolai (b. 1733).[30] The genre lay at the heart of *die Aufklärung* (the Enlightenment).

Just as important, literacy possessed by about 5 percent of the population in 1700, grew to 25 percent by the end of the century. Predictably, the number of every type of printed text also expanded: poetry, plays, operas, sheet music, and of course books. Reading societies proliferated, spreading even to the servant class. The proportion of Latin titles steadily declined, and by the 1770s secular titles had taken the place of the catechism as vehicles for shaping moral character. Most historians of the German Enlightenment credit the reading revolution with giving a defining identity to the middle class. Live theater further complemented this new persona, and Johann Schlegel (1719–49) wrote immensely popular plays, among them *Canut*, an exploration of enlightened absolutism that came close to glorifying a rebellious heroism.

The English theater influenced the German stage, and so too did themes drawn from the French philosophes. Voltaire's attack on the injustice rendered to Jean Calas made its way into a play of the same name (1774) written by Christian Weisse.[31] German language opera and musical performance in general flourished in the Berlin and Vienna courts but also in new musical halls where German composers came into their own. Out of these activities emerged the age of Bach, Haydn, Mozart, and Beethoven. Gradually, the German Enlightenment escaped the confines of its language; Wolff's writings appeared in French and so too did the plays and prose of Lessing. German opera began to rival that of Italy.[32]

While originating in the German courts and music halls, songs also became a vital part of enlightened culture in Vienna. Their origin lay much more in popular song and stage, not least in the songs used in masonic lodge meetings. While in disfavor with Queen Maria Theresa, her son and heir in 1780, Joseph II,

FIGURE 9. A meeting of a main Viennese masonic lodge, with Mozart
reputed to be the last figure on the right. Courtesy of Wikimedia.

embraced freemasonry and its culture. So too did Frederick
the Great in Berlin. Songs in lodges functioned like hymns in
church, used at the opening and closing of meetings and on
special occasions. Many of these appeared in the famous *Journal
für Freymaurer* during the 1780s, and by 1790 some took on
Jacobin political meaning—much to the horror of Emperor
Joseph. That Haydn and Mozart were active freemasons only
adds to the importance of masonic music before the repression
of the 1790s (figure 9). The songs glorified Joseph II and his
enlightened endeavors, and they also proclaimed the equality
of all brothers: as one song put it, "In the communal guild of
Freemasons the slave is as worthy as the king: here precedence
is justified solely by virtuous conduct."[33]

The Viennese lodges and cafes became homes for poets and writers, not just songwriters. The poet Gottlieb von Leon and his friends met in the Kramersches Kaffeehaus as well as in the lodge True Harmony, where eventually could be found Mozart and various government officials. Before 1785, Mozart preferred the more Catholic lodge Zur Wohltätigkeit ("For Beneficence"), but in that year Joseph II clamped down on the lodges, and within a year True Harmony disappeared. Some of the members then joined groups with democratic tendencies and were accused of engaging in conspiracy and arrested. Leon continued to write but turned increasingly toward Romanticism. After 1785, the days of Josephinism were remembered as a lost "golden age," when, it was believed, tolerance and the search for social harmony had dominated city life.[34] Before 1785, Joseph II had proclaimed religious tolerance for all orthodox Christians, gave some relief to Jews, brought the Austrian church under the control of the state, closed most of the monasteries, and loosened censorship of books and journals. After 1785, the more radical masonic lodges were suppressed and the entirety of Austrian freemasonry brought under the oversight of the state.

Much hyperbole surrounded the pre-1785 Viennese Enlightenment and its presumed leader, Joseph II. In the novel *Faustin*, thinly imitative of Voltaire's *Candide*, Johann Pezzl invented an imagined replica of the Habsburg emperor who presided over the century of philosophy. The tolerance of Faustin is matched only by his adulation of the French philosophes, while the surrounding clergy are depicted as book burners who jail people because of their heretical libraries. Everywhere he goes, this hero of the Enlightenment condemns belief in sorcery, the devil, and hell itself. Traveling to Italy, Faustin casts a particularly cold eye on the religious repression found there. The novel ends with

Faustin and a friend settled happily in Vienna, proclaiming that under Joseph II, reason and humanity reign.[35] Pezzl is a perfect representative of the extremes the Viennese Enlightenment could exhibit. His attack on monasticism and superstition, and his disdain for European colonialism, incurred the hostility of the church, yet Pezzl kept his deism private in the interest of public peace. So too did many other German philosophes, and like quite a few of them Pezzl was also a freemason, a member of Mozart's lodge. As one brother put it, "Similar to birds in a nest, Masons live as brothers in the House of Joseph."[36]

Joseph II, like his mother before him, was a believing Catholic who wanted his state and empire to be Catholic, but first and foremost subject to secular control. He also wanted Austrian culture to rival that of its northern, Protestant neighbors, and he accepted the influence of English and French texts as an inevitable part of the German cultural scene. Although Austria and France had long been political enemies, Joseph welcomed the influence of the philosophes before 1785, when he then disavowed them as atheists and materialists.

The 1780s in Central and Southern Europe were intellectually tempestuous. By the middle of the decade, it was clear to the absolutist monarchs and territorial princes that considerable discontent, often of enlightened origin, lurked in their cities. In Germany and Austria, the Illuminati—a secret and radical form of freemasonry—elicited a witch-hunt-like atmosphere, and hundreds were arrested by the authorities. In the Austrian Netherlands, Josephine reforms aimed against the church and aristocracy, often led by state officials who were freemasons, produced further discontent. By 1785–86, the Josephine regime concluded that the lodges were a threat to order, and consolidated them into only one for each of the three Belgian provinces. The reaction in some masonic circles was swift and threatening: "We wanted to imitate them; the Kings, the sovereigns, the magistrates . . . but alas! The power is without boundary, the authority without limits, the slavery absolute; & the Mason generally only finds the happy alliance of sovereignty and liberty in his lodges."[37] With the outbreak of the French Revolution in 1789, the situation in Austria became even more repressive. Censorship returned with a vengeance, as did the secret police who took charge of it.

A minor and moderate member of the Viennese Enlightenment, Mozart reacted to all these twists and turns. He resented being treated like a servant, which was the way his court employers treated him. Like Maria Theresa, he had been influenced by a reforming Catholicism of Italian origin. Of course, the papacy had condemned membership in the lodges in 1738 and 1751, and the effect had been to propel liberal-minded freemasons like Mozart into an anti-papal stance. He had applauded the Josephine reforms, and after 1785, like so many German thinkers, Mozart turned increasingly toward a mystical and magical version of freemasonry best described as Rosicrucian.[38] It was as if the German Enlightenment had rediscovered evil and sin; a darker and brooding vision overcame the intellectual life of many lodges, and Mozart participated in this turn to the mystical. This is best exemplified in his most famous and baffling opera, *The Magic Flute* (*Die Zauberflöte*), first performed in the autumn of 1791.

This opera's use of symbolism, much of it drawn from alchemy and Egyptology, sought to depict good and evil as residing in the same psyche, the same soul. The music draws out these conflicting emotions that are reconciled only at the end of the opera, when the sun triumphantly rises and the soul emerges into the light. The characters depict various virtues and vices and are searching for an apotheosis, a way forward toward the light. The opera may exemplify the so-called Catholic Enlightenment and should be seen as religious, not secular in its inspiration. It is perhaps a fitting end to the Austrian Enlightenment and its dependence on the indulgence of the emperor. *The Magic Flute* lived on nevertheless, and its themes were taken up by Goethe, who worked on plays inspired by it, yet possessing none of the mysticism and comedy so beloved by Mozart.[39]

The "High Enlightenment" in Germany

Traditionally, the "High Enlightenment" is associated with Paris after 1750, with the intellectual universe of heresy sampled by our traveling book dealer, the widow Stockdorff. Here, we may also associate it with the emergence of a vibrant culture graced by philosophes like Lessing, Herder (whom we met as an unknown young man in chapter 3), the Jewish philosopher Moses Mendelssohn, of course, and Friedrich Nicolai, as well as the brilliant Johann Wolfgang von Goethe, Friedrich Schiller, and Immanuel Kant. All were familiar with the writings of the French Enlightenment, looked to England as the model of enlightened politics, and made major contributions to German literature. Throughout much of the eighteenth century, France had a larger population than Germany, and its urban centers, beginning with Paris, were also much larger. Yet in the period 1750 to 1850, led by Georg Hegel and Karl Marx, German philosophy dominated Western thought. The steps along this path had been set by *Die Aufklärung*.[40]

Many leaders of the German Enlightenment came out of Lutheran backgrounds. Lessing's father had been a modest, provincial vicar with puritanical ideas about what his son should study and how he should live. His parents wanted Lessing to study theology, a plan from which he quickly rebelled, left university, and struck out for a career as a journalist and play writer in Hamburg. Lessing's dislike for the heavy hand of authority probably began at home and stayed with him his entire life. His intellect was remarkably precocious and he learned languages, both ancient and modern, with extraordinary skill. His writing style transformed the German language and he introduced plays that catered not to the elite or the titled, but to ordinary citizens. One of his earliest, *Miss Sara Sampson* (1755), depicted events as occurring in England, and dwelt upon issues of absolute virtues and vices. After dumping his mistress of many years and the mother of his child, a deeply flawed hero seduces Sara. Thus unfolds the tragedy as he becomes ensnared in a drama about their child and his own deep ambivalence about marriage, even to the young woman whom he now professes to love. The drama centers on the remorse of Sara, who, with her seducer, has fled her father's home, and the efforts she and her father make to reconcile. In the end, various characters meet death by murder or suicide, and the father is left with only the grandchild who is not his own but whom he decides to raise as if she were.

The father in *Miss Sara* is a paragon of virtue who forgives his daughter and her seducer; he is a practitioner of Christian virtue. The deeply flawed seducer is more weak than evil; as Sara's father puts it, "he was unfortunate rather than vicious." Sara is a version of Richardson's fictional Clarissa, a maiden beset by the whims and pleasures of her youth and inexperience. Lessing was inspired by the English novel of the same name as well as by various sentimental family dramas by Diderot. It is very difficult at this distance to imagine the Hamburg audience that sat spellbound, in the end weeping, but from all accounts, that was the effect of these morally infused characters, ordinary and beset by quandaries and character flaws from which they cannot escape. Lessing is also clearly struggling with patriarchal authority, here presented sympathetically. Diderot was so taken with the play that he commissioned a translation, but it was never published. In other of Lessing's plays—some still performed in German theaters—the father as prince is depicted as tyrannous.[41]

In his last tragedy, *Emilia Galotti*, conceived in the 1750s but completed only in the 1770s, Lessing chose to place it in an Italian principality and thus could argue that it was meant to have no contemporary political significance. Once again there is a father figure who is entirely sympathetic and—again—the deeply flawed suitor who has become the libertine and tyrannous prince of the territory. He is sinister and dangerous, and his pursuit of Emilia makes her so deranged that she persuades her father to kill her. What is remarkable about Lessing's tragedies rests in their failure to convince us that this is the best of all possible worlds. While in them religion is not dwelt upon, other writings by Lessing put him in the eye of the heretical storm and earned him a place as a freethinker, or worse in the eyes of his harshest critics, a Spinozist.

The charge was deeply fraught. After his death in 1677, Spinoza was systematically vilified. His enemies never missed the chance to point out that he had been a heretic and a Jew. Lessing knew his philosophizing well, but more to the point after he left home as a young man in search of a literary career, Lessing, now in Berlin, met and befriended Jews, among them the young—soon to become famous—Moses Mendelssohn. In the mid-eighteenth century, a sea change occurred in the reading and understanding of Spinoza. Partly under the impact of the new biological sciences, the appearance of French materialists at the Berlin court of Frederick the Great, and the reinstatement of Wolff in Halle, opinion about Spinoza shifted. Freethinking required an engagement with his philosophy, not its simple-minded rejection. At precisely this time, Lessing and

Mendelssohn came to their study of the greatest Jewish philosopher of early modern times.

A year before *Miss Sara Sampson*, Lessing provoked learned Germans in a play about Jews, *Die Juden* (1754). Amid the prevailing anti-Semitism found throughout Germany, a legacy that has been rightly implicated in the Holocaust of World War II, Lessing presented his audience with an entirely different image of the Jew from what had been commonplace. Rather than the reviled money-changer and trickster, Lessing's Jew is an honorable man, a selfless traveler who befriends a nobleman set upon by robbers dressed as Jews. The play hangs on the identity of the traveler and the robbers. Having been accosted, he thinks, by Jews, the baron's anti-Semitism is given a full airing, and he is so grateful to the traveler that he offers his daughter in marriage. Meanwhile, the robbers shed their costumes. The traveler reveals that he is an actual Jew and of course forbidden, by state law, to marry a Christian. Once again, true virtue is embedded in a single character—think Sara and Emilia—only this time, he is a Jew speaking perfect German (not the customary Yiddish), noble in character.

This theme is expanded upon in Lessing's most famous play, *Nathan der Weise*, first performed in 1783. Nathan, the Jew, is modeled upon Moses Mendelssohn, and he is a study in parental devotion to his daughter, who has been saved from their burning house by an itinerant Templar. He may have been inserted for the masonic element in the audience because many German freemasons believed that they were descended from the persecuted Knights Templar. Nathan exhibits only good will toward the Templar, and also toward his friend and chess partner, a Muslim. Lessing puts in the language of the Christian knight a fairly typical anti-Semitism. Eventually, after falling in love with Nathan's daughter whom he had rescued, the

Templar acquires the ability to think without prejudice. Not so the Christian Patriarch; living in Jerusalem where all the action unfolds, he shows only a doctrinaire hatred of Jews whom he would burn after finding them in violation of Christian law. Nathan is left to articulate the vision of Christianity, Judaism, and Islam as separate but equal.

Lessing wrote *Nathan the Wise* in the wake of his quarrel with Goeze, and it was as much a plea for religious equality as it was an attack on Christian heresy-mongering. Mendelsohn loved the play, as did many liberal thinkers in Germany into the twentieth century. In 1945, it was the first play to be performed after the German defeat. Critics have argued that Nathan is an abstraction, and we learn little about his practice of Judaism; it is hidden throughout much of the play, submerged and privatized in the face of a universalist humanism. However, it illustrates well the growing consensus among philosophes that religion should be a private matter, never assailed or enforced by church or state.

Amid all the journalism and play-writing, Lessing retained a deep interest in his first subjects of study, religion and theology. He was a seeker, an enemy of rationalizations who delighted in paradoxes, even contradictions. He sought a pure religion of the heart and mind and he was not afraid to sound heretical. His early writings display an even-handed interest in being historical and comparative about the three monotheistic religions.

When made librarian at the Duke of Brunswick's remarkable library at Wolfenbüttel—still one of the great European libraries—Lessing had the time and resources to pursue religious topics. In his essay *Leibniz on Eternal Punishments*, Lessing seems to endorse Christian orthodoxy (as does Leibniz), but read closely, the text argues for heaven and hell as relative places, not absolute states. Both good and evil in various degrees reside in everyone and hence both can be found among those who reside in either heaven or hell. Nothing stopped Lessing from embracing heresies, sometimes only temporarily. Being librarian gave Lessing access to an unprecedented amount of unpublished manuscripts, some of them in that state because they could never pass the censors. It also gave him the perfect cover if he decided to publish heretical material he deemed important. Having gotten such material from the daughter of the deceased Herman Samuel Reimarus (d. 1768), Lessing recognized its dangerous content and decided to publish fragments from it anonymously. He claimed to have no idea where the library had gotten "On the Toleration of the Deists: Fragment of an anonymous Writer" (1774), even suggesting that the author might have been J. Lorenz Schmidt (d. 1749), the translator of Spinoza into German, who spent time in jail for his publications and had to live in obscurity under various assumed names. The fragment argued for the toleration of rationalists and deists and it took issue with the veracity of biblical stories.

That Reimarus's daughter, Elise (b. 1735), supplied the heretical material should not surprise us. She was front and center in enlightened circles and an avid correspondent with Lessing, Mendelssohn, Jacobi, and others. Her family, both maternal and paternal, contained many academics, and in addition a financially advantageous marriage meant that her father could educate all his children, not simply his sons. Elise grew up in an enlightened household and, like so many women drawn to its ideals, led a literary salon that met in the Reimarus home. Although she possessed a deep affection for Lessing, she never married. In matters religious, she was, like her father, a deist. In the 1790s, she also expressed democratic sentiments, and the household was known for its anti-aristocratic views. Her own literary achievements were unexceptional, and largely poetic. After Lessing's death, she stopped writing poetry. Yet when she gave Lessing her father's manuscript, she clearly understood and approved its contents. Lessing's first published fragment went largely unnoticed; that would soon change.[42]

Seeming to fly under the radar, and against the counsel of his friends, Lessing published more fragments, far bolder than the first: the clergy should stop decrying reason because they need it to argue for the truth of Christianity; revelation cannot possibly speak to all men and salvation comes through the book of nature, by the natural religion possessed by all men; the Israelites could not have possibly passed through the parted Red Sea in one night, it would have taken nine days at least; revelation is full of contradictions and inconsistencies. As Reimarus sums it up:

> Now since it is apparent to everyone that these miracles are self-contradictory and truly impossible, they cannot have occurred. They must therefore have been made up and indeed so noticeably and crudely that one easily sees they come from an author who neither himself experienced this migration and saw everything that it would entail in the context of the Red Sea, nor had any clear conception adequate to what experience and the facts would require.[43]

A storm of criticism assaulted Lessing. At first patiently, and then with growing sarcasm and irritation, Lessing struck back. Recently widowed and grieving, he went after Goeze and wrapped himself in the mantle of Luther; his "spirit absolutely requires that no man may be prevented from advancing in the knowledge of the truth according to his own judgment." For his part, Goeze accused Lessing of being a disciple of the English deists, Tindal and Toland, while Lessing's employer, the duke of Brunswick, told him that now he must submit to censorship.[44] Furious, Lessing turned back to the genre of drama writing he had practiced so well; the result was *Nathan the Wise*.

In a letter of 1780, Lessing told his friend and fellow freemason Herder that he had intended to find a middle way between orthodoxy and radical deism. He was searching for a historical understanding of Christianity and a way of reading the Bible, not as divine word but as a fascinating historical record of the first centuries of Christian belief that preceded the writing of the New Testament. He distinguished between the "religion of Christ" and the Christian religion, which "is so uncertain and ambiguous, that there is scarcely a single passage which, in all the history of the world, has been interpreted in the same way by two men."[45]

There is no point in trying to depict Lessing as an orthodox Christian by the standard of his day. Similarly, while many believed that he had become a secret Spinozist, and hence by the same standard, an atheist, this is also unprovable. Rather, like so many of the philosophes, Lessing came to believe that religion was an entirely private matter and the enlightened search for truth about human destiny required soul searching, questioning, iconoclastic debunking, and a deep dislike for the system builders in theology. Convinced that the human soul is immortal, Lessing even entertained speculations about the possibility of metempsychosis or reincarnation. Struggling with the role of reason in relation to revelation, he sought allies among the educated and enlightened, but did not always find them.[46] Lessing had started out in the Leibnizian-Wolffian tradition, but toward the end of his life, natural religion and heretical philosophy appealed far more.

Lessing searched in many ancient and modern texts and social movements. He also looked in freemasonry, as did so many German literati. In his dialogue in *Ernst und Falk*, Lessing and late German seekers after true Enlightenment looked at the Prussian state and its discontents. As the freemason, he has his fictional character, Falk, tell his interlocutor, Ernst—in the 1778 dialogue

that bears their names—"deeds . . . good men and young men . . .
observe their deeds"—and let these speak for themselves. After reciting the many charitable actions undertaken by German
and Swedish freemasons, Falk extols the necessity of doing good
deeds "in the world." Throughout the dialogue of *Ernst und Falk*,
certain assumptions are basic: men and institutions require reform and renewal, religious differences separate humankind,
freemasons aim at social equality, but they will be no better or
worse than the civil society that surrounds them.[47] From the
wholehearted embrace of the secular, Falk inevitably turns to
the state. Because centered in "die bürgerliche Gesellschaft (civil
society)," Falk can ask, "Do you believe that men were created
for the state, or that states are for men?" He notes that states create divisions around wealth or religion; freemasons are the only
men capable of healing those divisions. This meditation on the
need for reform allows Lessing to return to freemasonry, and to
castigate the refusal of its German form to admit Jews.

By contrast, the French philosophe Mirabeau (d. 1791), inspired by the goals of freemasonry despite its many flaws, would
set up a parallel organization to aid all of humankind through
education and most importantly through the reform of law and
government. Its members must be freemasons and labor for
"the one object of the order of Freemasonry: THE GOOD OF
ALL MANKIND." As Mirabeau describes it, the second "great
object . . . is the correction of the actual system of law and government." This correction "may be special or general, gradual or
sudden, secret or open."[48] In contrast and in keeping with the
tenor of the German Enlightenment, Lessing was far less politi-
cally engaged and certainly no advocate of political revolutions.

There was plenty with which to fault the German lodges of the
eighteenth century. Falk finds objectionable the superstitions
about the Knights Templar, the recourse to the magical arts, the

play with words, gestures and symbols, and not least, the inability to promote true and absolute equality. Yet Falk clearly implies that there are freemasons who support the American Revolution.[49] *Ernst und Falk* directs the impulse for reform outward toward the state, then critically inward, toward the lodges of its day. Falk, speaking for Lessing, locates freemasonry as a state of mind, a way of being in the world, and not as the imperfect behavior that he so readily observed in everyday lodges. Some critics have argued that the fourth and fifth dialogues are more radical than the others, but there is an obvious continuity among them all. In advocating reform and renewal, Lessing was in tune with the discontents that permeated German freemasonry in the 1770s and 1780s. Like Christianity, freemasonry is deeply flawed, but participation, he argues, can lead to self-criticism, enriched friendships, and independent learning.[50]

Lessing's meditation on freemasonry resonated among reformers particularly in the wake of the French Revolution. In the 1790s, Herder offered his own meditation on freemasonry and the state, in the form of a dialogue that is clearly in dialogue with *Ernst und Falk*. He begins by embracing "all the good that has been done . . . in the world." Herder, himself a freemason, reiterates "in the world." He starts with Falk's question, are men created for the state, or the state for men? He then, like Falk, notes all the divisions that states impose upon men, and he ends by invoking his desire to have a society composed of all the thinking men in the entire world.[51] Herder's embrace of a cosmopolitan and utopian order is another example of masonic language being employed to investigate the ideal of civil society. This order, too, is perfectly in keeping with the logic of the secular impulse that fosters attention to civil society and the state.

Neither Herder nor Lessing, who died before the revolution, was willing, however, to intervene in the political workings of the state. They watched on the sidelines, hoping that someday the reform of human moral codes would inspire transformation in the mundane order. As Herder explains, "Every living force is active and continues active. Thus ... it progresses and perfects itself according to inner eternal laws of wisdom and goodness, which are urged upon it and inherent in it."[52] Herder never clearly defined what he meant by a force (*Kraft*).

While waiting for progress toward perfectibility, consolation could be found in cosmopolitan sociability. Lessing drew comfort from his deep friendship with Moses Mendelssohn (1729–86), a Yiddish-speaking Jew from a poor family who possessed a prodigious intellect and, like Lessing, a gift for languages. Mendelssohn in his youth learned the Talmud and became a brilliant German prose stylist as well as a critic of the French philosophes, the Newtonian Maupertuis, Rousseau, and having mastered English, of Pope and Burke. His intellectual passion, fed in part by his reading of Leibniz and Wolff, focused on philosophy and metaphysics. In 1754, he met Lessing, and their bond lasted until Lessing's death in 1781—indeed continued after it—as Mendelssohn sought to protect his friend's posthumous reputation. They shared an absolute commitment to religious toleration, to civil rights for Jews, and to the necessity of using reason as the key to unlock the mysteries of the monotheistic religions. Mendelssohn further believed in the absolute right of liberty of conscience, that the state had no right to use coercive power over it. He even extended the liberty to atheists.[53]

In 1783, Mendelssohn presented his understanding of Judaism and laid out a vision by which the man of reason could adhere to it. He argued in *Jerusalem*, "I recognize no eternal verities except those which can not only be comprehended by the human intellect but also be demonstrated and verified by human reason.... I believe Judaism knows nothing of a *revealed religion* in the sense in which Christians define this term." Mendelssohn would eliminate any belief that flies in the face of reason and it rests on laws: "Judaism is a *Divine legislation*—laws, commandments, statutes, rules of conduct, instruction in God's will and in what they are to do to attain temporal and eternal salvation."[54] Moses gave these laws to the Jews who are obliged to follow them. They are to be taught and followed but never imposed by force by either church or state.

Mendelssohn became the leading figure in the *haskalah*, the Jewish Enlightenment, and his influence extended into the twentieth century. Only poor health kept him from reading and writing more about philosophy and what he called "the truths of natural religion." By the 1780s, he came to believe that materialism haunted the Enlightenment and its sources extended back to Hobbes and Spinoza (d. 1677), and later Toland (d. 1722).[55] Mendelssohn also realized that the rabbis were capable of censoring enlightened Jews, of trying to turn the tide back to traditional education, in religious as opposed to secular subjects. Joseph II pushed in the opposite direction, wanting to see the Germanization of the Jews in his empire. By 1782, deep fissures within the Jewish community had become visible: freethinkers versus the rabbis afraid of change; the hyper-Orthodox Hasidim versus the followers of the Enlightenment; the revivers of the Kabbalah versus the rationalist philosophers like Mendelssohn.[56]

The writings of Spinoza accentuated these fissures and particularly troubled both the German and Jewish Enlightenments; his equation of God with Nature, hence his assumed atheism and materialism, could be used against any philosophe trying to put religion on a firm foundation of reason, or as Mendelssohn put it, on "the rational knowledge of God."[57] His critical responses—*Morning Hours* appeared in 1785, followed the next year by the posthumously published *To the Friends of Lessing*—constituted his defense of rational, providential theism. For the criterion for truth-seeking, Mendelssohn, like so many of the European philosophes, assumed that the new science inherited from Galileo and Newton had enriched "our knowledge beyond our every expectation."[58] Knowing from science that truth is attainable, he rejected the hypothesis that mere chance governs the world, and "we always search for a cause whenever we discern harmony and concord with diversity."[59] Mendelssohn takes his audience through general philosophy and epistemology because he is setting up the intellectual conditions by which he can prove the existence of God: "Without God, providence, and immortality, all the good things in my life are in my eyes worthless and contemptible . . . or as Voltaire says, without this comforting prospect we are all swimming in the deep . . . with no hope of ever reaching the shore."[60]

The reason for Mendelssohn's writing an entire defense of theism based upon rational argumentation, and then a defense of Lessing, lay in his desire to set the foundation for a truly tolerant person and to defend the memory of Lessing. In 1783, Lessing's acquaintance Friedrich Jacobi announced in a letter that Lessing had been a secret pantheist. Such a fatalistic Spinozism, Jacobi believed, was the only systematic philosophy compatible with reason, and he loathed it. Mendelssohn spied in his motives the desire to undercut the basis of a truly tolerant society. Two years later, Jacobi published the correspondence with Mendelssohn at the same time as he learned that Mendelssohn would publish his defense of providential theism. In the eyes of Mendelssohn, Jacobi had accused Lessing, "known to the world as the great and admired defender of theism and the religion of reason . . . of being a Spinozist, an atheist, and a blasphemer."[61] Thus ensued another crisis within *Die Aufklärung,* this one known as the *Pantheismusstreit* (the pantheism conflict).

The conflict made a deep impact on what became the final decade of the Enlightenment in Germany. The dispute turned very public, and Lessing's reputation was dragged through the streets for his supposedly being an atheist. Almost certainly he had defended Spinoza to Jacobi with the usual paradoxes and contradictions that were the hallmarks of Lessing's philosophical style. As Herder put it, "you know Lessing's way of turning things in such a manner as to show the absurdity of the absurd."[62] Jacobi missed the nuance and the jest; Lessing's relationship with Mendelssohn and Jews in general fed his prejudices. Anti-Semitism had always lurked beneath the surface in all of Lessing's disputes. Earlier, in the dispute with Goeze, a Viennese journal even accused Lessing of taking money from Amsterdam Jews to finance his publications. Only this time in the pantheism conflict, and despite calls for him to be punished, the duke of Brunswick stood by Lessing.[63]

Almost certainly, Lessing remained deeply influenced by his religious background, yet drawn to ideas that would undermine traditional, theological system building. Lessing enjoyed using the motto, "I am One and All," and from it Jacobi deduced that Lessing was a pantheist. Yet it is more likely that Lessing found the beings in creation as possessing a distinct plurality; the world is the best possible because it manifests God's self-replication. With such a formulation, a distinct, if eccentric, theism remains true to Lessing's understanding, and also demonstrates how it was possible, by the mid-eighteenth century, to think outside the box of traditional Christian philosophy. It was a position easily misunderstood.[64]

Just as controversy had exhausted the fifty-year-old Lessing and, almost certainly, hastened his death, Mendelssohn also suffered under its impact. His health had always been frail, and on a bitterly cold New Year's Eve, 1785, Mendelssohn rushed his manuscript defense of Lessing to the publisher and caught a bad chill from which he never recovered. In his final days, Lessing had believed that the present condition of Christianity—so enfeebled by theological controversy and the desire to persecute—would have to be changed. By early 1786, two of the most important religious thinkers in Enlightenment Germany, who might have assisted in such a reform, were gone. For her part, Elise Reimarus, who had been a go-between among the major participants of the pantheist crisis, withdrew and blamed herself from having facilitated the exchange about Lessing.

Intellectual leadership, with somewhat different agendas, passed to Johann Gottfried von Herder (1744–1803), and his university professor, Immanuel Kant (figure 10). When last he appeared, Herder was a young and unknown traveler setting off to visit France. When there, he personally met (or read) some of the great philosophes, and he encountered the fashionable vitalism, or vitalist materialism, found in those circles as well as in medical thought of the period. All led Herder back to the study of Leibniz and Spinoza. He came away with the impression that France as a country was in need of reform, but its intellectuals steered him in the direction of a vitalism that became fundamental to his thinking.

First as a schoolteacher, and then as a Lutheran minister, Herder believed in a graduated pantheism where a form of immortality is still possible, and where system building and intolerance receive no validation. The influence of Lessing and Mendelssohn on him is palpable, as is his commitment to reason and the advance of new ideas.[65] The number of disciplines that Herder helped establish is daunting: hermeneutics, linguistics, anthropology, and a secular philosophy of history. While Herder continued the deep interest in philosophy and religion so characteristic of the German Enlightenment, he also searched for

FIGURE 10. Kant, the greatest original philosopher of the period. Johann Gottlieb Becker (1720–82) (ID# 141114). Courtesy of Bridgeman Images.

ways to explain the human condition in history, in the use of language, and in the profound differences observed among the peoples of the world.

Herder was no slavish follower of religiously inspired ideas, and he was an avid reader of travel literature. He came to recognize that the peoples of the world were vastly different. First in their languages, which "do not point to a divine origin of language, but to the very opposite, namely, that language has its origin in our animal nature . . . [it] is not derived from symbols of a divine grammar, but from the primitive sounds of natural organs. . . . Hence, language is inherent in, or the natural corollary of, the very first act of human reasoning."[66] The sounds will vary inevitably; languages will develop in groups of people, "essentially, therefore, the first human thought prepares communication with other beings."[67] Language use is deeply social.

With impeccable logic, Herder surveyed the infinitude of synonyms found in multiple languages and then came to a conclusion that "each of these . . . is closely connected with the customs, character and origin of a people; and everywhere it reveals the inventive spirit of man."[68] Herder's understanding of the origin of language laid the foundation for his acceptance of the multiplicity of human cultures and the need to study them. He put in place the conceptual foundations for what would become anthropology, and he did so scientifically, by collecting "factual data about the human mind, about the organization of human nature, about the structure of ancient and primitive languages and the conditions under which they developed."[69] Herder saw the natural and human sciences as two sides of the same empirical coin.

Undergirding Herder's intellectual trajectory, pantheism played a critical role. His reading of Spinoza, Lessing, and Joseph Priestley, among others, led to the conviction that we cannot rule out "the possibility of thought or other spiritual powers being material. . . . We know of no spirit capable of operating apart from, or without, matter . . . we observe in matter so many powers of a spirit-like nature." We are composed of "organic powers, the finger of creative Divinity."[70] Herder insisted upon a pantheism that gave no ground to the materialists who would eliminate the soul and immortality. He was, however, after even bigger stakes, the foundation of a "possible philosophy of human history."

The powers of the universe reside in the human mind; they require only an organization, or a series of organizations to set them in action. Every human being goes through a process of constant change and transformation, "thus the history of man is ultimately a theater of transformations," which only God, "who animates these events and lives and feels Himself in all of them, can review." All of humankind is one and the same species upon the earth. There are no races, only communities or nations, and their complexity forms "different shades of the same great picture which extends through all ages and all parts of the earth. Their study, therefore, properly forms no part of biology or systematic natural history but belongs rather to the anthropological history of man."[71] Space and time, having been stripped of qualities and attributes, now unbounded and absolute, can be filled by human action: "is it not feasible to assume that the combination of matter and power is capable of undergoing a series of mutations from its original state to a more developed and subtle organization?"[72] In Herder's vision, transformations in time arise from "mind and matter, and all the powers of matter, of attraction and repulsion, of motion, of life, originally from one single entity."[73]

Herder's understanding of the human condition is deeply democratic and temporal. Human actions fill secular time and space; human beings in their complexity, in their communities or nations, make history. The laws of physics are at work in space and time, and "no living power can stand still or retreat in the realm of nature, it must push forward, it must progress." This understanding of time as progressive, supported by the laws of nature, provides the key "to the wonderful phenomenon of man and hence also to a possible *philosophy of human history.*"[74]

Herder's intellectual move takes up an idea also found in Toland, that force resides within the very matter of the universe of which space and time are entities. The laws of attraction and repulsion govern "the history of our species . . . by the many attempts and enterprises that man has undertaken, and by the events and revolutions that have overtaken him." The human mind contains the powers of the universe, and only organization, or a series of organizations, can "set them in action." Space and time are "empty concepts" that the mind transcends, and fills.[75]

This transcendence occurs among individual minds that are bound together in communities. The social is essential for the human forces to work in space and time, to make history. Separated from their country or tribe, human beings are hopelessly adrift. From the abstractions of space and time, of mind and forces, Herder turns to the social condition of human beings, what is necessary for them to be engaged in making history. What would it be like to be devoid of such a communal, social condition?

Herder launches into a diatribe against slavery: "what gives you the right, you despicable slave-drivers, you inhuman brutes, even to approach the lands of these unfortunates, let alone to tear them away from it by cunning, fraud and cruelty?" The treatment of American natives receives an equally stern rebuke. All have been denied their free ability to make history.[76] For Herder, like Lessing, freedom is basic to human dignity and the capacity to make one's own history.

Residing in the Holy Roman Empire, Herder has nonetheless cast his historical vision globally. Slave trading and empire building were not the preserves of eighteenth-century Germans, yet Herder's passion is as powerful as that of the French Huguenot Benezet. Herder's deep interest in the injustices of empire building puts us in touch with one of the hallmarks of enlightened thinking, with cosmopolitanism. Although Herder, perhaps echoing Rousseau, casts aspersions on "the idle cosmopolite"—in contrast to the hospitable savage—his anti-imperialism depends upon a universal humanism founded in nature: "the very thought of a superior European culture is a blatant insult to the majesty of Nature."[77]

Herder bequeathed to us the ability to think about historical forces, unleashed by free individuals bound in communities or nations. Given the forces of attraction and repulsion, historical forces operate dialectically. They throw up a status quo—a thesis—that is pushed against by a contradictory force—the antithesis—and out of that struggle emerges a new order, a synthesis. In time, it becomes its own thesis, and the historical forces once again throw up contradictory forces. If this sounds familiar, it is because, although Herder did not use these terms, those who took up his understanding of historical forces created this dialectical understanding of world historical forces. There is a path that leads from Herder, via many twists and turns, to Hegel and Marx. They, however, never subscribed to Herder's anti-imperialism.

In addition, Marx was resolutely a materialist and Herder was decidedly not. His idealism, his emphasis on forces and their implied immateriality, is antithetical to Marx's economically rooted materialism. In Herder's struggle to escape the impoverished rationalism he associated with a certain of type of enlightened thinking, he had gone back to the seventeenth-century roots of the Enlightenment. He resurrected both Leibniz and Spinoza (as had Lessing), and in so doing brought Spinoza into the mainstream of Western philosophy, a dramatic rehabilitation, a rejection of decades wherein Spinoza had been dismissed as an atheist. In the middle of the pantheist conflict, in the mid-1780s, Herder wrote his most important philosophical and theological work, *God, Some Conversations* (1787).

It is a searching attempt to rehabilitate Spinoza and to explain his philosophy:

> The substances of the world are all maintained by divine power, just as they derived their existence from it alone. Therefore they constitute, if you will, appearances of divine powers, each modified according to the place, the time, and the organs in, and with which, they appear. . . . [Matter] is not dead but lives. For in it and conforming to its outer and inner organs, a thousand living, manifold forces are at work.

Herder anchors his argument for forces at work in nature by appealing to recent advances in science, particularly in the discovery of magnetic and electrical forces. The forces within nature make us "as limited beings we swim in space and time," but "no part of the world can also be a part of God."[78]

Herder's elevation of Spinoza took enlightened philosophy firmly away from the mechanistic materialism so prevalent in the French school of Enlightenment. Suddenly, a way of thinking that seemed to endorse nothing more interesting than atheism transformed itself into a dynamic approach to the study of humankind, of languages and histories. The invigoration of Spinoza's legacy by a believing Christian made the dismissals—generally offered by the devout—less tenable. Herder provided a philosophical foundation for the study of humankind progressing through time and space, developing language, making history. The foundation had been laid for anthropology as well as linguistics.

None of Herder's innovations occurred in a historical or personal vacuum. For starters, in 1785 his old friend and former teacher Kant delivered a blistering critique of *Ideas for a*

Philosophy of the History of Mankind.[79] Part of the issue was probably jealousy, as the master watched his star pupil ascend in public recognition. Kant also felt that his philosophical insights had been overlooked. But there were real philosophical and ideological disagreements between them, and Kant decided that these needed to be aired. He also spied in Herder's text veiled criticisms of his own thinking. Kant believed that human happiness ultimately came at the end of history and through the institutions of the state. Herder believed that every living creature takes delight in its life and the state exists to foster that state of well-being. He also spied in Kant's thinking a bias toward Europe, where it was assumed that the state was a more highly developed entity.[80]

There were so many areas in which the two thinkers were in agreement. Both saw the pursuit of human happiness as a fundamental right and goal. Both believed in the laws of Newtonian science and in the purposefulness of the universe. Kant put it this way: "human actions, like every other natural event are determined by universal laws." Nature endowed human beings alone with reason and the freedom of the will, accordingly "man was not to be guided by instinct, not nurtured and instructed with ready-made knowledge; rather, he should bring forth everything out of his own resources."[81] Nature did not make things easy for humankind; striving must be constant.

Whereas Herder saw a basic sociability in humankind, Kant's vision was darker, closer to Hobbes than to Rousseau. Human striving is fraught, as Kant put it, "Nature demands a constant striving, a struggle to achieve, for heartless competitive vanity, for the insatiable desire to possess and to rule!" Given the propensity to warfare, only the state and civic constitutions can protect us. Even then, the natural bellicosity of states leads to warfare, and this can be prevented only by the establishment of a "league of nations."[82] Living in relative peace within the state,

ideas of inferiority and superiority that were—to use our modern term—blatantly racist. They were not much better on the subject of gender superiority and inferiority. For his views on men and women, Kant received rough treatment from the modern philosopher, Jacques Derrida (d. 2004). Kant's "anthropobotany," as Derrida called it, allowed him to imagine that men love domestic peace, that women possess certain essential characteristics; put in a phrase, Derrida read in Kant and "his analysis of the feminine perversion, the complex system of phallogocentrism."[85] While it is rather hard to imagine Kant being particularly phallic about anything, the indictment resonated with modern-day feminist critiques of masculinist discourse—however enlightened it might claim to be.

By the 1780s, Kant had changed. In his *Idea for a Universal History with Cosmopolitan Intent* and his essay asking "What is the Enlightenment?"—both from 1784—he suggests a more open mind, one searching for the universal meaning of human aspirations. Then the French Revolution intervened. By every contemporary account in 1789, Kant was transfixed by the news coming from Paris. He thought that he now could die in peace because he had heard news so stirring and important. Unlike many Europeans, after the Terror Kant never repudiated the revolution. He also endorsed the American Revolution and the Irish uprising of the late 1790s. He was a devoted supporter of the young republics. Yet in his published works of that decade, he declared that a people have no right to revolt. Was he trying to stay on the good side of the Prussian authorities, or did he think that revolution would not work anywhere in Germany? Did he reason that its people did not possess that level of political sophistication?[86]

Various explanations have been offered to explain the discrepancy between Kant's private views as a citizen and his philosophical arguments. What is important is to see that in the 1790s, Kant repudiated imperialism and the racism that was used to justify it. Instead, he sought to articulate a cosmopolitan vision by which nations might live in peace, perpetually, and through justice, safeguard human rights.[87] Kant offered justifications that remain valid to this day. We may not forgive him his earlier views—commonplace though they were—but we need to understand what made him the greatest philosopher of the eighteenth century.

Kant published prolifically, and when his *Critique of Pure Reason* appeared in 1781, it was his longest and most difficult book. Among the first reviews written by his friend (and suppressed so as not to offend), Johann Hamann saw Kant as trying to find a middle way between Leibniz and Locke, bringing appearances and concepts—sensibility and understanding—together into a "transcendental something," where both are in danger of disappearing altogether. He accuses Kant of proceeding "arse-first" and using "weapons of light" to spread obscurity. Hamann hopes that the book will be praised by some, well known, and "as a mark of the highest authorship understood by bloody few." We can see why he chose not to publish it in his lifetime.[88]

In short, Kant is not easy to understand. It is, however, the case that his *Critique* sent Western philosophy into an entirely new direction, laid the foundation for what became known as German Idealism, and established Kant as one of the most important philosophers ever to put pen to paper. Like so many of the leading German philosophes, Kant came from a humble background, his father was an artisan and his mother was deeply pious, having been brought up as a Pietist who wanted the same education for her son. He in turn rebelled against its emotionalism and all his life saw reason as his guiding star.

So too did the other German philosophes. They could be remarkably audacious, and in 1792, the relatively unknown Carl Friedrich Bahrdt, just out of prison for having published a scandalous play against the Prussian prime minister, published *Rights and Duties of Rulers and Subjects in Relation to the State and Religion*, wherein he argued for the right of sexual satisfaction. It is on par with the right to life, to food and drink, to property, and "society is culpable if it obstructs this choice and pleasure."[89] All of these positions were enveloped in a lengthy work of three volumes.

Bahrdt's argument had little impact at the time, possibly because he was associated with advocacy for revolution. Yet it added another arrow in the bow of the enlightened search for human freedom. The German philosophes never escaped the confines imposed by the absolutist principles central to their political structure. They bequeathed to the nineteenth century a set of abstract ideals that made the search for democracy in Germany ever elusive until it was imposed by the conquering Allies in 1945. That history gives a tragic dimension to what had been sought but never attained after the death of the philosophes.

7

Naples and Milan

TO REACH ITALY BY LAND, one must cross the Alps. In the eighteenth century, the passage felt as much psychological as physical. The traveler arrived in cities and principalities that were independent from one another yet for the most part belonging to the Austrian Habsburgs or the papacy. Everywhere these lands were Catholic, and the heavy hand of the Counter-Reformation was still visible. With roots in the sixteenth century, the Jesuits and the Inquisition enjoyed an almost hegemonic influence over cultural and intellectual life throughout Italy.

For an opening example, we need only examine the persecutions inaugurated in Naples during the 1690s. These were intended to rid the schools of atomism, atheism, and the excessive freedom that the clergy saw pervading these educational institutions. All these natural philosophical positions were denoted by the term "Modern philosophy," said to be inspired by Descartes, and by the 1690s Naples was its capital. Its method was experimental, and its bias was against the Aristotelianism of the schools. In medicine, the Moderns were highly critical of contemporary practices such as blood letting, and they argued that complete freedom of inquiry was necessary for medicine's improvement. They also had access to some of the best libraries in Europe, where could be found works by ancient atomists as well as by modern philosophers such as Spinoza. Fatefully, the Neapolitan authorities chose to use the methods of the Roman Inquisition—constant interrogation, secrecy, public condemnation—and they imprisoned atomists for years on end, generally without a public trial.

The head of the Jesuit school in Naples, Giovan De Benedictis, denounced the freedom that prevailed everywhere, and he blamed the new science of Descartes and Gassendi, among others, as the cause of this profound threat to Catholic beliefs. Similar accusations were brought against proponents of the new science in the Republic of Venice. Writing from Naples in 1693, one Jesuit explained to a colleague, "The News from here is that the atomists were almost all discovered to be atheists. Two recanted and twelve are in prison."[1] For their part, the Modern philosophers believed that atomism had been transmitted by the ancient Hebrews, and they read avidly among the English proponents of the new science such as Robert Boyle. Unimpressed, De Benedictis believed that Descartes's *cogito* licensed a subjective individualism and privileged imagination over truth. Descartes's proclamation, "I think therefore I am," licensed the will to explore any idea and his notion of corpuscles as the building blocks of nature left the Scholastic doctrine of form meaningless. Atomism ineluctably led to atheism.[2]

By contrast, in this same decade in London, a close associate of Isaac Newton named Richard Bentley presented—from the prestigious London pulpit of St. Martin-in-the-Fields—an explanation of atomism that he said bolstered the anti-materialism of Newtonian metaphysics. He denounced the materialism of Epicurean atomism and substituted the immaterial force of universal gravitation at work amid the atoms in the vacuum of space. A few years later, a similar argument was elaborated upon by

Samuel Clarke, and between them these Newtonian lectures were translated into various European languages.[3]

From the time of Galileo (d. 1642) onward, the new science was ill understood on the Italian peninsula. The heresy hunters stood guard against a system that they believed led to atheism and materialism and, not incidentally, undermined the Scholasticism derived from St. Thomas Aquinas's interpretation of Aristotle. Aquinas's interpretation was used to explain the Catholic doctrine of transubstantiation, among others. In the face of opposition from the Scholastics, some of the Moderns settled for "quietism," the belief that Christianity can be embodied in a few doctrines and that the true follower should strive passively for an inner spiritual peace that eschews external demonstrations of faith.

The breakthrough toward Enlightenment came in Rome in 1707, when Celestino Galiani (1681–1753) and his coterie began experiments in Newtonian optics. Still, Galiani had little confidence that the new science would thrive in an Italian setting; in 1705, he wrote to a friend, "What is to be feared is not so much the Inquisitor as the beliefs of men who hold [scientific experiments] to be little more than tricks of acrobats."[4] But he persevered and accepted the atomic hypothesis that lay at the heart of Newtonian optics. The Inquisition reserved its opprobrium for explicit endorsements of Copernicanism for which, nearly a century earlier, it had convicted Galileo. At that time, his covert atomism was one of the doctrines that alarmed the Church authorities. Newton's commitment to atomism and heliocentrism was basic but implicit.

Italian Newtonianism owed a significant debt to the notices that appeared in the Leipzig Latin journal, *Acta eruditorum*. From it, Leibniz, who was visiting in Rome, learned in detail about Newton's science and affirmed his Copernicanism. His extensive contact with Catholic intellectuals put them under suspicion for having such close interactions with a Lutheran. Out of these encounters, however suspect, emerged the first stirrings of the Italian Enlightenment, and Celestino Galiani, with his close friend Antonio Niccolini, was at its center. The latter came under suspicion after he had journeyed to England, returned to Florence and became a freemason, and with Galiani, read deeply in English and French thought.

Impoverished as a young man, Galiani became a monk and then in Rome enjoyed an academic life that gave him mastery of both philosophy and science. He accepted a bishopric in 1731 and became the leader of Neapolitan educational life. He paid a heavy price for his prominence. In the face of the Inquisition, he decided never to publish, quietly abandoned "the Aristotelians' meaningless words and occult qualities," and scoured the writings of Descartes. From being a Cartesian, Galiani migrated to Newtonianism, and there he remained, a fervent believer in physico-theology as explicated by Bentley and Clarke, among others. Galiani's associate in these scientific circles, the abbé Antonio Conti, had actually met Newton in London and read widely in the philosophical disputes associated with materialism and the English freethinkers. He tried valiantly to pull Galiani away from his belief in divine providence, but to no avail. However, the circle developed a complete familiarity with the writings of Spinoza, Hobbes, Toland, and the other Newtonian explicators such as David Gregory and Willem s'Gravesande. The point is that by the 1720s, the new enlightened culture with its European sources had arrived in Italian intellectual circles, despite the best efforts of the Inquisition to suppress it.

As we have seen elsewhere, urban centers possessed a distinctive intellectual vitality. Though we have chosen to focus on Naples and Milan, other cities in the peninsula merit a brief mention. Rome was a place where bright young men, often en route to a clerical career, could find an excellent education. Of course, the city, capital of the Papal States, was dominated by the papacy and its apparatus of censorship. The area was also almost entirely passive in economic matters and manufactured virtually nothing. In the 1740s, Pope Benedict XIV reformed the main university, and it began to teach the new science, with chemistry and physics as experimental practices. And just as in Naples and Milan, economic issues arose in need of reform and they required innovative political and economic approaches.[5]

In contrast to the glory of Rome, Turin, which was in the north (Piedmont-Savoy) and bordered on the west with France, had been a place of little distinction until 1563, when it was named the capital of the Savoyard state. In the process, it acquired the famous burial garment, the Holy Shroud of Christ, and its dukes undertook a series of architectural improvements that made its center into the elegant eighteenth-century city that it is today. By 1700, its population had grown to about 44,000—about the size of Edinburgh. Its form of princely absolutism rested on the power of the region's landed aristocracy, but the city itself had become a vital part of the state's financial structure.[6]

By the 1730s, Turin possessed the most powerful and absolutist of the various Italian principalities, and it imposed its authority with little opposition. By the 1780s, it had a vibrant version of enlightened academic culture and could hold its head high in relation to other Italian and European cities. This had not always been so. In the 1730s, Turin incarcerated people whom other states or the papacy had deemed a menace. Such was the fate of the Neapolitan jurist and historian Pietro Giannone (1676–1748). After being kidnapped, Giannone languished in a Savoyard prison for twelve years as punishment for his derogatory treatment of the Church in his massive history of Naples from ancient times to the present.[7]

Giannone had castigated the Church for its corruption and its interference in the political life of the state; he also had little use for the Spanish and their treatment of Naples when it was under their control. Following Hobbes, Pufendorf, and Spinoza, he urged the sovereign to use all of his authority to preserve the independence and rights of Naples, thus ensuring the stability of the government. Giannone's *Civil History* appeared in 1723. Within a few years, it was translated into English and French, and in 1758 into German. Giannone went from obscurity to fame and notoriety. Swiftly, his book made the Index of Forbidden Books and he and his printer were excommunicated. Mobs protested against him, and he had to flee in disguise.[8]

In Vienna, he had been warmly received by the Austrian court, but in every Italian state that Giannone visited, his reputation put him in jeopardy. The Austrians lost Naples to the Bourbons in 1734, and hence Giannone fled to Venice, where he was abducted by the Venetian Inquisition and, after a brief trial, expelled. He was tricked into crossing into Italian territory from Protestant Geneva, where he had sought refuge, and was arrested in the middle of the night by armed guards sent by the king of Savoy. The Savoyards imprisoned him. Significantly, Giannone's history of Naples, complete with its attack on the Church and feudalism, was republished in 1770. The issues it raised had still not been resolved.

Giannone had even been expelled from Venice, one of the freer city-states, which was famous for its printing presses. Venice was not without interference from the Inquisition, as when Beccaria's book on crime and punishment was banned (figure 11), placed on the Index of Forbidden Books. Yet Venice nurtured a vibrant form of enlightened Catholicism that accepted the

FIGURE 11. Beccaria, the first to forcibly attack the use of
torture in judicial proceedings. Cesare Bonesano de Beccaria
(1884–90) (ID# 1002350). Courtesy of Bridgeman Images.

limitations of reason and the necessity for revelation. The leading
liberal Catholic of the period, Ludovico Muratori (b. 1672, near
Modena), was a devout Catholic priest, and his thinking on the
reform of politics affected dukes and princes in various Italian
principalities, among them Venice.[9] Again, the aim was to liberate

secular authority from the interference of the papacy. Muratori also wanted the ruler to encourage commerce and industry, and his impact was very real in the Austrian territories. His most important treatise, *Della pubblica felicità* (*On public happiness*, 1749), argued that reform had to originate with the prince. Even private luxury should be tolerated if its benefits could be directed at public needs. The impact of his thought was greatest in Naples.[10] Muratori saw moral education as the necessary prelude to political action.[11]

Giannone's anti-Catholicism had doomed his chances of enjoying personal freedom. Flight was the only choice in the face of imprisonment, as Alberto Radicati di Passerano (1698–1737) of Turin learned in the course of his tumultuous career. Radicati came from a distinguished noble family, long famous in the region. From an early age, he was rebellious; his first marriage was fraught, and he embarked on a labored intellectual trajectory that began in Protestantism and ended with free-thinking and materialism. Called upon for advice, he tried to convince Victor Amadeus II (duke of Savoy, who became king of Sicily and then Sardinia) that he should emulate the great European monarchs and downgrade the power of the Church and the Inquisition in his territories. His proposals echo those of Giannone and the far less heretical Muratori, but they were far too radical for Victor Amadeus, who opted instead to make peace with the papacy. Having lost the argument and convinced that reform in Piedmont-Savoy was impossible—even that he might be subject to the Inquisition's wrath—Radicati chose exile. In 1730, if not earlier, he was penniless in London, where he began to publish in English.

Clearly inspired by Montesquieu's *Persian Letters*, Radicati anonymously published *Christianity Set in a True Light* (1730), in which he assumed the voice of a Muslim forced to convert to paganism, by which he meant the Catholic Church. His guide through the process is a dervish, and he observes in passing that all the priests of his new faith are magicians.[12] The footnotes contain various references to his home city of Turin, and the whole is a satirical send-up of Catholicism. The Dutch reviews immediately identified the true author, and Radicati was launched on his English literary career. He followed *True Light* with an explication of Islam written by a Muslim for a Jewish rabbi. It takes up the theme of Moses as an impostor, which by 1732 had made its way through European circles of freethinkers.[13] Lest there be any doubt as to which school Radicati then belonged, in his most outrageous treatise, *Dissertation upon Death* (1732), the publisher advertised Toland's complete works.[14]

The *Dissertation* advocated the right of human beings to commit suicide. Written as a hymn to "the Goddess Nature," it also made perfectly clear Radicati's debt to Toland's pantheism: "Motion is to Matter as essential as is Heat to Fire. [They] are of an eternal Co-existence, since it is not possible that they should be derived from Nothing. . . . This Matter, modified by Motion into an infinite Number of various Forms, is that which I call NATURE."[15] Materialism, combined with advocating suicide—a wickedly unchristian combination—finally did it for the authorities. The bishop of London wrote to the secretary of state, who arranged for the arrest of Radicati, his publisher, and his printer. They were eventually released, but Radicati was charged the staggering sum of 400 pounds for bail. Someone—we do not know who—stepped forward and paid the fee to secure his freedom.

Although sick and impoverished, Radicati continued to advertise his treatises. Then suddenly, in the winter of 1734–35, he fled again, this time to the Dutch Republic. There, he had many of his writings translated into French and repeated his pleas for a strong monarch to unite all of Italy. In 1734, he cast his lot with Charles of Bourbon, the new king of Naples, and Radicati became one of the first to call for Italian unification. He also renewed his assault on the clergy. Still poor and stricken with tuberculosis, Radicati apparently had a change of heart in matters religious. Under the influence of French-speaking Protestant clergy in the Republic, Radicati repented, and he died while reconciling himself to the Reformed Church.[16]

Radicati had said he wanted a civic religion overseen by the secular authorities, and Italy unified under a strong sovereign. The second goal did not materialize until the nineteenth century. The first never did, although dedication to the Italian Catholic Church has fallen markedly since 1945.

Naples and the Necessity for Reform

When Austrian rule ended in 1734, Radicati was not the only political thinker to be excited by the sudden prospects for Neapolitan reform under a new king. Charles III settled in Naples, the capital of the Kingdom of the Two Sicilies, and embarked on various reform and building projects: the digging of the archaeological site of Herculaneum, a new theater, a reorganization of the university. The Spinelli family, princes of the Holy Roman Empire, also built a palazzo filled with works of art, books, and scientific instruments, some purchased from Dutch craftsmen. They designed the palazzo to be the "Temple of Minerva," a cosmopolitan center for learning meant to celebrate the new reign of King Charles and the grand supporting family, the Spinelli.[17] It sponsored a new academy that met on the grounds of the palazzo. In time and in the face of Neapolitan social problems, the Temple came to seem like a frivolous display of wealth where little learning actually occurred. Other reforms instituted by King Charles sought to eliminate some of the privileges enjoyed by the nobility and to curtail clerical interference in state affairs; these did little to alleviate the chronic poverty of the peasantry or the laboring class.

With a population of 200,000 in 1700, Naples was the largest city in Continental Europe after Paris. By 1750, its population had grown by another 100,000 and would continue on that path well into the next century. Mount Vesuvius loomed over its skyline and returned to its volcanic activity throughout much of the eighteenth century. The sight was both spectacular and terrifying. Letters between Naples and London took about three or four weeks, or longer in bad weather or wartime. And not least, the city and the surrounding countryside were marked by enclaves of extreme poverty, criminality, or disease. Nevertheless, the vitality of its musical and artistic life attracted visitors from much of the rest of educated Europe; Mozart, father and son, played for the British ambassador in 1770. A socially active Neapolitan connoisseur of culture could spend two nights a week at the theater, another two holding concerts at home, and finally an evening of conversation with nobility and friends at a learned academy.[18] Yet the social and political problems of Naples were endemic and needed to be addressed.[19]

Predictably, the university in Naples came to play an important role in these reforming efforts, and once again Newtonianism provided an intellectual catalyst, with Celestino Galiani in the lead. At this optimistic moment entered the young Antonio Genovesi. Galiani recognized his extraordinary philosophical talent and Genovesi proclaimed his Newtonianism, displaying a singular familiarity with the English debates about matter and motion. Galiani thought so highly of Genovesi that he was given the task of teaching metaphysics in the university.

He also coveted the chair in theology but was blocked by powerful adversaries. Undaunted, Genovesi turned his formidable skills toward worldly problems, of which the extreme poverty of Southern Italy was the most challenging. In 1754, he was rewarded with the newly created chair of political economy, the first of its kind in any European university. In the tradition of British and Dutch Newtonianism, Genovesi sought to improve both agriculture and manufacturing through the informed application of science. He had been inspired by Muratori, but he also devoted himself to English and French thinkers. Agriculture had to be reformed, and manufacturing had also to be encouraged.[20] Even luxury had its place, if homegrown; it promoted the circulation of money and a certain level of refinement. Although denounced by the clergy, the value of luxury became one of the main theoretical points put forward by the new science of political economy.

The period after 1734 became the great age of Neapolitan academies. They provided an intellectual home for members of the various professions such as medicine and also a place to discuss the current political and religious climate. For this reason, they were regarded as highly suspect, and the Church authorities watched them closely. They also sought to take over academic culture as various bishops sponsored their own academies. During the archbishopric of Serafino Filangieri, uncle of Gaetano, the famous author of *La scienza della legislazione* (to which we shall return), the goal was to give the clergy the necessary intellectual tools to combat the freethinkers. Filangieri's term brought about the integration of the new scientific paradigms into Catholic culture. Celestino Galiani chose this archbishop to occupy the chair in experimental physics in the University of Naples. Filangieri was a committed Newtonian and fluent in the ideas of John Locke. He gave his support to a new theological academy, that of San Michele, founded in 1782. Through the renewal of apologetics, this academy sought to produce an educated theologian suitable for the Age of the Enlightenment.[21] However, it did not help the religious reputation of the Neapolitan academies that many were allied with masonic lodges in the city. By contrast, Milan possessed a more vibrant lay religious culture dedicated to specific saints and religious feasts.[22]

Predictably, Muratori's reforming ideas made an impact in Naples. Out of his circle came a new voice in economics, Ferdinando Galiani (b. 1728, and nephew of Celestino). He cut a dashing figure in the cultural and political life of Naples and received considerable attention for his *Della Moneta* (*On Money*), published anonymously in 1751. He was a mere twenty-three years old when word spread that he was the author. He argued that money was simply a spontaneous institution. Its value depends upon individual, subjective evaluations in determining the desirability of any item; utility and scarcity then play into the calculation of value. The treatise showed the application of Newtonian principles: the "desire for gain; or to live happily" is comparable in the moral sciences to gravity in the physical. It also showed the way to the subjective theory of value based on utility; "utility is anything that produces a true pleasure." Gold and silver, because they are valuable, are used as money, and the universal desire we have for the admiration of our fellow human beings requires our striving for superiority. Gold and silver can bring the desired adulation.[23]

On Money was almost instantly famous, although at first few knew who had actually written it. Courts, both papal and secular, opened to find and receive him. Once again, Galiani began with a history of monetary practices—he pointed out the impact of American silver and gold brought back to Europe by the Spanish and lauded the effects of prosperity in promoting wealth and happiness. He even praised luxury as an unavoidable result of good government. He granted that one man's riches may lead to a reduction in another's wealth, but he accepted this as the inevitable outcome of peace and prosperity.[24] A decade later, a similar argument appeared in Diderot's *Encyclopédie*. Though Italian political economy owed debts to English, Scottish, and French thinkers, it was the Italians, aided by Galiani, who first put in place this secular study of the state in relation to economic development.[25] Like so many of the philosophes, Galiani also studied the travel literature to shed light on ancient practices still extant among "savages and Indians" of his day.[26]

That Galiani's theories of political economy were known in Paris was hardly accidental. King Charles was a Bourbon and wanted an intimate knowledge of what was happening at the French court. In 1759, he chose Galiani to represent him personally and sent him to Paris. Galiani cut a bizarre figure: four and a half feet tall, a tonsured monk, speaking French with a Neapolitan accent. He in turn was miserable: "things are very hard. Bad, heavy air, poisonous water, an incredibly strange climate . . . no fruit, no cheese, no good seafood—everything does violence to the Neapolitan temperament."[27] But Galiani persevered and eventually became a Francophile.

Suddenly, Galiani's luck turned. King Charles had to abdicate to take up the throne of his recently deceased half-brother in Spain; Galiani was promoted to a higher office in Paris and at the same time entered enlightened society escorted by the abbé Morellet. Now everyone who was anyone in the circles of philosophes knew Galiani: Diderot, D'Holbach, Grimm, Helvétius and Madame Helvétius, Madame Necker, various women who ran prestigious salons, and Madame d'Épinay, who had been at one time the lover of Rousseau. Galiani became the trusted friend of Diderot and Grimm, and his economic ideas were now more widely known. He and Genovesi had introduced economic thinking into the higher reaches of Italian intellectual life; little had changed, however, in the Neapolitan economy, and famine returned in 1764. It was followed by an epidemic. Agricultural reform seemed remote if not impossible. When Genovesi died in 1769, his chair at the university was abolished. In Paris, the circle around Morellet continued its interest in politics and economics, and he translated the Milanese reformer, Beccaria into French.

Galiani produced another economic text, *Dialogues on the Grain Trade* (1770). In it, he took to task "the economists," many of them French, who would allow the price of grain to adjust to the market, regardless of the hardship inflicted on the people. He asserted his commitment to follow reason and experience and began with the assumption—commonplace at the time—that agriculture is the basis of the riches of all countries. Ordinary people think that the management of grain is a political matter; the great think it is purely a matter of commerce. Galiani would place it somewhere between, neither completely without regulation nor with prices fixed by the state. His examples were drawn from throughout Europe, and he paid particular attention to those from England and the Dutch Republic.

With the departure of Charles to Spain, reform now depended upon his son and successor, Ferdinand. Ferdinand had been badly educated, and disliked books and intellectuals. Yet curiously enough, he became a reformer of sorts; he wanted to reduce the power and wealth of the Church. Taking his cue from other Catholic states such as Portugal and France, one night in 1767, Ferdinand rounded up the Jesuits and shipped them out of the kingdom. Their schools and their rich treasuries were declared secular, to be run by the state. Inspired in part by the reforms in Austria and influenced by the writings of Filangieri (1752–1788), Galiani, and others, King Ferdinand, aided by his prime minister, the anti-clerical Bernardo Tanucci (1698–1783), reduced the power of the Church in education, reformed the academy of science and literature, and upgraded the university. Masonic influence at court and in elite circles increased as the queen, Carolina from Vienna, encouraged an expansion of the lodges and thus their respectability.[28] The king cared about the power of the state, and those who sided with the Enlightenment cared about secular reform.

Among the secular reformers was Mariangiola Ardinghelli, a Newtonian who translated the writings of the English Newtonian Steven Hales and became an informal but important correspondent with the Paris Academy of Science.[29] Her salon in Naples rose to prominence as a place to learn about the latest scientific news. There she met the abbé Jean Nollet, one of the main scientific lecturers on the Continent. Through him, she joined the "republic of letters" that connected her with philosophes in several countries. Unlike Laura Bassi of Bologna, who became the first woman in Europe to hold a position as university professor, Ardinghelli followed the custom of many learned European women of the time and preferred anonymity.[30] Her most important achievement, undertaken through private correspondence, rested on the depth and breadth of her cultural and intellectual exchanges. These linked Naples with the French Enlightenment and hence more generally with what became, by the 1770s, an international republican conversation.

Filangieri

The most important Italian contributor to the conversation was Gaetano Filangieri, with his five-volume *Science of Legislation*

(*La scienza della legislazione*, Naples, 1780). The work went through numerous Italian editions and was translated into every major European language. Over the centuries, and even within ten years of its first edition, *Science* fell into a historiographical quagmire not of its own making. The American Revolution was very much on the mind of Filangieri when he wrote; the French Revolution began in 1789, and Filangieri died, while still a young man, in 1788.

The French Revolution set off an immense revision of French and European history, creating the split between right and left with which we remain familiar. Suddenly, Filangieri's masterpiece was read as a Jacobin work *avant la lettre*, to be praised or condemned accordingly. Then, as we shall see, revolution broke out in Naples in 1799, followed by a short-lived republic. Filangieri was enlisted as its hero, and then repudiated by its enemies. Only in the post–Cold War era has an effort been made to read *Science* in relation to its intellectual context, the Italian Enlightenment in the late 1770s.

After 1734, the entire effort of King Charles, and after him his son, Ferdinand, aimed at reforming the institutions inherited from the Middle Ages. Their focus was on the abuses of the Church and the inordinate power of the nobility in their role as landowners and judges. The 1770s became critical. Before publishing *Science*, Filangieri had intervened in a dispute about the arbitrary behavior of these judges and argued that the philosophe must act to ensure that justice serves the rights of humanity. He was already established as an enlightened reformer before *Science* appeared. It is important to realize that in Naples, it was possible to learn of events just about anywhere in Europe.[31]

The Italian newspapers followed the American Revolution almost day to day, with a two-month gap.[32] Filangieri did not need to leave the Italian peninsula to participate in the international republican conversation. In 1782, events in the American colonies so inspired him that he wrote to Benjamin Franklin to ask if he could come to the new United States and contribute to the formation of "the great codes of laws that is being prepared ... laws ... which must decide not only the fate [of the states], but also of this new hemisphere."[33] Franklin gently reminded the young philosopher of the hardships to be found in the struggling republic, especially difficult for someone of noble background. The United States represented to Filangieri a possible future model for the whole of the Western world. On one issue he castigated the new States: slavery. As he remarked, "only Pennsylvania does not have slaves," and he heaped praise on William Penn. In the same breath, like Herder, he condemned European imperialism.

Filangieri was among the first—if not the first—to theorize the meaning of constitutionalism for the new American republic. A republic need not be small, as the ancients had assumed, and to accommodate its growth, it needed to be a representative democracy. The ancient constitution, insofar as it privileged monarchy and aristocracy, had to be replaced by a system of representation in which the legislative body is capable of amending the constitution, but only with considerable difficulty. It must be a written document and must distribute power among the legislative, executive, and judicial bodies without endowing any one element with sovereignty or greater power. In the new constitutionalism theorized and schematized by Filangieri, no governing entity can marginalize another, and all rest upon the ideal of human equality. The most recent and insightful historian of Filangieri's legacy argues that he drew from his lived experience of enlightened culture particularly as he found it in the Neapolitan masonic lodges and their participation in the international circulation of ideas.[34]

Filangieri was not the only enlightened reformer to be so moved by the experience of brotherhood: witness Lessing and Herder. However, anyone with any sense, as they both candidly noted, knew that all sorts of privilege and mystical mumbo-jumbo could be found in the lodges. Also, the Italian lodges played at palace intrigue, aided and abetted by Queen Carolina, who, as an Austrian, saw them as allies against Spanish influence.[35] Yet where else in Italy could be found an ideology of meeting as equals, elevated not by birth but by merit?

In the 1780s, not a decade before the French Revolution, King Ferdinand, ever the huntsman and play soldier, began a social experiment to reward his decommissioned officers and a little colony of silk manufacturers. He spared no expense, granting them good salaries, medical care, education, and a reformed legal code. Contemporaries believed that Filangieri had inspired these almost utopian reforms, and that had the revolution not intervened, Ferdinand would have become a great reformer.[36] This fantasy was made all the crueler, when ten years later actual revolution erupted in Naples, only to be destroyed by the British navy in conjunction with the Bourbons, the Church, and aristocracy. They betrayed the revolutionaries who had been promised a pardon, an act of betrayal that followed Lord Nelson, the British commander, to his grave. The Bourbons never recovered from their reputation as tyrants.

When alive, Filangieri was not interested in fomenting revolution. Rather his concerns centered on the notion that "despotism in the magistrates, the nobility, or the sovereign, is equally despotism." He would not accept ancient usage or charters that "give to the magistrates, the nobles, or the monarch, any right contrary in its nature to the liberty of the people, the security of the individual, the general interest of the nation, or the public happiness, which is the first object of all laws."[37] Those are the purposes of good government. Absolute dominion, "unlimited and boundless authority, which many princes have possessed, or wished to possess . . . is no other than a two-edged sword, that wounds the idiot who seizes it." Neither in Vienna, nor Berlin, nor Madrid would Filangieri offer kings much solace. Filangieri wanted a nation with a central power that would protect property and individual rights and ensure the enforcement of laws and contracts.[38]

In addition, Filangieri is critical of the British system of government and its unwritten constitution. There, in certain circumstances, the king can ally with the parliament, as did Henry VIII, and thereby effect his will: "how many outrages against the liberty of his people" did he not commit?[39] Even in his criticism, Filangieri makes clear his general admiration for British accomplishments, as did so many of the European philosophes. He did not advocate the abolition of monarchy or aristocracy but their fundamental reform: "by giving every citizen the right of admission into the class of nobles, whenever he should unite the merit and qualifications recognized and directed by the laws."[40] Similarly, he raised a stern voice against the abuses of the Church and the Inquisition. He was repaid when the Inquisition put *Science* on the Index of Forbidden Books. He had been schooled in the writings of Giannone, Genovesi, the French philosophes, and English freethinkers.[41] Most of them had also incurred the Inquisition's condemnation. During the eighteenth century, Naples had been plagued by many problems that were only compounded by the privileges of the clergy.

Milan and Political Economy

Landlocked, isolated from constant contact with foreigners, and much smaller than Naples, the duchy of Milan began the century more religiously devout than many other European cities. With a population of about 110,000, it was also half the size of Naples.[42] Taken from the Spanish by the Austrian Empire in 1706 and during the War of Spanish Succession, Milan remained a part of Austrian Lombardy, with the exception of the Napoleonic occupations, until 1859. It was bounded on the north by the Alps and the Swiss confederation, on the south by the river Po, on the west by Piedmont, and on the east by the Republic of Venice. Lombardy was a net exporter of grain, and the subject of its control vexed Milanese theorists just as it had the Neapolitans.

As with Naples, Milan's problems demanded recourse to the new science of political economy. From midcentury onward, new economic theories from Paris called for the removal of all controls over the price of grain. In Milan, the debate was intense, and its major participants included Pietro Verri (1728–97) and Cesare Beccaria (1738–94). With them, we enter the heart of the Milanese Enlightenment. Put schematically, the Austrian authorities favored free market pricing, which they believed would permit agricultural growth, increase the tax base, and strengthen the power of the Viennese court at the expense of local patricians who favored price controls. Maria Theresa and Joseph II governed through plenipotentiaries who received their orders directly from Vienna. Lombardy's financial situation was fragile, and from the 1740s onward, reform became the order of the day. As in the Austrian Netherlands, Kaunitz in Vienna played a key role in the reform of the tax base and in establishing the Supreme Council of the Economy. It was filled by non-Milanese and was intended to lessen the power of the local patricians. The non-Milanese were, however, at a distinct disadvantage. As Pietro Verri explained, they "were unable to speak the language, unacquainted with customs and the system . . . which was an intricate labyrinth in which even the nationals were often adrift."[43] Aided and abetted by the clergy, the nobility who controlled the courts had been able to stifle reform into the 1760s.

As with so many of the philosophes, the Enlightenment entailed a personal break with family and tradition. Verri rebelled against his patrician father, as did Beccaria, and with a group of like-minded friends, he established the Accademia dei Pugni (the Academy of Fists), in which debate and controversial ideas held sway. It had no clerical members, nor was there a comparable group of Catholic intellectuals capable of offering an alternative vision. Pressed by the Austrian authorities, the Church in Milan spent its time trying to secure its property and privileges. The nobility had been empowered by the Spanish and jealously guarded their power even to the point of invoking Montesquieu and the authority he vested in noble intermediaries.[44] Of course, the enlightened reformers also engaged with Montesquieu and commented extensively on his ideas. Unlike their fathers who were jurists, the new Milanese reformers turned to economics as the key to the improvement of Lombardy.

The bonds of friendship that made the Academy of Fists possible, and the sheer precociousness of these young reformers, reminds us of Jean-Jacques Rousseau and the group that formed around the plan for a new encyclopedia. Everything should be questioned for the purpose of reform. Among these friends, the painfully shy Beccaria found purpose and direction to his life and a way to become what he desperately wanted to be: a philosophe. As a jurist and advocate for the less fortunate of humankind, Beccaria took a cold look at crime and punishment as it occurred in his society and the result was his masterpiece, *Of Crimes and Punishments* (*Dei delitti e delle pene*, 1764; see figure 11). The book landed like a bolt of thunder in European intellectual life. Within months, Beccaria was the talk of the town, not just in Milan but also in Paris and elsewhere.[45] The abolition of torture in both Austria and Russia can be traced to his influence, and the book's translation into all the major European languages occurred rapidly. Under its influence, Maria Theresa abolished torture in the Austrian empire in 1776, although it took a long time for the reform to become universal.

Beccaria took his point of departure from Hobbes: "Laws are the condition by which independent and isolated men, tired of living in a constant state of war . . . unite in society."[46] Human passions are such that we seek to extend our liberties at the expense of others; a "gravity-like force . . . impels us to seek our own well-being" and the lawgiver must "oppose the ruinous course of gravity."[47] Hence the necessity for laws and "the sovereign's right to punish crimes." Only the law can dispense punishments for crimes: "this authority can only rest with the legislator, who represents all of society united by a social contract." The contract establishes that both the sovereign and "the greatest and most wretched of men" are bound by it. Enlightened reason forbids "excessively severe punishments" that are "contrary to justice and to the nature of the social contract itself."[48] Judges must administer the law but not interpret it. When governed by "fixed and immutable laws, then, citizens acquire personal security."[49]

Beccaria turned "enlightened reason" on the topic of crime and punishment, a topic seldom addressed by other philosophes. He did not invoke notions of sin or man's fallen nature to explain criminality, and neither did he embrace the determinism that accompanied the fashionable materialism of the French Enlightenment. Human beings and their passions begin with "total and universal freedom of action," but must sacrifice some of it to ensure their security and liberty. His approach was egalitarian:

"the greater the number of people who understand the sacred law code ... the less frequent crimes will be." Printing and literacy are on the side of lawfulness; they make "the entire public, not just a few people, the depository of the sacred laws." The greatest crimes are committed against security and liberty by both "the common people, but also ... by nobles and magistrates." In the final analysis, crimes against society are the essence of criminality, of which the greatest is high treason, and after it "come those crimes which violate the security of private persons."[50]

A curious development came out of reading Beccaria, and it is found in the writings of his clerical opponents. One of the insults they hurled at the author and his circle was that they were "socialists," a word invented by his enemies. They associated Beccaria with Rousseau and the other utopian thinkers of the age who placed their faith in the benevolence and progress possible in the contractual relations among people in society. This is not our modern meaning of the word, but its first appearance signals one of the legacies bequeathed by the more radical thinkers of the Enlightenment. The assertion of human equality inevitably raises the issue of social and economic inequality. It deeply troubled the Italian architects of political economy. The desperate inequality evidenced by the rural and urban poverty of Italy could be seen to a degree in every European country, with the possible exception of the Dutch Republic.[51] The writings of Genovesi and Muratori had indeed influenced Beccaria, and the issue of economic inequality moved Pietro Verri to publish his *Meditations on Political Economy* (1771). Penal reform could not be separated from the disorders caused by injustice and despotism, especially as found in the behavior of those "holding a more exalted station."[52]

Judgment of one's peers is a most useful law, because "those sentiments which inequality inspires," fear and envy, can be eliminated. Punishments should also be the same "for the first citizen as for the least." Beccaria had no doubt that the law was more favorably imposed on the rich and titled than on the poor. The response to the behavior of the criminal, the purpose of punishment, "is not to torment and afflict a sentient being or to undo a crime which has already been committed." Beccaria proclaimed that punishment should "dissuade the criminal from doing fresh harm to his compatriots and to keep other people from doing the same." Brashly he advised that "punishments and the method of inflicting them should be chosen that . . . will make the most effective and lasting impression on men's minds and inflict the least torment on the body of the criminal."[53]

The advice struck many of Beccaria's contemporaries as ludicrous. In every European society, the death penalty could be imposed for crimes affecting property—horse theft in England, for example. Torture was still used in many countries to establish guilt or innocence (figure 12). Trials for certain crimes and their punishment were held in secret: for sodomy in the Austrian Netherlands as one example.[54] So too, accusations could be made in secret, as witnessed at the office of the Roman Inquisition. Beccaria used his most pejorative language for the use of torture: "a cruel practice . . . what right . . . other than the right of force, gives a judge the power to inflict punishment on a citizen while the question of his guilt or innocence is still in doubt?" Finding truth through the infliction of pain means that "the criterion of truth lay in the muscles and fibers of a poor wretch." There is also the enormous risk of torturing an innocent person. The notion that someone convicted of "infamy" must have his bones broken "should not be tolerated in the eighteenth century." Some courts required a confession of guilt before conviction, and Beccaria denounced the practice

FIGURE 12. Picart's depiction of torture. Bernard Picart
(ID# 1748817). Courtesy of Bridgeman Images.

as having originated in the confessional where the confession
of sins is an essential part of the sacrament. He further notes
that a man will confess to anything to get rid of the pain that is
being inflicted.[55]

Beccaria is not afraid of imposing harsh penalties for crimes.
For stealing property, the convicted should lose some or all of
his own property. An atrocious crime merits banishment or the
confiscation of all one's property, and punishments that are "inevitable" are far more effective than ones that are cruel. Where
Beccaria draws the line is at the use of the death penalty. "By
what alleged right can men slaughter their fellows?" He goes
through all the arguments that have been advanced to justify it
and presents objections to each. He argues that a life sentence
is just as great a deterrent. After rehearsing a set of arguments

then in use and still trotted out in countries, such as the United States, that execute criminals, Beccaria states:

> Capital punishment is not useful because of the example of cruelty that it gives ... it appears absurd to me that the laws, which are the expression of the public will and which detest and punish homicide, commit murder themselves, and, in order to dissuade citizens from assassination, command public assassination.[56]

At this point, we might expect Beccaria to take a page from Rousseau's book and endorse democracy. To the contrary, he argued for an increase of the authority of "beneficent monarchs [now] seated on the thrones of Europe.... This is a reason for enlightened citizens to desire more ardently the continued increase of their authority."[57] We misjudge Beccaria if we imagine him as a representative of the radical Enlightenment. Like Verri, he was an aristocrat, and while he distrusted the power of the clergy, he was not against religion. He also saw the power of local elites and their efforts to thwart reform, and he enthusiastically endorsed the Austrian regime and its efforts to reform everything from the grain trade to the privileges of the clergy.[58] He read the materialists and was lauded in person by D'Holbach, among others, but he did not embrace their determinism or their atheism.[59] Yet his impact in enlightened circles and at the various European courts was nothing short of astounding.[60]

The collaboration of Beccaria and Verri extended from the reform of the penal system to the principles of political economy. Both saw the poverty that plagued the lower classes and both thought that solutions could be found through an accurate description of their plight and reforms that only the state could enforce. Verri, like the Neapolitan theorists, began his science of political economy with the nature of money and its purposes, and then described the economic situation in which wealth is enjoyed only by the few. He registered the discontent and idleness that plagued the poor and advocated the abolition of the single heir, instead advocating the distribution of land and goods among all the children, male and female.[61] In addition, his defense of luxury was entirely secular and eschewed moral considerations. It was the engine that fostered economic development. Borrowing a concept from Newtonian science, Verri argued that equilibrium, a balance between national consumption and production, would slowly but surely translate into widespread prosperity.

Beccaria and Verri's collaboration, which included Verri's younger brother, also produced the leading and enlightened journal of Milan, *Il Caffè*. Publishing for only two years in the mid-1760s, the journal focused on economic reform and innovation, "all directed towards public utility." Beccaria proclaimed that he saw "a stronger impulse towards equality that did not obtain in the past." This was at a time when 2,000 families out of a total of 30,000 in Milan divided over half of the net product among themselves. Half to two-thirds of working class families lived at or below subsistence level.[62]

Nevertheless, the Lombardy economy gradually improved in the second half of the century and became entirely agriculture based. Local industry and manufacturing did not stand a chance in the face of international competition. Prices for agricultural products, mainly cereals, rose by 50 percent in the last decades of the century, and this new prosperity was credited to the Austrian-imposed land reforms. Both Verri and Beccaria participated in these reforms and exercised influence with Kaunitz. They were rewarded with state positions, making them among the few philosophes in Catholic Europe to play official roles. Beccaria taught in the school intended for future state administrators, and he embraced agriculture and the division of labor as the way forward for Lombardy. Verri's notions of luxury and its role in stimulating commerce played into the economic vision being put forward by the Milanese political economists. Only in one area did they condemn luxury: as found in the Church.

Envy and temperamental differences doomed the friendship of Verri and Beccaria. Although in Milan they were universally seen as bonded, the international fame of Beccaria far exceeded that of Verri; hence the envy. Toasted, read, and pondered in Europe, *On Crimes and Punishments* also had a remarkable impact in the American colonies and on Franklin and Jefferson, in particular. Jefferson had been trained in the law, and he transcribed large portions of Beccaria into his legal commonplace book. He came to believe that capital punishment should be used only in cases of treason or murder. Franklin too wanted to vastly curtail its use; he and his good friend Benjamin Rush, also inspired by Beccaria, worked to abolish slavery and (in Rush's case) capital punishment as well.[63] Beccaria's book made its way to almost every state in the new United States, where its work woefully still remains to be done.

8

The 1790s

At a period when the Kingdoms of the earth are shook upon
their settled foundations—when Kings are humbled to
the dust by those they are born to govern . . . it is not very
wonderful that the physical economy and organization of the
human body should, in many instances, experience something
of sympathetic and similar revolutions.[1]

CONVENTIONALLY, we end the Enlightenment at 1789
and the outbreak of the French Revolution. Europe and the
new American Republic became fixated on events in Paris and
beyond, then on the ensuing tension—finally war—between
Britain and France. By the mid-1790s, the French Revolutionary
Army was on the move, invading and occupying the Low Countries and eventually reaching into Germany, Italy, and Russia.
And revolution broke out in 1799 Naples, but it was brutally
suppressed.

Two years before 1789 in Paris, Amsterdam and Brussels
became centers of revolutionary ferment. By 1789 to 1790, the
ten Belgian provinces had declared their independence from
Austria and modeled manifestoes, although not their politics,

on the American Declaration of Independence.[2] This document was also widely publicized by the Italian press. In Britain, religious Dissenters looked with some sympathy on the American rebels and saw them as heirs to the English revolutionary tradition.

By 1790, the writings of the philosophes, new enlightened attitudes among the educated, and the expansion of secular space and time seemed like old stories, less compelling than the revolutionary events emanating from Philadelphia, Brussels, and Amsterdam, and most dramatically from Paris. Time itself seemed to accelerate. As the foundations of states and kingdoms shattered, so too an emotional transformation occurred in the lives of the men and women inspired by these political traumas. The transformations also owed a debt to the intellectual ferment of the previous hundred years, to the Enlightenment. During the 1790s, it offered the intellectual tools for the creation of a new persona—a thinking and critical person guided by secular principles—that informed the emotional identity of revolutionaries and reformers. Among those who self-defined as enlightened, some opposed the democratic revolutions, but they were in the minority.

Thus cultural movements, and sound ideas more generally, do not die abruptly, nor do ideals lose their relevance. Rather, they are transformed. During the 1790s, French, British, German, Dutch, Italian, and American intellectuals and sympathizers with both enlightened and revolutionary ideals had to come to terms with a revolution that veered off into the Terror and the rise of Napoleon, and then ended in 1815 with a profound reaction against its ideals. Although battered, the Enlightenment lived on, particularly among writers and intellectuals, often described as Romantics, whose psyches were shaped by the bold ideas of the eighteenth century. As president of the United

FIGURE 13. Thomas Jefferson, philosophe and radical revolutionary.
Rembrandt Peale (1778–1860) (ID# 258634). Courtesy of Bridgeman Images.

States, Thomas Jefferson (figure 13) affirmed his dedication to
Enlightenment principles when he wrote to Joseph Priestley, a
fellow revolutionary, about their enemies: "the barbarians really
flattered themselves [that] they should be able to bring back the
times of Vandalism, when ignorance put everything into the

hands of power and priestcraft. All advances in science were proscribed as innovations . . . this was the real ground of the attacks on you."[3]

There were those who had personally experienced the French Revolution and sought for calmer times. Writing from Paris to Jefferson in late 1792 about the course of the revolution, Condorcet explained that some of its supporters now hoped to "return it to the slow and soft action of the Enlightenment."[4] Yet all who lived through the events of the late 1780s and into the 1790s knew that they had changed personally, that the revolutions had shaped them profoundly.

After 1789, return was not possible. As the anti-Jacobins argued, "the principles of Infidelity transferred from *books* to *men*; from *dead* characters to *living* subjects," now gathered in ominous groups. It was alleged that Voltaire, Volney, and D'Holbach prepared the way for Thomas Paine and the London Corresponding Society. With biased logic, the opponents of the French Revolution argued that the good deist of the Enlightenment became the good democrat of the revolution.[5]

The French Revolution asserted democracy and the end of absolutism in church and state in ways that forever put these ideals on the agenda of the Western world. In the 1790s, Paris became not only the center for dramatic political changes but also an emotional cauldron of frenzied expectations and debilitating fears. From one day to the next, the aspirations of reformers and revolutionaries rose and fell. Political events were experienced as emotional highs and lows; the creation of the democratic citizen required personal transformation, a subjective and unique experience, often transgressive of customs and mores.[6] This was nowhere more the case than for men and women who identified with enlightened values—who came out of the decades after 1750 immersed in books that advocated

unleash the extremes of atheism and what he saw as its companion, unnatural passions. One of his followers argued that all sacred laws and doctrines had been abolished by the revolution.[9]

Burke may have been right, but it was for the wrong reasons. He detested the revolution and everything he imagined that it stood for. Those Britons drawn to it, by contrast, saw the possibility of rethinking laws and mores, the chance to create a liberated, even democratic subject. In Britain and Ireland, sympathy for revolution, first the American and then the French, ran most commonly among non-Anglican Protestants—that is, Dissenters. In the 1790s, radicals from the Dissenting tradition formed coteries and clubs often in the principal cities of the kingdom. Leaders included Joseph Priestley in Birmingham, William Godwin in London, George Dyer in Cambridge, and William Drennan in Belfast. They were in league with men whose fame as Romantic poets continued into our own time—William Wordsworth, Samuel Taylor Coleridge, and Robert Southey—as well as those who were equally as important then but are now less well-known—John Thelwall, Charlotte Smith, Anne Plumptre, Mary Hays, and Mary Robinson.[10] Many of them congregated regularly for tea with the Priestleys in London as the family packed to depart for Pennsylvania.[11] An antirevolutionary mob had devastated their household and laboratory in Birmingham, and flight seemed the better part of valor.

Perhaps Godwin captured the new radical impulse most daringly. His *Enquiry Concerning Political Justice* (1793) argued that only the moral reform of his readers would make genuine political change possible. Writing against the geographical determinism of Montesquieu, Godwin wanted to inspire human transformation through the use of reason. As he wrote, his distrust of government grew more pronounced. Gradually, he came to the view that it could be replaced, that the existing forms of law and property needed to be dismantled. Amid the signs of economic progress (referencing steam engines, he asked, "Who shall say where this species of improvement must stop?"), Godwin answered oddly by denouncing the institution of marriage as "a system of fraud." The certain and unremitting laws of the universe show us that "the supposition that I must have a companion for life, is the result of a complication of vices." Even wanting to know the actual father of every child results from "aristocracy, self-love and family pride."[12] Children should not be a form of property. Godwin's logic, that took him from machines to marriage, assumed that economic improvement depends upon moral and personal reform.

This sort of secular moralizing owed a great deal to Godwin's religious background as a Dissenter. His *Enquiry* was an expensive book when first published, but soon cheap copies were pirated and could be found in Ireland and Scotland. It was even read aloud by its devoted fans. In subsequent editions, Godwin placed a greater emphasis on sympathy and affection, an approach he adopted from his reading of Adam Smith. Despite being denounced as a seditionist and an atheist, or perhaps because of it, Godwin had a wide following among nineteenth-century socialists. In fact, he had produced the bible for an anarchist movement.

Economic and social issues were uppermost in the conversations of radical literary circles. George Dyer never failed to raise the subject of the poor and became one of the guiding lights for a utopian project to be established in Pennsylvania, "pantisocracy." The Romantic poets planned to leave England to join it; Priestley, they thought, would be one of its guiding spirits. Although it never came to fruition, the communitarian experiment remained a goal into the first decade of the new century. Followers mourned its failure.[13] Dyer believed that an entirely secular version of benevolence "is the hope and guide of more enlightened periods," born out of "rational conviction" possessed by all independent beings.[14]

Social radicalism matched personal, unconventional experimentation. In 1800, Dyer was on the verge of bringing out a collection of his poetry, but had it suppressed. The only known copy contains an ode to a male friend, "Oh! May I view again with ravish's sight, / As when with thee, Anderson, I stray'd, / And all the wonder-varying scene survey'd."[15] As Burke would have predicted, the circle of Dyer, Wordsworth, Coleridge, Southey, and others bent the heterosexual norms of friendship and the erotic.[16]

In these circles, conversations about social institutions invariably turned to marriage and the education of women. One pious Anglican observer thought that the French Revolution had resulted from men and women being too far apart.[17] Radicals like Godwin questioned the entire institution, while Southey and his friends talked about projects that would put women to work.[18] Their enemies reserved special scorn for women with "a democratic twist," an expression used by an acquaintance about the writer Charlotte Smith in 1792 and 1793. She had developed a devotion to the French Revolution that was dampened by the Terror, but never repudiated.

The long-suffering Smith referred to herself as nothing more than "a legal prostitute," having been in effect sold to her husband, "This monster."[19] She bore him twelve children and he died in debtor's prison. Periodicals dedicated to the causes of reform and revolution routinely carried long essays on the abilities of women and made frequent reference to the feminist writings of Mary Wollstonecraft, the wife of Godwin, who died in childbirth. They rejected any idea that women were mentally inferior. These publications also excoriated the institution of slavery.[20]

Although in sympathy with the plight of French émigré exiles, Smith believed in the principles of the Revolution: liberty and equality. She also read among the philosophes, even carrying on her travels a French edition of Bayle's *Dictionnaire*.[21] Among her radical peers, John Thelwall sang her praises, saying that her sonnets "display a more touching melancholy, a more poetical simplicity . . . a greater vigour and correctness of genius, than any other English poems that I have ever seen."[22]

For the younger generation, particularly those from industrial families, the French Revolution played into their disdain for the British ruling and landed classes. The acknowledged leaders of the new industrial ventures were Josiah Wedgwood, of pottery fame, and James Watt, who perfected the steam engine. Wedgwood approvingly described events in Paris as "a glorious revolution."[23] Their sons had become friends. In early May 1791, Josiah Wedgwood Jr. wrote to James Watt Jr. and revealed the depth of his alienation and the need for a general enlightening of the people:

> For my part I do not believe that any of our leading men in the H. of Commons have pure notions of liberty, at least if they have they dare not avow them for both parties are under influence, one of the crown and the other of a powerful aristocracy. There are no hopes of reform in this country but from the people and they are far from being sufficiently inlighten'd. I believe that John Bull who has so long been proud of his liberty has possessed only the shadow, and he has so long been content with that, that he has no desire for and does not wish to know the substance. I hope however our french neighbours affairs will go on prosperously and that John having their example always before him will at length mark the difference between their situation and his own.[24]

For many British radicals and sympathizers with the revolution, disillusionment came in the wake of the Terror. In 1794, Josiah Jr. wrote again to James Jr.: "France would have been the country, but Dame Guillotine has been so busy . . . that no one will venture to settle there until time shall have cooled the passions of the people and demonstrated the safety of a residence among them."[25] Every British proponent of republicanism had to come to terms with the revolution, make peace with its failures, or in some cases repudiate the cause entirely.

British, Irish, and Welsh provincial cities such as Edinburgh, Norwich, Belfast, Carmarthen, and Bristol nurtured the radicalism found particularly in the circles of Dissent. Norwich had long enjoyed a reputation as a Whig stronghold, with a strong Presbyterian, Unitarian, and Quaker intellectual life. Out of it came the Plumptre sisters—also frequenters of London coteries—who were fascinated by the possibilities for freedom unleashed by the revolution. Anne Plumptre even enlisted foreign writers into the agenda of British radicals. As translator of the German playwright and diplomat Augustus von Kotzebue, Plumptre found ideas to praise in his prolific writings. In one play, Kotzebue depicts a Jew as the sole giver of charity and has a liberal baron proclaim, "a marriage without love is absolute slavery."[26] In another widely translated and performed play of 1791, *Bruder Moritz, der Sonderling* ("The Odd Brother"), Kotzebue argues for the complete equality of all peoples, classes, men, and women. The anti-Jacobins mercilessly attacked the penchant of radical writers for German literary productions.[27] As a novelist, Plumptre further bent gender stereotypes and took up the cause of women's intellectual attractiveness. In her novel of 1801, it is the men who are the letter writers and romantics.[28]

Plumptre's lack of concern for organized religion mirrored the metaphysical sentiments found in these radical and enlightened circles. Materialism universally appealed. Priestley's is well documented, and George Dyer wrote jestingly to their mutual friend Mary Hays that "I have not a rhyme pass through my *organized matter* a long time."[29] At the same time, Hays defended the materialism of Helvétius and used it to argue that men and women do not possess different "natural powers, aptitudes and dispositions."[30] A few years earlier, she had been seen as a Unitarian, but it is likely that she retreated even further from her original theism or deism. George Dyer wrote to her sometime in the mid-1790s and passed along "my respects to any of yr friends, who enquire after me, whether they are disciples of Helvetius, or like your good mother, continue true and faithful to Jesus Christ."[31]

John Thelwall, an intimate of the Wordsworth-Coleridge circle, leaves little doubt about his commitment to a materialist creed. In verse, he proclaimed:

The Laws of Nature up to Nature's Cause, Thro all their mazy labyrinths, we descry How in eternal revolution urg'd, Obedient to the first impress'd command, The Protean atoms thro their whole extent In infinite mutation interchange—[32]

Thelwall was imprisoned for his politics and spent much of his life after release as an itinerant lecturer. When he died in 1834, he left his widow and three-year-old child impoverished. Only in the last twenty years, partly as a result of the discovery of his many lost writings, has his reputation at the center of 1790s radicalism been restored.

In the same period, Southey saw himself as a follower of the pagan and stoic Epictetus, as did Coleridge. Mourning the loss of a close friend, Coleridge said, "he was clay and stuff of my moral being—a sort of second conscience. . . . He it was who taught me to lay aside Rousseau for Epictetus."[33] Jefferson also ascribed great value to reading him, writing to his daughter in the spirit of the ancient Stoic that "it is part of the American character . . . to surmount every difficulty by resolution and contrivance."[34] Epictetus (born in the 50s CE) laid great emphasis on human choice and freedom; he was also a former slave. He believed that human beings can shape their circumstances and impose order and design on nature.

The pagan naturalism of Epictetus easily complemented a commitment to the materialism derived from the new science. A leading radical publication of the 1790s, produced anonymously, printed excerpts from Helvétius.[35] An anonymous catechism of 1794 proclaimed that "as men have been free, they have been virtuous."[36] Plumptre in turn translated the correspondence of Grimm and Diderot, those great friends of Beccaria.[37] And true to the spirit of the leading French philosophes, radicals like Henry Yorke called out the clergy for usurping "the opinions and judgments of all other men, from whose Breasts they expel Reason. . . . The history of the Church, or of the dominion of Priests . . . is the record of Farce over Truth, of Superstition over Reason."[38] By contrast, Charlotte Smith had a soft spot in her heart for the exiled clergy, but not for the aristocracy.

Such sentiments frightened and angered the authorities, who watched and finally persecuted—not always with success— various societies that sprang up in London, Edinburgh, Dublin, and many provincial cities. Yorke belonged to one in both London and Sheffield. The London and Welsh societies provided a network that answered the needs of Welsh supporters of the Revolution. The corresponding societies aimed to establish a national and international network of republicans in touch with their French counterparts.

It is important for the story of the 1790s and the Enlightenment that those societies included an unprecedented number of literate artisans or middling folks with a smattering of formal education. Such was the Welsh writer Iolo Morganwg (Edward Williams, 1747–1826), who was a stonemason, a radical, and a Unitarian. Like so many English supporters of the French Revolution, Iolo took up the cause of African slavery and wrote fierce denunciations of it. In his shop, he refused to sell sugar from the slave plantations of the West Indies, as did many other evangelical opponents of slavery. Once again in the Welsh anti-slavery movement, we see the influence of Protestant Dissent as well as the principles of the Enlightenment. The movement only gained force in the early decades of the nineteenth century.[39]

Enemies of the radical artisans said that amid "the lower orders of society . . . credulity is ever the strongest."[40] The most famous of these English artisans is, of course, William Blake—poet, radical, artist of remarkable talent. Like Thomas Paine in his *Rights of Man*, Blake used a forceful and direct form of address so that his poetry could reach a large audience, a practice that was democratic in both form and content. Blake willingly expropriated biblical texts and imagery to show how the American and French Revolutions were the ultimate fulfillment of biblical prophecy.[41]

The corresponding societies were outlawed in 1799; by then "habeas corpus" had been suspended. Prison for sedition became an ever-present possibility in Britain. Repressive laws, surveillance of suspected Jacobins, and monitoring of the Continental press continued into the 1820s, by which time war and revolution had largely disappeared from the scene. The issue of poverty had also fed into British discontent, and from the 1790s onward, various parliamentary reports made fitful efforts to address the condition of the poor.[42]

The situation in Scotland and Ireland was not as easily policed as that in England. As we saw in chapter 5, one of James Watt's sons, Gregory (d. 1804), attended the university in Glasgow in the 1790s, and his circle included young radicals as well as men with a penchant for the homoerotic. Gregory no doubt knew of the intense political struggle in Scotland among radical clubs taking inspiration from the French Revolution, and a British government intent upon suppressing them. In 1793 and 1794, leading Scottish radicals were routinely spied upon. Most of the professors at Glasgow University opposed the French Revolution, but Gregory studied with the minority who supported it, among them Robert Cleghorn in chemistry, George Jardine in logic, Archibald Arthur in moral philosophy, Thomas Reid, and John Millar. His tutor, Thomas Jackson, was blocked from an appointment as professor of natural philosophy in 1796 because of his political opinions.[43]

Gregory's student notebook from 1793 shows that teaching at Glasgow must have been contentious, for it followed enlightened and even pro-revolutionary lines. In it, Gregory, apparently influenced by his teachers and possibly his brother James, registered his approval of regicide: "The haughty Tyrant seated on his gorgeous Throne . . . dreaded and obeyed by an abject people is for the time considered . . . at the Zenith of human glory. The hand of Death cuts him short in his career, he perished in the midst of his splendor."[44] Travel, ill health, and scientific interests may have saved Gregory from deeper involvement in radical circles. In the early 1790s, James Jr. had thrown himself into the Jacobin cause, gone to Paris, and been denounced by Burke from the floor of Parliament.

While in the south of England for his health (he died in 1804 of tuberculosis, as did his sister before him), Gregory Watt met the young Humphry Davy. The Watt circle of Gregory's father launched Davy on his career in science; Davy, who isolated nitrous oxide and invented a mine safety lamp, became internationally famous and president of the Royal Society of London.

His Tory enemies assailed him for effeminacy and dandyism, claiming that his wife wore the pants in their childless marriage. The fact that Davy consorted with known radicals such as the chemist Thomas Beddoes and Coleridge, to whom he administered nitrous oxide, was a red flag in anti-Jacobin circles. Careful not to invoke the materialism of Erasmus Darwin, Davy nevertheless made clear his debt to the Enlightenment and his belief in the great age of the earth.[45]

As he developed, Davy gave the government little cause to worry about his politics. Yet the interconnectedness of other Scottish, English, Welsh, and Irish radicals must have caused the authorities growing alarm. While discontent was visible in most urban settings, only the Irish rose in actual rebellion in 1798. Theirs was by far the most dangerous and violent result of the revolutionary fervor put in motion in the British Isles by the events of 1789. The outcome was between 20,000 and 30,000 casualties, many of them Irish peasants.

The Irish Rebellion was led by the United Irishmen, a Presbyterian-dominated club, but it became a Catholic uprising as well. Massacres and atrocities fed the passions of the day, accompanied by government-approved executions and wanton violence by the rebels. A desperately needed French invasion landed but was seriously undermanned and lasted only a few weeks. It finally failed, as did the rebellion.

Among its sympathizers—and forlorn because of its defeat—Thomas Moore (b. 1779) narrowly escaped being rounded up after the failed uprising; he became a famous poet and songwriter. His friend, Robert Emmet, was executed for his part in yet another rebellion in 1803. In 1799, Moore, a Catholic who had managed to matriculate at Trinity College in Dublin, left for London; there he socialized in Whig circles and among supporters of Catholic Emancipation.

Moore is another radical whose eroticism is not easily classified. Although an Irish Catholic and a nationalist, at the Protestant bastion of Trinity he received a liberal and classical education. His reading of the ancient bisexual poet Anacreon was simply part of a boy's education and seems to have been fairly commonplace.[46] But Moore did more than read his poems. He put in his English translation a poem written by the ancient poet to a young man, Bathyllus, which even Coleridge condemned as completely unacceptable.[47] Over a decade later, Moore and Lord Byron became very close friends; Byron was godfather to Moore's daughter. Moore wrote his biography, in the process downplaying or even obscuring Byron's bisexuality, about which he may very well have known. Southey, having turned to conservatism, labeled them "the Satanic School." Byron and Moore came to despise Southey as a turncoat who succumbed to honors and wealth. The point here is not the Moore-Byron friendship but rather the values they shared: both admired the French Revolution; both had democratic inclinations and shared a willingness to trespass on conventional mores; both despised the fashionable and what they saw as the inauthentic, supported Catholic emancipation and the rights of the oppressed in Ireland.[48] They likewise took a dim view of organized religion.[49]

While his translation of Anacreon brought Moore fame, a volume of his own poems was met with prudish disdain. Yet he wrote some of the most popular poems and songs of the time, many of them known to this day by any Irish nationalist.[50] Byron offended public sexual mores and died in Greece a patriot for its revolution. His life especially displays "something of sympathetic and similar revolutions" inspired by the political events of the 1790s.

None of these affectations, transgressions, or beliefs were missed by the rabid anti-Jacobins. Their literature, distinctive to that decade, claimed detailed knowledge of an "Infidel Society" wherein reigns a "degeneracy of principle and practice" in which men drown "in the stagnant pool of French Atheism . . . like the deadly lake of Sodom . . . mortal to the taste."[51] The anti-Jacobins postulated a clandestine genealogy of immorality, where domestic vice or disappointment, or the fear of succumbing to secret and homosexual desire, fueled political allegiances.[52] Gregory and his mates, Coleridge and company, Moore and Byron may have been exploring the "virtues and vices of Nature," but the anti-Jacobin pundits said that, in their clubs, men were "degraded mortals who pride themselves in being nothing more than mere organizations of matter." They were not simply deists or democrats—they were atheists and materialists.

The advocates of democracy had a harder time in Ireland. Its Catholic population had long been subjected to inequities, and rural poverty was endemic, as was distrust between Protestants and Catholics. Taxation fell unfairly, and among Protestants, Anglicans but not Dissenters had access to political power. The radicals who espoused democracy were also invariably nationalist, and they rejected the dominance of king and church. Irish agitation for reform began in the 1780s, failed, and returned with renewed vigor after events in France.

William Drennan and his society, the United Irishmen, accompanied by Theobald Wolfe Tone, waged the most sustained campaign for independence and drew upon the principles articulated in the American Declaration of Independence. Addressing fellow countrymen as slaves, they argued in Rousseauian terms that it is possible to throw off the injustices of British government and become free. They also invoked the English republican tradition of the mid-seventeenth century.[53] Their vision of complete religious toleration embraced the call for democracy and hence a radical reading of Enlightenment texts.[54]

For a time, Tone fled to Philadelphia, as did many Irish radicals, but he was uninspired by what he saw in the new world. In the 1790s, when all hope of peaceful reform seemed impossible, Tone wrote as a Protestant to his Catholic fellow countrymen, arguing that "no reform is honourable practicable or just which does not include as a fundamental principle the elective franchise of Roman Catholics."[55] He became the leader of the 1798 rebellion and a martyr to the cause of Irish independence. He died in prison in Dublin in 1798.

In the Irish litany of abuses, the need for religious equality joined with the demand for economic equality with Britain. In 1803, another short-lived rebellion, led by Robert Emmet, laid emphasis on Irish economic grievances; the issue smoldered throughout the nineteenth century. Whatever the issues, the first rebellion entered the collective imagination as a story of murder and mutilations committed by both sides. The level of atrocities colored the telling of Irish history well into the twentieth century; indeed, that dark legacy still affects parts of Northern Ireland to this day. It should be remembered that many United Irishmen who fled to the new American Republic were avowed democrats.

The New American Republic

Of the various versions of enlightened thought that we have examined in this book, it is the Scottish one that arguably had the greatest impact on American thinkers.[56] The concern for agricultural improvement, for an accommodation of religion with science, and not least, for the nature of progress and the forms of social organization that best promote it, make Scottish thinkers and American colonists obvious interlocutors. Yet the colonies had one element unknown in Scotland: slavery. Some have argued that enlightened texts aided and abetted the plantation owners and never the slaves. This argument confuses the way a work is read with the intentionality of the author. Few whom we have identified as belonging to the Enlightenment—with the possible exception of David Hume and the early Kant—wanted their learning or theories to encourage human bondage.[57] A slave owner who fathered children with his slave/mistress, Thomas Jefferson saw the paradox that he himself lived:

> What a stupendous, what an incomprehensible machine is man! who can endure toil, famine ... imprisonment, & death itself in vindication of his own liberty, and the next moment be deaf to all those motives whose power supported him thro' his trial and inflict on his fellow men a bondage, one hour of which is fraught with more misery than ages, of that which he rose in rebellion to oppose.[58]

It is also the case that once the American Revolution had been fought and won, the troubled 1790s witnessed a backsliding from its most radical and liberating principles. As an example, after spending many years in England and revolutionary France, in 1802 Tom Paine returned to his adopted New World home. His reputation preceded him, and nary a Baltimore tavern would serve a man said to be both a Jacobin and an atheist. When Paine arrived, being seen as a democrat had become highly controversial, in good measure because of the reaction to the extremes of the French Revolution. Recall that years earlier, Jefferson had praised his ideas as "sound and pure." The French Revolution and its aftermath had refueled a trans-Atlantic, international republican conversation that involved most of the European languages.[59] It was aided in part by the hundreds of

British, Irish, and French immigrants who had directly experienced the political events of the 1790s. The leading American deist of the decade, Elihu Palmer, celebrated the Fourth of July by pointing out that the French Revolution had been inspired by the American one, and how French soldiers returned home with the will to deliver a destructive blow to despotism: "In vain have the despots of the earth combined to strangle in its birth the child of Freedom."[60]

The conversation about freedom and despotism predated the American and French Revolutions by several decades; it was an inherent part of the Enlightenment. The readings and writings of Benjamin Franklin from midcentury onward exemplify how an educated American could participate in republican thought, deism, freemasonry, science, and the search to become an educated person, capable of political action and meritorious because imbued with useful learning.[61] Franklin, like so many other experimenters of the period, sought to understand the nature of electricity and to channel it in useful directions.[62] He also wanted to forge a consensus around the enlightened search for a reformed religiosity, one that could serve the needs of a virtuous and free people.

In 1782, we find Franklin as *Le Venerable*, the master of the Lodge of the Nine Sisters in Paris. For a few decades after his initiation in a Philadelphia lodge, Franklin had been an active freemason and a leader within the lodges. Very shortly after Franklin joined St. John's Lodge in Philadelphia, according to his *Autobiography*, he decided: "There seems to me at present to be a great Occasion for a united Party of Virtue, by forming the Virtuous and good Men of all Nations into a regular Body, to be governed by suitable good and wise Rules, which good and wise Men may probably be more unanimous in their Obedience to, than common people are to common Laws." To these ends, Franklin later remembered, he had spent much of that period of his life trying to discover what every religion had in common so that it could serve as the foundation for a universal, natural religion to which all could agree. Of the ethical principles he recalled, the most striking and most relevant was "That the most acceptable service of God is doing Good to Man."

Franklin drew more from freemasonry than the search for a universal, natural religion. He also learned lessons in group behavior and political organizing. In 1774, he co-founded with David Williams the Society of 13, a deistic circle that included in its original membership Franklin, Williams, Major Dawson, Thomas Bentley (assistant to Josiah Wedgwood), James Stuart, John Whitehurst, Thomas Day, and Daniel Solander. The Society of 13, echoing the masonic model of a secret society of learned men, kept the masonic tradition of limiting the membership of lodges in persecuted countries, in this case to 13. All the men in the group associated with it were radical Whigs and republicans; they were not entirely wrong in thinking themselves persecuted.

Richard Price, Joseph Priestley, Benjamin Vaughan, J. R. Forster, Edward Bancroft, Thomas Paine, and David Hartley were among the big names associated with the society. Vaughan corresponded extensively with Franklin, particularly on matters of moral philosophy, and was more familiar than most with Franklin's attempts at elucidating an ethical, largely secular system. All of these men supported the American Revolution, and the group served, above all else, to conduct English and French radicals safely and secretly across the Atlantic.

Even though his temperament was not for secret societies and philosophical liturgies, Jefferson nevertheless knew of the group, corresponded with its members, and as a deist shared their views on religion and politics. Franklin, Price, and Priestley were associated with another British radical organization that was obviously descended from masonic influence: the Grand Lodge of the Constitutional Whigs, which traced its origins back to the principles of the Glorious Revolution of 1689 and the preceding years of opposition political thought.[63]

The ferment of ideas around the nature and origins of religion, when combined with new forms of social solidarity, galvanized attention on government, particularly on its absolutist forms. Later in the century, this unwelcome attention was particularly visible in France and Germany but was also seen in the Austrian Netherlands and Italy. We do not think about enlightened challenges to Christian orthodoxy as having much to do with the democratic revolutions of the late 1780s. We should think again.

In 1765, John Adams believed the settlement of America opened up "a grand scene and design in Providence for the illumination of the ignorant." Other Americans in the 1790s thought that the new nation was the "most enlightened" in the world.[64] They were capable of identifying with an international and cosmopolitan movement while still professing loyalty to the nation. Paradoxically, they imagined themselves as equal yet at the same time excluded blacks and indigenous people from citizenship. American prosperity reinforced this righteous sense of being enlightened.

The philosophes were also on the minds of colonial political thinkers. In 1765, amid the Stamp Act crisis, Samuel Adams invoked Montesquieu when he argued that political liberty depends upon "a tranquility of mind."[65] He further described that state of nature in Rousseauian terms: "no man in the state of nature can justly take another's Property without his consent."[66] Likewise Samuel Adams believed that "the present age is more enlightened than former ones. . . . Such an age . . . will view the utility of universal Education in so strong a light as to induce sufficient national patronage and support."[67] By 1794, he saw the French as having repudiated "the absurd and unnatural claims of hereditary and exclusive privileges ... [they] suddenly awoke, from their long slumber, abolished the usurpation, and placed every man upon the footing of equal rights."[68]

Such favorable judgments did not prevent a growing hostility between the French and American governments. In 1798, the Alien and Sedition Acts attempted to tamp down radical and potentially rebellious movements in the new United States. Led by the Federalists, the opponents of democracy sought to demote the revolutionary tradition that was now both American and French. How far should the revolution be taken? To slaves? Women? The impoverished? Therein lay the tension, present since the seventeenth century, and caused by self-proclaimed "freeborn English men" who both practiced and profited from slavery.

Thomas Jefferson laid out these tensions in a frank letter to Richard Price regarding Price's 1784 pamphlet, *Observations on the Importance of the American Revolution*. People south of the Chesapeake, Jefferson says, will not accept its condemnation of slavery; a little farther north they will accept it in theory but "not have the courage to divest their families of a property which however keeps their consciences inquiet." In the area north of Maryland, where fewer and fewer slaves are kept, opponents will be found largely among the young. Jefferson thought that the decision to abolish slavery might still be possible, "but will not be so long."[69] In their darker moments, the heirs of the democratic revolutions may have realized that only war would one day settle the issue of slavery.

At the beginning of the American Revolution, the rebels were also frightened. So Jefferson wrote, to console those Americans who had actually witnessed the bloody events in Paris and were at times frightened. But according to Jefferson, they too would need to "pass successively thro' it, and happy if they get thro' it and as soon and as well as Paris has done."[70] Revolutionaries like Jefferson believed that each generation had the right to forge its own consensus, customs, and laws. Writing some years after his time in Paris and as president of the United States, Jefferson believed that no experiment of forming and governing a new republic "can be more interesting than that we are now trying, and which we trust will end in establishing the fact that we are now governed by reason and trust."[71] He spoke like the philosophe he had become.

Germanic Lands

The response to the French Revolution varied considerably in the German- and Dutch-speaking lands. The German lands were run by princes, and even the most liberal of them, the small duchy of Saxe-Weimar and Eisenach, officially displayed no support for foreign revolutions. It even made money by selling inmates from the local jails to the British, who put them to work as soldiers against the American colonists. The poet Goethe, in his capacity as a government official, actively engaged in the practice. The duchies were run in the manner of absolutist monarchies, and revolutions were not on their list of approved political actions. Even in Weimar, every effort was made to shield the population from contact with revolutionary ideas, and this was especially true in the wake of the French Revolution.[72]

In the German-speaking lands, the stage for this negative reaction had been set by the emergence of a radical secret organization, the Illuminaten, and the publication of its secret papers in 1786/87. The hysterical reaction by the German authorities in every province merged with the growing fear—put forward as early as the autumn of 1789 by French opponents of the Revolution—that the Revolution had been the work of a secret conspiracy of philosophes and freemasons. We saw in Scotland how John Robison latched on to this conspiracy theory (chapter 5) and helped make it an indelible part of far-right political philosophy well into our own time. In reality, we now believe that there were about 600 Illuminati in the whole of Germany. To repeat: Conspiracy theories never depend upon facts.

The Weimar duchy also feared that the bellicose French might invade, a fear that was particularly acute because local peasants and students began to display an affection for their revolution. Various repressive tactics were tried against the press and the university, and discontent went largely underground. Clearly, the authorities in every German principality—Prussia and Saxony, for example—were worried, and in Weimar the duke even enlisted Goethe to write against the revolution.[73] Weimar intellectuals were not uniformly anti-revolutionary, but under the circumstances they kept a very low profile.

Independent port cities such as Hamburg became relatively open to events as they unfolded in France. The journal *Minerva* appeared there, and it brought news from France and the French Caribbean as well as discussions of economic matters, all of interest to the city's merchants. In the 1790s, German periodicals exploded with over one thousand publications in press. Many contributors, such as Friedrich Schiller, tried to maintain their aesthetic sensibility and to avoid politics altogether. Their enlightened German predecessors had long practiced such abstinence. But others ventured their support for events in Paris, at least up until the execution of Louis XVI in September 1793.

In the decades before the French Revolution, various German-speaking states and territories had effected reforms inspired by enlightened principles. In the Habsburg Empire in 1776, Maria Theresa abolished the use of torture in judicial proceedings, a move supported by her reforming chancellor of state, Prince Wenzel Kaunitz, who had been directly influenced by the writings of the Italian philosophe, Beccaria. His 1764 *On Crimes and Punishments* became a point of reference for all who found European prisons, and the use of torture, barbaric. Kaunitz and the empress (d. 1780) had begun reforms and building projects in the Habsburg territories, including the Austrian Netherlands (today Belgium). Her son, Joseph II, inherited these enlightened impulses.[74]

Joseph II (d. 1790) came to exemplify what has been called "enlightened absolutism." With all the contradictions inherent in the phrase, it came to be associated with Joseph's principles and his desire to bring the Enlightenment to the Habsburg territories. In this activity, he was aided by Viennese masonic lodges and their Western European brethren.[75] Joseph's instincts for limited religious toleration and a relaxation of censorship awakened similar impulses among the lower classes, who resented the privileges and arrogance of the clergy and aristocracy. In Naples, as we saw, Queen Caroline had also used the masonic lodges to enhance the power of the court and to point its interests in the direction of the Habsburgs. In Milan, Josephine reforms privileged lay authority in the educational system and strengthened the education of students aspiring to liberal professions such as law and medicine.[76]

Then came the French Revolution. Its impact was felt throughout the Habsburg territories, especially in Hungary. Even the peasantry responded to the news coming from Paris, and the floodgates opened with tracts against the papacy and against clerical and aristocratic privileges in general. Joseph II had no alternative, as he saw it, but to pull back from enlightened reform as he witnessed cobblers, tailors, and female cooks taking sides against the privileged. The trouble brewing in the western Habsburg lands predated the French uprising, and revolution had broken out in Brussels in 1787. By that year and slightly before, Joseph had instructed the secret police to be vigilant, and at his death in 1790, reaction against enlightened principles had become the norm.

His successor, Leopold II, sought to restore public order in Belgium, to strengthen the monarchy while sustaining peasant objections to the power of the nobility. While offering his services, one Hungarian professor summed up Leopold's policies: "The Americans and the French have made good laws as a result of much bloody violence. Your Majesty makes good laws, which all enlightened men admire . . . without any revolution."[77] The Enlightenment was back on the political agenda as Leopold limited the secret activities of the police. He was dead in 1792, succeeded by his son, Francis II, who abandoned, once again, the policies of enlightened absolutism. War against the French, whose army had advanced on the Low Countries, now became inevitable. Censorship, secret police, and the closing of independent presses became the order of the day.

By 1793, the masonic lodges had ceased to meet. Now forced to meet in private, opposition groups circulated the French translation of Thomas Paine's *Rights of Man* and sang French revolutionary songs, while handwritten democratic pamphlets passed among sympathizers and Rousseau's *Social Contract* was translated into Hungarian. The Ministry of the Police decided that a Jacobin conspiracy had been established, while the Austrian army suffered one defeat after the other at the hands of the French. In the summer of 1794, the police struck out against the imagined Jacobins. Anyone suspected of atheism was arrested, cautioned, or in some cases pilloried or imprisoned. In 1795, the

Hungarian courts sentenced eighteen "Jacobins" to be hanged, while in both parts of the kingdom large prison sentences were imposed. In the Habsburg Empire, the anti-Enlightenment had won.

Upheaval in Naples

It is worth remembering that Queen Carolina was an Austrian and the sister of Marie Antoinette, wife of the French king, who was famously guillotined in October 1793. No place in Europe was more alarmed by the events in Paris than the Neapolitan court. As news came from France, royal police and spies multiplied, as did the surveillance of the population, and especially of anyone with French sympathies. Somehow, an Italian translation of the *Declaration of the Rights of Man* came to be circulated, while the court refused to receive the new ambassador from the French Republic. The French sent a fleet to the harbor in Naples and demanded an explanation, and the court caved in to its demands.

Repression returned, while at the same time clubs formed that demanded "liberty or death," even "A Republic or Death." Secret judges met, dozens of people were arrested, and three young students were condemned to death. A court-sponsored reign of terror commenced, and it predictably provoked a backlash. In the person of Napoleon and his army, the French Revolution came to Naples. Its supporters declared a republic, and for a brief period it looked as if Naples might become the second new republic in Europe. Then the British fleet commanded by Lord Nelson arrived. By the end of 1799, the Neapolitan Republic ceased to exist, the French were defeated, and the British and Austrians emerged victorious. So too had the Italian Enlightenment, at least for a time, been defeated.

The Dutch Republic

After its independence from Spain was legally secured in 1648, the Dutch Republic remained an independent nation until it was invaded by the French Revolutionary Army in 1795. The Army left only in 1813, and at the Congress of Vienna the House of Orange was restored as a monarchy in place of the inherently weaker stadtholderate. The economic history of the Dutch eighteenth century reveals a state of decline from its spectacular prosperity of the seventeenth century, the co-called *Gouden Eeuw* (Golden Century).

I have argued elsewhere that the Enlightenment began in the late seventeenth century in England and the Dutch Republic. The relatively free presses in both places made possible the publication of foundational texts by Spinoza, Hobbes, and Locke. Not least, the Dutch presses specialized in the clandestine, which encompassed everything from the risqué to the pornographic and the blasphemous. Yet the vibrancy of the period before 1750 was not visible in the second half of the century. Dutch trade in the Atlantic declined markedly and, beginning with the Revolution of 1747–48, instability plagued the Republic. As was the case among French and German reformers, Dutch enlightened opinion began to turn away from imperialism. In 1769, Onno Zwier van Haren's play, *Agon, Sultan van Bantam*, cast the Dutch East India Company (VOC) as the villain; the play is hostile to the entire enterprise of empires and colonies.[78] By that decade, widespread discontent in the Republic was commented upon by foreign visitors.

An uprising in 1787 would have transformed the state radically, but it was stopped in its tracks by a Prussian invasion.[79] Its leaders, *Patriotten*, fled to France, and many of them returned with the victorious French army. Their inspiration had come first from the American Revolution and then the French, and whatever their differences they remained committed to revolutionary principles.

Among the patriots who fled to France, J. A. Craÿenshot had been the orator in the prestigious Amsterdam masonic lodge, La Bien Aimée. He had published radically anti-Orangist pamphlets, and his lodge brothers were international merchants, sea captains, bankers, surgeons, professors, and artists. The lodge must have been a remarkable meeting place. The yet-to-be-famous Jean Paul Marat and the soon-to-be-infamous Casanova were among the visitors, as were brothers from Philadelphia, Edinburgh, and Moscow. Consistently, the orations given in the lodge speak of the brothers as freedom loving. In 1782, the lodge concluded a treaty with its American counterparts. Thirteen years later when the French army invaded, the brothers greeted it by singing "La Marseillaise." The corridor from Amsterdam to Paris had witnessed the Enlightenment and then embraced the democratic revolutions of both the Americans and the French.[80]

tinkered with their liturgy to express an egalitarian discontent with Anglican hierarchy and orthodoxy.[1] Decades earlier, Voltaire had championed the Unitarians' cerebral version of religiosity. He could not imagine anything as irrational as democracy; by the 1760s, however, Rousseau showed little restraint when he dreamed of it. By the 1770s, it was clear to the enlightened that in the Western world the American colonies had embarked upon a rebellion that could usher in just such an experiment.

Since the late 1680s into the 1790s, all sorts of people tried to break with tradition and find alternatives to absolutism in church and state. Someone like Isabella de Moerloose (chapter 3) turns up almost by accident. Early in the century in the Dutch Republic, she taught school while taunting the local clergy and writing passionately about sexual freedom. She landed in prison for her trouble, and there she seems to have succumbed to madness. A few decades later in the republic, the Huguenot refugee Jean Rousset de Missy became a revolutionary, and after events in 1747–48 he was exiled. Like English, American, and French revolutionaries, he enlisted John Locke to justify his rebellious battle.[2] The Italian theorist of republics, Filangieri wanted to join Franklin in the new American Republic so that he could assist at its establishment, while several years later Irish radicals and republicans flocked to the new republic, where many remained.

Then as now, the political has often been personal. Seekers after alternatives to absolute monarchies and their churches filled civil society, dwelt in its cafés, coffee houses, salons, eating clubs, and lodges. There they could find the like-minded, or the pugnacious, even the outrageous and the subversive. Not least, their shelves offered free newspapers and journals. The century ended with revolutions—Brussels, Amsterdam, Paris, Belfast, Dublin, Naples—that focused minds on making new institutions, new laws, new hopes and dreams. All of them in this world, in time to be lived. Sin, hell, and salvation became less real, or to be attended to less urgently. Consumption became easier for the urban educated and employed; books, clocks, and watches to measure the time spent reading were more plentiful. In some minds, the clergy could be disdained, churches avoided or viewed only for their physical beauty; even the founders of the great monotheistic religions could be mocked. By 1800, space and time on earth were filled by fewer miracles, saints, and prophecies than had been the case in 1700. The secular with which we still live had become all pervasive, even if offensive to the religiously observant. In the United States, nineteenth-century evangelical Protestants still longed for a great awakening that would restore the faithful to their Godly covenant. In some quarters in our own time, such dreams remain possible, yet curiously unattainable or tainted by political involvements. The eighteenth-century philosophes, despite their disagreements, shared a universal distrust of organized religion and the priests who enforced it. We have sought here to recall the contours of their thinking and the social and political settings that gave rise to it. This historical account seeks not to return to the past but to bring the best of the secular Enlightenment with us into the future.

GLOSSARY OF NAMES

Adams, John (1735–1826)—American statesman, lawyer, and political theorist. The second president of the United States.

Adams, Samuel (1722–1803)—American statesman and political philosopher. One of the Founding Fathers of the United States.

Adanson, Michel (1727–1806)—Eighteenth-century French botanist and naturalist.

Aikenhead, Thomas (1676–97)—Scottish student from Edinburgh. The last person in the British Isles to be executed for blasphemy.

Anacreon (582–485 BCE)—Greek lyric poet.

Anderson, John (1726–96)—Scottish natural philosopher and liberal educator. A leader in the application of science and technology in the Industrial Revolution.

Aquinas, St. Thomas (1225–74)—Italian Dominican friar, Catholic priest, and Doctor of the Church.

Ardinghelli, Mariangiola (1728–1825)—Italian Newtonian who translated the writings of the English Newtonian Steven Hales and became an informal but important correspondent with the Paris Academy of Science.

Aristotle (384–322 BCE)—Ancient Greek philosopher.

Arpe, Peter Friedrich (1682–1740)—German lawyer, historian, and legal writer.

Arthur, Archibald (1744–97)—Scottish Enlightenment philosopher. Active at the University of Glasgow, where he worked as an assistant to Thomas Reid before taking over his teaching duties in 1796.

Bacon, Francis (1561–1626)—English philosopher and scientist. An advocate of the scientific method. His *Novum Organum* is an important work in Europe's scientific revolution.

Bahrdt, Carl Friedrich (1741–92)—German biblical scholar, theologian, and polemicist. A highly controversial figure in his day.

Bancroft, Edward (1745–1821)—American-born physician and chemist. During the American Revolution, he was a double agent, spying for both the United States and Great Britain.

Barruel, Augustin (1741–1820)—French publicist and Jesuit priest. Famous for his *Memoirs Illustrating the History of Jacobinism*, where he argued that the French Revolution was planned and carried out by secret societies.

Bassi, Laura (1711–78)—Italian physicist and academic. One of the first female university graduates and professors in Europe, she helped spread Newton's ideas in Italy.

Baxter, Andrew (1686/87–1750)—Scottish metaphysician.

Bayle, Pierre (1647–1706)—French philosopher, Huguenot refugee, and writer best known for his *Historical and Critical Dictionary*.

Beccaria, Cesare (1738–94)—Italian criminologist, jurist, philosopher, and politician. Best known for his treatise *On Crimes and Punishments* (1764), which condemned torture and the death penalty.

Beddoes, Thomas (1760–1808)—English physician and scientific writer.

Bekker, Balthazar (1634–1698)—Dutch minister, philosopher, and theologian. Defended reason and opposed superstition, which he attacked in his best known work, *De Betoverde Wereld*, or *The World Bewitched*.

Benedict XIV, Pope (born Prospero Lorenzo Lambertini) (1675–1758)—As Pope of the Catholic Church from 1740–58, he promoted scientific learning.

Benezet, Anthony (1713–84)—French Huguenot reformer. An abolitionist and educator active in Philadelphia, he founded one of the world's first anti-slavery societies, the Society for the Relief of Free Negroes Unlawfully Held in Bondage.

Bentley, Richard (1662–1742)—English classical scholar and theologian. Master of Trinity College, Cambridge.

Bentley, Thomas (1731–80)—English manufacturer of porcelain. Known for his partnership with Josiah Wedgwood.

Bernard, Jacques (1658–1718)—French theologian and publicist who worked in the Dutch Republic.

Bernard, Jean Frederic (1680–1744)—French writer and translator.

Black, Joseph (1728–99)—Scottish physician and chemist. Known for discoveries of magnesium, latent heat, specific heat, and carbon dioxide.

Blake, William (1757–1827)—English poet, painter, and printmaker. Although little appreciated during his lifetime, he is now considered a seminal figure in English Romanticism.

Boyer, Jean-Baptiste de (Marquis d'Argens) (1704–71)—French philosopher and writer.

Boyle, Robert (1627–91)—Anglo-Irish natural philosopher and scientist. Regarded as the first modern chemist.

Bruno, Giordano (1548–1600)—Born Filippo Bruno. An Italian Dominican friar, philosopher, mathematician, and poet. Burned at the stake by the Church.

Burke, Edmund (1730–97)—Irish statesman, author, political theorist, and philosopher. Whig Member of Parliament in the House of Commons.

Byron, George Gordon (Lord Byron) (1788–1824)—English nobleman, poet, and leading figure in the Romantic movement.

Calas, Jean (1698–1762)—French merchant. A Protestant executed in Catholic France, he is remembered as a victim of religious intolerance.

Casanova, Giacomo (1725–98)—Italian adventurer and social commentator and critic. His *Story of My Life* is regarded as one of the most authentic sources of the customs and norms of eighteenth-century European social life.

Cassirer, Ernst (1874–1945)—Neo-Kantian German philosopher. Attempted to theorize an idealist philosophy of science.

Chaptal, Jean-Antoine (1756–1832)—French chemist, physician, agronomist, statesman, and philanthropist.

Châtelet, Madame du (1706–49)—French natural philosopher, mathematician, and physicist. Famous for her translation and commentary on Newton's *Principia*.

Clarke, Samuel (1675–1729)—English philosopher and Anglican clergyman.

Cleghorn, Robert (1755–1821)—Scottish physician and pharmacologist.

Cleland, John (1709–89)—British writer.

Coleridge, Samuel Taylor (1772–1834)—Arguably the most famous of the English Romantic poets.

Collins, Anthony (1676–1729)—English philosopher and proponent of deism.

Conti, Antonio Schinella (1677–1749)—Known by his religious title as Abbé Conti. An Italian writer, translator, mathematician, philosopher, and physicist.

Craÿenshot, J. A (dates unknown)—Amsterdam freemason.

Cullen, William (1710–90)—Scottish physician and chemist. One of the most important professors at the Edinburgh Medical School.

Curchod, Louise-Suzanne (1737–94)—French-Swiss salonist and writer. Hosted one of the most famous salons of the *ancien régime*. The mother of Madame de Staël and the wife of finance minister Jacques Necker, her married name was Suzanne Necker.

Dampier, William (1651–1715)—English explorer and navigator. The first Englishman to explore parts of Australia, and the first person to circumnavigate the world three times.

Darwin, Erasmus (1731–1802)—English physician, natural philosopher, and abolitionist. One of the major thinkers of the Midlands Enlightenment.

Davy, Humphry (1778–1829)—Cornish chemist and inventor. Best remembered for isolating a series of substances for the first time, including potassium, sodium, calcium, strontium, barium, magnesium, and boron.

Day, Thomas (1748–89)—British author and abolitionist. Known for his book *The History of Sandford and Merton*, which emphasized Rousseauian educational ideals.

De Benedictis, Giovani (1641–1706)—Jesuit of Naples, also known as Benedetto Aletino. A professor of philosophy at the College of Naples.

d'Épinay, Louise (Madame d'Épinay) (1726–83)—French writer, salonist, and woman of fashion.

Derrida, Jacques (1930–2004)—French philosopher. Best known for his method of analysis called deconstruction, and one of the major figures associated with post-structuralism and postmodern philosophy.

Desaguliers (1683–1744)—French-born British natural philosopher, clergyman, engineer, and freemason. Elected to the Royal Society in 1714 as experimental assistant to Isaac Newton.

Des Périers, Bonaventure (1500–1544)—French author.

Dewey, John (1859–1952)—American philosopher. His ideas have been influential in educational and social reform.

D'Holbach, Paul-Henri Thiry (Baron) (d. 1789)—French-German author, philosopher, encyclopedist. Born Paul Heinrich Dietrich, he was a prominent figure in the French Enlightenment.

Dickenson, Samuel (1733–1823)—English clergyman and botanist.

Diderot, Denis (1713–84)—French philosopher. Best known as the co-editor (with Jean le Rond d'Alembert) of the *Encyclopédie*, a collection of all the world's knowledge.

Dodsley, Robert (1704–64)—English bookseller, poet, and playwright.

Drennan, William (1754–1820)—Irish physician, poet, and political radical. One of the chief architects of the Society of United Irishmen.

DuLaurens, Henri (1719–93/97)—Defrocked French monk. Later became a political satirist and novelist.

Dunoyer, Anne-Marguerite (1663–1719)—Famous early eighteenth-century journalist.

Durand, David (1680–1763)—Huguenot French and English minister and historian.

Dyer, George (1755–1841)—English classicist, poet, and editor.

Effen, Justus van (1684–1735)—Dutch author who wrote chiefly in French. Also made important contributions to Dutch literature.

Emmet, Robert (1778–1803)—Irish nationalist and Republican, orator, and rebel leader. Led an abortive rebellion against British rule in 1803, for which he was captured and executed for high treason against the British king.

Epictetus (55–135 CE)—Greek Stoic philosopher.

Eugene of Savoy, Prince (1663–1736)—General of the Imperial Army and statesman of the Holy Roman Empire and the Archduchy of Austria.

Evelyn, John (1620–1706)—English writer and diarist. His rival was Samuel Pepys, who also chronicled seventeenth-century English society.

Evelyn, Mary (1665–1685)—Daughter of John Evelyn. Believed to be the pseudonymous author of *Mundus Muliebris*.

Ferguson, Adam (1723–1816)—Philosopher and historian of the Scottish Enlightenment.

Filangieri, Gaetano (1752–88)—Italian jurist and philosopher.

Filangieri, Serafino (1713–82)—Italian archbishop.

Forster, Johann Reinhold (1729–98)—Reformed Calvinist pastor and naturalist of Scottish descent. Made early contributions to ornithology, and accompanied James Cook on Cook's second Pacific voyage.

Francke, August Hermann (1663–1727)—German Lutheran clergyman, philanthropist, and biblical scholar.

Franklin, Benjamin (1705–1790)—American polymath and one of the Founding Fathers of the United States.

Frederick III (1657–1713)—First king of Prussia (1701–13) and Elector of Brandenburg.

Frederick the Great (1712–86)—King of Prussia from 1740–86. A patron of the arts during the Enlightenment.

Frederick William I (1688–1740)—King of Prussia and Elector of Brandenburg from 1713 until his death. Father of Frederick the Great.

Fréret, Nicolas (1688–1749)—French scholar.

Furly, Benjamin (1636–1714)—English Quaker merchant and friend of John Locke.

Gaime, Abbé Jean-Claude—Credited by Rousseau as the model for his Savoyard Vicar.

Galiani, Celestino (1681–1753)—Italian archbishop.

Galiani, Ferdinando (1728–87)—Also known as the abbé Galiani. An Italian economist.

Galileo, Galilei (1564–1642)—Italian polymath. Together with Copernicus, Kepler, and Newton, he is a central figure in the transition from natural philosophy to modern science.

Gassendi, Pierre (1592–1655)—French philosopher, priest, astronomer, and mathematician. Clashed with his contemporary Descartes and attempted to reconcile Epicurean atomism with Christianity.

Gay, Peter (1923–2015)—Born in Germany, he fled when the Nazis came to power. Living in the United States, he became of one the most important European historians of his generation.

Genovesi, Antonio (1713–69)—Italian writer, philosopher, and political economist.

Giannone, Pietro (1676–1748)—Italian historian. Had an open conflict with the Catholic Church and papacy.

Godwin, William (1756–1836)—English journalist, political philosopher, and novelist. Considered one of the first exponents of utilitarianism and the first modern proponent of anarchism. He attacked existing political institutions and class structures in *An Enquiry Concerning Political Justice* and *Things as They Are; or, the Adventures of Caleb Williams.*

Goethe, Johann Wolfgang (1749–1832)—German writer and statesman.

Goeze, Johann Melchior (1717–86)—Lutheran pastor and theologian.

Gottsched, Johann (1700–1766)—German philosopher and literary critic.

Gottsched, Luise (1713–62)—German poet, playwright, and essayist. Considered one of the founders of modern German theatrical comedy.

Gregory, David (1661–1708)—Scottish mathematician and astronomer. A professor of mathematics at the University of Edinburgh and later of astronomy at Oxford University. He was a follower of Newton.

Grimm, Friedrich Melchior (Baron von Grimm) (1723–1807)—German-born French-language journalist, art critic, diplomat, and contributor to Diderot's *Encyclopédie.* His ideas on aesthetics were particularly influential.

Grotius, Hugo (1583–1645)—Dutch jurist. Helped lay the foundations for international law based on natural law.

Gueudeville, Nicolas (1652–1721)—Benedictan monk who became a journalist and historian after being defrocked.

Haller, Albrecht von (1708–77)—Swiss anatomist, physiologist, naturalist, and poet. Often referred to as the "father of modern physiology."

Hamann, Johann Georg (1730–88)—German philosopher whose work was influential in Germany's pre-Romantic *Sturm und Drang* movement.

Haren, Zwier van Onno (1713–79)—Dutch statesman and playwright.

Hartley, David (1705–57)—English philosopher and founder of the Associationist school of psychology.

Haydn, Joseph (1732–1809)—Austrian composer of music's Classical period. Widely considered the "father of the symphony."

Hegel, Georg Wilhelm Friedrich (1770–1831)—German philosopher and an important figure in German idealism.

Helvétius, Claude Arien (1715–71)—French philosopher, materialist, and freemason.

Hennepin, Louis (1626–1704)—Roman Catholic priest and missionary of the Franciscan Recollet order. Explored the interior of North America.

Herder, Johann Gottfried von (1744–1803)—Born to devoutly Lutheran parents, he became one of the leading German intellects of the period.

Hobbes, Thomas (1588–1679)—The founder of modern political theory, Hobbes lived through the English civil wars. His most important book is *Leviathan* (1651).

Hogarth, William (1697–1764)—English painter, printmaker, and social critic.

Home, Henry (Lord Kames) (1696–1782)—Scottish judge, philosopher, and writer. A central figure of the Scottish Enlightenment and a founding member of the Philosophical Society of Edinburgh.

Horne, George (1730–92)—English churchman, writer, and university administrator.

Hume, David (1711–1776)—Scottish empiricist philosopher, historian, and essayist. He was a major figure in the Scottish Enlightenment.

Hutcheson, Francis (1694–46)—Irish philosopher. Born to a Scottish Presbyterian family, he became one of the major figures in the Scottish Enlightenment.

Hutchinson, John (1674–1737)—Anglican high-churchman.

Hutton, James (1726–97)—Scottish geologist, physician, and naturalist. Known as the "father of modern geology," he made fundamental contributions to geology, including the theory of uniformationism, which explains the features of the earth's crust by means of natural processes over geological time.

Huygens, Christiaan (1629–95)—Diarist and scientist. Fought alongside William III.

Huygens, Constantijn (1596–1687)—Dutch poet, composer, and royal secretary.

Jacobi, Friedrich Heinrich (1743–1819)—German philosopher and writer. Popularized the term "nihilism."

Jardine, George (1742–1827)—Scottish minister of religion, philosopher, academic, and educator.

Jefferson, Thomas (1743–1826)—One of the Founding Fathers, and the third president of the United States.

Johnson, Samuel (1709–84)—Highly influential English writer and poet.

Joseph II (Joseph Benedikt Anton Michael Adam) (1741–90)—Holy Roman emperor from 1765–90, and emperor of the Habsburg lands from 1780–90.

Kant, Immanuel (1724–1804)—German philosopher, and a central figure in modern philosophy. Famously defined the Enlightenment as "man's emergence from his self-imposed immaturity."

Kaunitz, Wenzel Anton (Prince Wenzel Kaunitz) (1711–94)—Austrian and Czech diplomat and statesman in the Habsburg Monarchy. A proponent of enlightened absolutism.

Keill, John (1671–1721)—Scottish mathematician, academic, and author. An important disciple of Isaac Newton.

Kotzebue, Augustus von (1761–1819)—German dramatist and writer. Also worked as a consul in Russia and Germany.

Labat, Jean Baptiste (1663–1738)—French clergyman, botanist, and explorer. Made religious missions in the French possessions in the Caribbean.

Lafitau, Joseph (1681–1746)—French Jesuit and naturalist. Worked in Canada.

Lange, Johann Joachim (1670–1744)—German Protestant theologian and philosopher.

Lavoisier, Antoine (1743–94)—French nobleman and chemist. Widely considered the "father of modern chemistry."

Leclerc, Georges Louis, Count de Buffon (1707–88)—French naturalist and mathematician. His works influenced the next two generations of naturalists, including Jean-Baptiste Lamarck and Georges Cuvier. His most important work is *Histoire Naturelle*.

Leibniz, Gottfried Wilhelm (1646–1716)—German polymath and philosopher. Developed differential and integral calculus independently of Isaac Newton.

Leon, Gottlieb von (1757–1830)—Austrian writer and librarian.

Lessing, Gotthold Ephraim (1729–81)—German writer, philosopher, and art critic. Widely considered to be Germany's leading writer of dramatic plays.

Levier, Charles (dates unknown)—Publisher anonymous in The Hague. Produced the first edition of the *Traité des trois imposteurs* under the title of *La Vie et l'Esprit de Spinoza* (1719). A member of the Knights of Jubilation.

Locke, John (1632–1704)—English philosopher and physician. Widely regarded as one of the most influential figures of the Enlightenment and the tradition of political liberalism.

Louis XIV (1638–1715)—King of France. Known as the Sun King, he reigned from 1643–1715.

Lovell Edgeworth, Richard (1744–1817)—Anglo-Irish politician, writer, and inventor.

Machiavelli, Niccolò (1469–1527)—Italian Renaissance political philosopher and historian.

Maclaurin, Colin (1698–1746)—Scottish mathematician. Made important contributions to geometry and algebra.

Madison, James (1751–1838)—An American statesman and a Founding Father of the United States. One of the most important contributors to the U.S. Constitution.

Maillet, Benoît de (1656–1738)—French diplomat and natural historian. Formulated an evolutionary hypothesis to explain the origin of the earth and its contents.

Malthus, Thomas (1766–1834)—English cleric and scholar. Best known for his 1798 *An Essay on the Principle of Population*, a book of political economy and demography.

Marat, Jean Paul (1743–93)—French political theorist, physician, and scientist. Best known for his role as a radical journalist and politician during the French Revolution.

Marchand, Prosper (1678–1756)—French bibliographer and member of the Knights of Jubilation.

Maria Theresa (Queen) (1717–80)—Holy Roman empress from 1745–65, and arch-duchess of Austria from 1740–80.

Marie Antoinette (1755–93)—Last queen of France before the French Revolution. Executed during the revolution.

Marshall, John (1961–)—Contemporary British historian. Has written extensively on John Locke and toleration.

Marx, Karl (1818–83)—German philosopher, economist, historian, political theorist, sociologist, and journalist. Heavily influenced by Hegel, his works *The Communist Manifesto* and *Capital*, among others, have been very influential in left-wing political thought.

Mendelssohn, Moses (1729–86)—German Jewish philosopher. A seminal figure in the *Haskalah*, or Jewish Enlightenment.

Mercier, Louis-Sebastien (1740–1814)—French dramatist and writer.

Millar, John (1735–1801)—Scottish philosopher and historian. A professor of civil law at the University of Glasgow from 1761–1800.

Mirabeau (Count) (1749–91)—Political leader in the early stages of the French Revolution.

Moerloose, Isabella de (1660/1–1712)—Dutch writer. Penned an autobiography.

Monro, John (1716–91)—English physician and specialist in insanity.

Montesquieu (1689–1755)—French man of letters and political philosopher. His full name was Charles-Louis de Secondat, Baron de La Brède et de Montesquieu.

Moore, Thomas (1779–1852)—Irish Catholic, poet, songwriter, and entertainer.

Moreau de Maupertuis, Pierre-Louis (1698–1759)—French mathematician, philosopher, and man of letters. Director of the Académie des Sciences and the first president of the Prussian Academy of Science.

Mozart, Wolfgang Amadeus (1756–91)—Austrian composer of music's Classical period, and freemason.

Muratori, Lodovico Antonio (1672–1750)—Italian historian and Catholic reformer. Best known for his discovery of the Muratorian fragment, the earliest known list of New Testament books.

Necker, Jacques (1732–1804)—Banker of Genevan origin who became French statesman and finance minister for Louis XVI.

Nelson, Horatio (Lord Nelson) (1758–1805)—Officer in Britain's Royal Navy. Played an important role in his country's military efforts during the Napoleonic Wars.

Newton, Isaac (1642–1726/7)—English physicist, mathematician, and astronomer. His book *Principia Mathematica* (1687) was seminal in the Enlightenment.

Niccolini, Antonio (1701–69)—Italian abbot, jurist, and scholar. A leading cultural figure in Tuscany.

Nicolai, Friedrich (1733–1811)—German writer and bookseller.

Nollet, Jean Antoine (1700–1770)—French clergyman and physicist. As a priest, he was also known as Abbé Nollet.

Paine, Thomas (1737–1809)—English-born American political activist, and political theorist. One of the Founding Fathers of the United States, his ideas were influential during the American Revolution.

Palmer, Elihu (1764–1806)—American author and deist.

Parny, Évariste (1753–1814)—French poet.

Pepys, Samuel (1633–1703)—English navy administrator and Member of Parliament. Most famous for his diary, which is one of the best primary sources for the English Restoration period.

Pezzl, Johann (1756–1823)—German writer and librarian.

Picart, Bernard (1673–1733)—French engraver.

Pitcairne, Archibald (1652–1713)—Scottish physician.

Plumptre, Anne (1760–1818)—English writer and translator.

Pope, Alexander (1688–1744)—English poet. Best known for his translation of Homer. A great stylist, he is second only to Shakespeare as the most quoted writer in *The Oxford Dictionary of Quotations*.

Price, Richard (1723–91)—Welsh moral philosopher, preacher, and mathematician. Active in radical causes, such as the American Revolution.

Priestley, Joseph (1733–1804)—English Unitarian theologian, natural philosopher, chemist, and political theorist. Credited with the discovery of oxygen, although others have strong claims.

Pufendorf, Samuel (1632–94)—German jurist, political philosopher, economist, statesman, and historian.

Radicati di Passerano, Alberto (1698–1737)—Italian historian, philosopher, and freethinker.

Raynal, Abbé (1713–96)—Also known as Guillaume Thomas Raynal. A French writer during the Enlightenment and a fierce critic of imperialism.

Reid, Thomas (1710–96)—Scottish philosopher. A contemporary of David Hume, a founder of the Scottish School of Common Sense, and an important figure in the Scottish Enlightenment.

Reimarus, Elise (1735–1805)—German writer, educator, translator, and salon-holder. Sister of Johann Albert Reimarus, and daughter of Hermann Samuel Reimarus.

Reimarus, Hermann Samuel (1694–1768)—German philosopher. A deist who denied the supernatural origin of Christianity and the divinity of Jesus.

Rey, Marc Michel (1720–80)—Influential publisher in the United Provinces. He published many of the works of the French *philosophes*, including Jean-Jacques Rousseau.

Rich, Mary, Lady Warwick (1625–78)—Seventh daughter of Richard Boyle, First Earl of Cork, and his second wife, Catherine Fenton.

Robertson, William (1721–93)—Scottish historian, minister in the Church of Scotland, and principal of the University of Edinburgh.

Robison, John (1739–1805)—Scottish physicist and mathematician. A professor of philosophy at the University of Edinburgh.

Roche, Daniel (1935–)—Contemporary French social and cultural historian.

Rousseau, Jean-Jacques (1712–78)—Francophone Genevan political philosopher and writer. His *Social Contract* (1762) was influential in the Enlightenment and French Revolution.

Rousset de Missy, Jean (1686–1762)—French Huguenot writer and historian.

Rush, Benjamin (1745–1813)—American physician, politician, social reformer, and educator. A Founding Father of the United States.

Ryder, Joseph (1695–1768)—Devout Protestant of the mid-eighteenth century. Wrote one of the longest diaries of the period.

Schiller, Friedrich (1759–1805)—German poet, philosopher, physician, historian, and playwright. Had a close personal and intellectual relationship with Goethe.

Schlegel, Johann Elias (1719–49)—German critic and dramatic poet.

Schmidt, Johann Lorenz (1702–49)—German theologian during the Enlightenment.

s'Gravesande, Willem Jacob (1688–1742)—Dutch mathematician and natural philosopher. Mostly remembered for his experimental demonstrations of the law of classical mechanics. As a professor at Leiden University, he propagated Isaac Newton's ideas in continental Europe.

Simon, Richard (1638–1712)—French priest and Oratorian. An influential biblical critic.

Smith, Adam (1723–90)—Scottish economist and philosopher. A pioneering figure in political economy, and key in the Scottish Enlightenment. He is best known for two works: one on political economy, *An Inquiry into the Nature and Causes of the Wealth of Nations*, and the other on moral philosophy, *The Theory of Moral Sentiments*.

Smith, Charlotte (1749–1806)—English Romantic poet and novelist.

Solander, Daniel (1733–82)—Swedish naturalist.

Southey, Robert (1774–1843)—English poet of the Romantic school. He was one of the so-called Lake Poets, together with William Wordsworth and Samuel Taylor Coleridge.

Southwell, Sir Robert (1635–1702)—Diplomat, secretary of state for Ireland, and president of the Royal Society from 1690 to 1695.

Spinoza, Baruch (1632–77)—Dutch philosopher of Sephardi/Portuguese origin. His ideas laid the philosophical foundation of the Enlightenment and modern biblical criticism.

St. John, Henry, First Viscount Bolingbroke (1678–1751)—English politician and political philosopher. Leader of the Tories.

Staël, Madame de (1766–1817)—French woman of letters of Swiss origin. Her work was influential in European Romanticism.

Tanucci, Bernardo (1698–1783)—Italian statesman. Brought enlightened government to the kingdom of the Two Sicilies of Charles III and his son, Ferdinand IV.

Tavernier, Jean Baptiste (1605–89)—French merchant and traveler. His journeys were financed by Louis XIV.

Taylor, Jeremy (1613–67)—Cleric in the Church of England. A writer during the protectorate of Oliver Cromwell.

Thelwall, John (1764–1834)—Radical British orator and writer.

Thomasius, Christian (1655–1728)—German jurist and philosopher.

Thoresby, Ralph (1658–1725)—Antiquarian and fellow of the Royal Society. Widely regarded as the first historian of Leeds, England.

Tindal, Matthew (1657–1733)—English deist author.

Toland, John (1670–1722)—Irish philosopher. His works were early expressions of the Enlightenment.

Tone, Theobald Wolfe (1763–98)—Leading Irish revolutionary figure. A founding member of the United Irishmen, and leader of the 1798 Irish Rebellion.

Vanini, Lucilio (1585–1619)—Italian philosopher, physician, and freethinker.

Vaughan, Benjamin (1751–1835)—British political radical.

Venturi, Franco (1914–94)—Italian historian and journalist. A scholar of the Italian Enlightenment, and active in the anti-fascist Resistance during World War II.

Verri, Pietro (1728–97)—Italian philosopher, economist, historian, and writer.

Victor Amadeus II (1666–1732)—Duke of Savoy from 1675–1730. Had a considerable cultural influence in Turin, remodeling the Royal Palace of Turin, among other buildings.

Volney (Constantin Francois de Chasseboeuf, Count of Volney) (1757–1820)—French philosopher, abolitionist, historian, and politician.

Voltaire (1694–1778)—French writer and philosopher. Helped introduce Newtonian science in France. His full name was Francois-Marie Arouet.

Vries, Simon de (1570/75–1628/29)—Dutch engraver.

Watt, Gregory (1777–1804)—Son of James Watt and Ann MacGregor. Became a geologist and mineralogist.

Watt Jr., James (1769–1848)—Scottish engineer, businessman, and activist.

Wedgwood, Josiah (1730–95)—English potter and entrepreneur. Credited with the industrialization of the manufacture of pottery.

Weisse, Christian Hermann (1801–66)—German Protestant religious philosopher and professor of philosophy at the University of Leipzig.

Whitehead, Paul (1710–74)—British satirist and a secretary of the infamous Hellfire Club.

Whitehurst, John (1713–88)—English clockmaker and scientist. Made significant contributions to early geology and was an influential member of the Lunar Society.

Wilkes, John (1725–97)—English radical and journalist. Supported the American rebels during the American War of Independence.

Williams, David (1738–1816)—Welsh philosopher and political polemicist. Also an ordained minister.

Williams, Edward (Iolo Morganwg) (1747–1826)—Welsh poet, antiquarian collector, and literary forger. Forged a number of manuscripts of Welsh literature, but nonetheless played a major role in reviving Welsh culture.

Windham, William (1750–1810)—British Whig statesman.

Wolff, Christian (1679–1754)—German philosopher and polymath.

Wollstonecraft, Mary (1759–97)—English writer, philosopher, and advocate of women's rights. Best known for *A Vindication of the Rights of Woman* (1792), where she argues for gender equality.

Wordsworth, William (1770–1850)—Major English Romantic poet. His joint publication of *Lyrical Ballads* with Samuel Taylor Coleridge helped to launch the Romantic Age in English literature.

Wyndham, Henry (1736–1819)—British Whig Member of Parliament.

Yorke, Henry Redhead (1772–1813)—English writer and radical publicist.

NOTES

Prologue

1. See the opening, "Introduction: Times Like These," in Janet R. Jakobsen and Ann Pellegrini, *Secularisms* (Durham, NC, and London: Duke University Press, 2008). Also see the introduction in Hasse Hämäläinen and Anna Tomaszewska, eds., *The Sources of Secularism* (New York: Palgrave Macmillan, 2017), pp. 1–20.

2. This is a vast subject. See Giorgio Agamben, *Homo Sacer: Sovereign Power and Bare Life*, translated by Daniel Heller-Roazen (Stanford, CA: Stanford University Press, 1998); Talal Asad, *Formations of the Secular: Christianity, Islam, Modernity* (Stanford, CA: Stanford University Press, 2003); Jürgen Habermas, *Religion and Rationality: Essays on Reason, God, Modernity*, edited by Eduardo Mendieta (Cambridge, MA: MIT Press, 2002), and see also his dialogue with Ratzinger, *Dialectics of Secularization: On Reason and Religion*, Joseph Cardinal Ratzinger and Jürgen Habermas, translated by Brian McNeil (San Francisco: Ignatius Press, 2006); Mark Lilla, *The Still-Born God: Religions, Politics and the Modern West* (New York: Knopf, 2007); Tomoko Masuzawa, *The Invention of World Religions, or How European Universalism Was Preserved in the Language of Pluralism* (Chicago: University of Chicago Press, 2005); Charles Taylor, *A Secular Age and the Turn to Religion* (Baltimore, MD: Johns Hopkins University Press, 1999), and *Religion and Violence: Philosophical Perspectives from Kant to Derrida* (Baltimore, MD: Johns Hopkins University Press, 2001).

See also Marcel Gauchet, *The Disenchantment of the World: A Political History of Religion*, translated by Oscar Burge (Princeton, NJ: Princeton University Press, 1997); Dale Van Kley, *The Religious Origins of the French Revolution: From Calvin to the Civil Constitution* (New Haven, CT: Yale University Press, 1996), and *The Jansenists and the Expulsion of the Jesuits from France* (New Haven, CT: Yale University Press, 1975); Denis Crouzet, *Dieu en ses royaumes: une histoire des guerres de la religion* (Seyssel: Chap Vallon, 2008), *La genèse de la réforme française vers 1520–1562* (Paris: Belin, 2008), *La nuit de la Saint-Barthélemy; un rêve perdu de la Renaissance* (Paris: Fayard, 1994), and *Les guerriers de Dieu: la violence au temps des troubles de religion* (Seyssel: Champ Vallon, 1990), in addition to numerous other works;

Thomas Kselman, *Death and the Afterlife in Modern France* (Princeton, NJ: Princeton University Press, 1993), and *European Christian Democracy: Historical Legacies and Comparative Perspectives*, edited by Thomas Kselman and Joseph A. Buttigieg (Notre Dame, IN: University of Notre Dame Press, 2003). And not least, "Introduction," in Sanja Perovic, *Sacred and Secular Agency in Early Modern France: Fragments of Religion* (London and New York: Continuum International Publishing Group, 2012).

3. Described in greater detail in Margaret C. Jacob, *Living the Enlightenment. Freemasonry and Politics in Eighteenth-Century Europe* (New York: Oxford University Press, 1991), pp. 188–89.

4. Lynn Hunt, Margaret Jacob, and Wijnand Mijnhardt, *The Book That Changed Europe. Picart and Bernard's Religious Ceremonies of the World* (Cambridge, MA: Harvard University Press, 2010).

5. London, George Allen and Unwin, 1981, now available from Cornerstone Books, Santa Ana, CA; its title then used by J. Israel, *Radical Enlightenment: Philosophy and the Making of Modernity 1650–1750* (Oxford: Oxford University Press, 2002).

Chapter One. The Setting: Space Expanded and Filled Anew

1. Margaret C. Jacob, *The Newtonians and the English Revolution* (Ithaca, NY: Cornell University Press, 1976).

2. John Dewey, *Experience and Nature* (New York: Dover, 2013), a reprinting of the 1958, second edition, pp. 173–76, and introduction. I owe this citation to the late John Slifko. I am indebted to James W. Carey, *Communication as Culture: Essays on Media and Society* (New York: Routledge, 1992 reprint of 1989 edition).

3. P. P. Boucher, *Cannibal Encounters: Europeans and Island Caribs, 1492–1763* (Baltimore, MD: Johns Hopkins University Press, 1992).

4. See http://digital2.library.ucla.edu/picart/index.html (accessed May 4, 2017). The rest of the title page reads "représentées par des figures dessinées de la main de Bernard Picard, avec une explication historique, & quelques dissertations curieuses" (Amsterdam: Chez J. F. Bernard, 1723–).

5. Point well made in C. John Sommerville, *The Sacralization of Early Modern England* (New York: Oxford University Press, 1992), ch. 2.

6. See Georges Gurvitch, *The Spectrum of Social Time* (Dordrecht: Reidel, 1964), p. 3.

7. British Library, ADD. MS 6185, "Memoirs of the Society for the Incouragement [*sic*] of Learning," f. 1. The society began in 1736 and ended for financial reasons in 1747.

8. British Library, ADD. MS 30 866, f. 6, and f. 11v, f. 15 from 1770 for the Bill of Rights and others; f. 17 and f. 37v for Dr. Franklin.

9. *The Spectator*, March 11, 1711. See also http://www.gutenberg.org/files/12030/12030-h/12030-h/SV1/Spectator1.html#dedication (accessed March 4, 2018).

10. Dorothée Sturkenboom, *Een verdeelde verlichting: stemmen uit de spectators* (Amsterdam: Athenaeum-Polak & Van Gennep, 2001).

11. Bruce Granger, ed. *Proteus Echo (1727–18)* (Delmar, NY: Scholars' Facsimiles & Reprints, 1986), pp. 32–36.

12. Federico Barbierato, *The Inquisitor in the Hat Shop: Inquisition, Forbidden Books, and Unbelief in Early Modern Venice* (Burlington, VT: Ashgate, 2012).

13. For the reception of proselytes, see Prefecture of the Police, Paris, Aa/4/205 arrest of Simon Langlois, 1706.

14. Craig Koslofsky, "Parisian Cafés in European Perspective: Contexts of Consumption, 1660–1730," *French History*, vol. 31, 2017, pp. 39–62.

15. Robert Collis, "Jolly Jades, Lewd Ladies and Moral Muses: Women and Clubs in Early Eighteenth-Century Britain," *Journal for Research into Freemasonry and Fraternalism*, vol. 2, no. 2, 2011, pp. 202–35.

16. Allison Blakely, *Blacks in the Dutch World: The Evolution of Racial Imagery in a Modern Society* (Bloomington: Indiana University Press, 1993), pp. 225–27.

17. Theo van der Meer, *De wesentlijke sonde van sodomie en andere vuyligheeden. Sodomietenvervolgingen in Amsterdam 1730–1811* (Amsterdam: Tabvla, 1984), p. 103.

18. For the books, see L. La Haye and H. de Radiquès de Chennevière, *Inventaire analytique des pièces et dossiers contenus dans la correspondance du Conseil provincial et du procureur général de Namur* (Namur: Douxfils, 1892), p. 303; for the merchant, see Th. Pisvin, *La Vie intellectuelle à Namur sous le Régime autrichien* (Louvain: University of Louvain, 1963), pp. 202–3. I wish to thank Julie Godinas, assistant, Archives de l'Etat à Namur, Boulevard Cauchy, 41, B-5000 Namur.

19. Dossier on "Vie de Louis Robert Hipolithe de Brehan comte de Plelo," where "de tribus impostoribus" is mentioned as a source for the ideas of the priest; see Archives Nationales, Paris, MS L10, dossier IV, no. 2–3, ff. 19–21; and S. Berti, "Unmasking the Truth: The Theme of Imposture in Early Modern European Culture, 1660–1730," in James E. Force and David Katz, eds., *Everything Connects: In Conference with Richard H. Popkin* (Leiden: Brill, 1999), pp. 21–36.

20. Staatsarchiv Dresden, Geheimes Konsilium, Loc. 7209, cited by Martin Mulsow, "Freethinking in Early Eighteenth-Century Protestant Germany: Peter Friedrich Arpe and the *Traité des trois imposteurs*," in Silvia Berti, Françoise Charles-Daubert, and Richard H. Popkin, eds., *Heterodoxy, Spinozism and Free Thought in Early-Eighteenth-Century Europe* (The Hague: Kluwer, 1996), p. 220.

21. Prefecture of the Police, Paris, AA/5/215 for Galoche; ff. 443–642, multiple examples of the books sought by the authorities; AA/7/297–303, and ff. 351 for Priapus, and f. 363, for [Anon.] *Histoire de Dom Bougre, Portier des Chartreux*, 1741.

22. Prefecture, AA/5/642 for injuries to the government; f. 650, satires against the king; f. 756 from 1752–56, satires against king and his mistress and also works against religion; AA/7, f. 756 and f. 766, for the captain.

23. From the 1723 *Constitutions* as reprinted by Benjamin Franklin, and available at http://digitalcommons.unl.edu/cgi/viewcontent.cgi?article=1028&context=library science (accessed July 10, 2017).

24. Bibiothèque Arsenal, Paris, MS 11556, f. 347, dated February 5, 1746.

25. Andreas Önnerfors and Robert Collis, eds. *Freemasonry and Fraternalism in Eighteenth-Century Russia* (Sheffield, UK: Sheffield Working Papers, 2009).

26. Bibliothèque nationale de France, FM 4 149, ff. 167–68.

27. Prefecture, AA/7/ f. 461; f. 541, 1747, printer of prohibited books, Claude Crespy; f. 565, 1748. For the shutdowns, see Bertrand Diringer, "Franc-Maçonnerie et Société à Strasbourg au XVIIIéme siècle," Memoire de Maitrise, Université Marc Bloch, Strasbourg, 1980, pp.10–11; for absolution, p. 37; pp. 42–52. For enlightened priest-freemasons, see Bibliothèque Nationale de Universitaire, Strasbourg, MS 5437, ff. 43–54.

28. Petri Mirala, "Masonic Sociability and Its Limitations: The Case of Ireland," in James Kelly and Martyn J. Powell, eds., *Clubs and Societies in Eighteenth-Century Ireland* (Dublin: Four Courts Press, 2010), p. 327.

29. [Anon.], *Lettre ecrite par un maçon à un de ses amis en province* (n.p., 1744), written from Paris, pp. 6–7.

30. Kenneth Loiselle, *Brotherly Love: Freemasonry and Male Friendship in Enlightenment France* (Ithaca, NY: Cornell University Press, 2014), pp. 14–15.

31. Margaret C. Jacob, "Newton and the French Prophets: New Evidence," in *History of Science*, vol. XVI, 1978, pp. 134–42.

32. Werner Alexander, *Apologie oder Schutzschrift für die vernünftigen Verehrer Gottes*, vol. 2 (Frankfurt: Insel Verlag, 1972), pp. 350–60.

33. Prefecture, Paris, AA/4/ ff. 636–38, and f. 902 for a long list of Jansenist works.

34. For such a dossier, see Bibliothèque Arsenal, MS 11455, dated 1740, and MS 11213; see MS 11556, ff. 283–85, house-to-house searches for masonic activities, aided by the local curé in Paris; f. 328 for the masonic pope.

35. Bibliothèque Arsenal, Paris, MS 12398, a dossier concerning a widow-publisher in Strasbourg who had extensive dealings in Maastricht: "Il est temps statuer chez cette nation Republicaine un exemple capable d'intimider les malheuveuse qui s'y refugient dans l'espoir de l'impunite." See also Robert Darnton, *The Forbidden Best-sellers of Pre-revolutionary France* (London: Harper Collins, 1996), p. 12.

36. Anthony J. La Vopa, "Herder's *Publikum*: Language, Print, and Sociability in Eighteenth-Century Germany," *Eighteenth-Century Studies*, vol. 29, no. 1, 1996, pp. 5–24.

37. Günther Vogler, "Eugen von Savoyen—Begegnung mit aufgeklärten Ideen und Persönlichkeiten," in Michael Benedikt, Reinhold Knoll, Endre Kiss, and Josef

Rupitz, eds., *Verdrägter Humanismus. Verzögerte Aufklärung*, vol. 1, part 2 (Klausen-Leopoldsdorf: Verlag Leben-Kunst-Wissenschaft, 1997), pp. 571–77.

38. Austrian National Library, *Bibliotheca Eugeniana. Die Sammlungen des Prinzen Eugen von Savoyen* (Vienna: Holzhausens, 1986).

39. Abraham Ortelius, *Theatrum Orbis Terrarum* (Antwerp: C. Plantin, 1579).

40. Bibliothèque Nationale, Enfer 233. Probably published in 1729.

41. Wolf. QuN 1013.2; Jacques Sadeur, *Nouveau Voyage de la terre australe* (Paris: Claude Barbin, 1693 [almost certainly a false imprint]), pp. 70–72; next to the Australian voice in the text, someone wrote "Gabriel de Foigny." This text is bound with tracts published by "Pierre Marteau," *Voyage d'Espagne*, 1667, and *Relation de l'Estat et Gouvernement d'Espagne*, 1667; also in same volume, Madame d'Aunoy, *Memoires de la Cour d'Espagne* (The Hague: Moetjens, 1695).

42. *L'Infidélité convaincu, ou les avantures [sic] amoureuses* (Cologne: Pierre Marteau, 1676); bound with *Hattige ou les Amours du Roy de Tamaran nouvelle* (Cologne: Simon l'Africain, 1676) [attributed to Gabriel Brémond].

43. [M. Heliogenes], *A Voyage into Tartary* (London: T. Hodgkin, 1689), p. 60. Cf. Gordon K. Lewis, *Main Currents in Caribbean Thought: The Historical Evolution of Caribbean Society in Its Ideological Aspects, 1492–1900* (Baltimore, MD: John Hopkins University Press, 1983), p. 87.

44. Jörg Baten and Mikolaj Szołtysek, "A Golden Age before Serfdom? The Human Capital of Central-Eastern and Eastern Europe in the 17th–19th centuries," MPIDR Working Paper WP 2014–008, August 2014; see http://econpapers.repec.org/scripts /search/search.asp?ft=poland+&ftp=false&adv=true&wp=on&art=on&bkchp =on&soft=on&pl=&auth=on&mh=100&sort=rank&lgc=AND&aus=&kw =&kwp=false&jel=&nep=nephis&ni=&nit=epdate (accessed April 30, 2017).

45. Richard Butterwick, "Catholicism and Enlightenment in Poland-Lithuania," in Ulrich L. Lehner and Michael O'Neill Printy, eds., *A Companion to the Enlightenment in Catholic Europe* (Leiden: Brill, 2010), p. 311. See Jerzy Snopek, *Objawienie i Oświecenie. Z dziejów libertynizmu w Polsce* [*Revelation and Enlightenment: On the History of Libertinism in Poland*] (Warsaw: Ossolineum, 1986). Made available to this author by the kind translation services of Anna Tomaszewska.

46. Boghos Levon Zekiyan, *The Armenian Way to Modernity* (Venice: Supernova, 1997), pp. 64–71.

47. *Archivo Histórico Nacional (Madrid)*, Inquisición-legajos: Legajo 4473, no. 5, cited in Patricia Manning, *Voicing Dissent in Seventeenth-Century Spain: Inquisition, Social Criticism and Theology in the Case of El Criticón* (Leiden: Koninklijke Brill NV, 2009), p. 83.

48. Thomas Jefferson, *The Life and Morals of Jesus of Nazareth, Extracted Textually from the Gospels in Greek, Latin, French, and English*, with an introduction [by Cyrus Adler] (Washington, D.C.: U.S. Government Printing Office, 1904).

49. Ezio Vailati, *Leibniz and Clarke: A Study of Their Correspondence* (Oxford: Oxford University Press, 1997), pp. 47–52.

Chapter Two. Time Reinvented

1. As detailed in UCLA, Young Research Library, MS 170/16.4, completed in 1765 and taking three hours and thirty-five minutes.

2. British Library, ADD. MS 30866, f. 39, diary of John Wilkes in July 1773.

3. Morgan Kelly and Cormac Ó Gráda, "Speed under Sail during the Early Industrial Revolution," January 2018; see https://voxeu.org/article/speed-under-sail -during-early-industrial-revolution (accessed June 26, 2018).

4. For the impact of the Reformation in England and the sense of time, see C. John Sommerville, *The Secularization of Early Modern England: From Religious Culture to Religious Faith* (New York: Oxford University Press, 1992), ch. 2.

5. From Bodleian Library, Oxford, Locke MS 16.25, p. 18, and cited in Victor Nuovo, "Locke's Proof of the Divine Authority of Scripture," in Ruth Savage, ed., *Philosophy and Religion in Enlightenment Britain: New Case Studies* (Oxford: Oxford University Press, 2012), p. 68.

6. Jed Z. Buchwald and Mordechai Feingold, *Newton and the Origin of Civilization* (Princeton, NJ: Princeton University Press, 2013), ch. 4. The quotations were kindly supplied by Stephen Snobelen and taken from Newton, "Quaestiones quaedam philosophiae" ("Certain philosophical questions," Cambridge University Library, ADD. MSS. 3996, f. 27r.) On Christ's reign forever, see Yahuda MSS 1.3, ff. 64r–65r, Jewish National and University Library, Jerusalem.

7. Raymond Gillespie, "The Circulation of Print in Seventeenth-Century Ireland," *Studia Hibernica*, no. 29, 1995–97, p. 34. Irish Catholics in the 1640s actually desecrated the Bible.

8. Cosme Bueno, *El conocimiento de los tiempos, efemeride del año de 1794, segundo despues Bisiesto: en que van puesto, los principales aspectos de la luna con el sol: calculados para el meridiano . . . de Lima . . . ; con el calendario de las fiestas, y santos . . . ; va al fin La disertacion sobre los antojos de la mugeres preñadas* [Lima, 1793]. Cf. Laura Delbrugge, ed. and intro., *Reportorio de los Tiempos* (London: Tamesis, 1999).

9. Alison A. Chapman, "Marking Time: Astrology, Almanacs, and English Protestantism," *Renaissance Quarterly*, vol. 60, no. 4 (Winter 2007), pp. 1257–90. And see Rienk Vermij, "The Marginalization of Astrology among Dutch Astronomers in the First Half of the 17th Century," *History of Science*, vol. 52, no. 2, 2014, pp. 153–77.

10. William Donaldson, *The Jacobite Song: Political Myth and National Identity* (Aberdeen: Aberdeen University Press, 1988), pp. 45–47.

11. [Anon.], *Almanach des Honnêtes Gens. L'an du premier regne de la raison, pour la présente année*. No place or date is given for publication, but the accompanying

Arrêt de la cour du Parlement is dated January 7, 1788. See pp. 18–19 for the accusations and p. 14 for the author's defense. Sylvain Maréchal did time in prison for this particular almanac.

12. For an extreme example of the Catholic attitude toward time, see *Almanach ecclésiastique, contenant la Succession Chronologique des Papes...* (Paris: Chez Duchesne, 1755). For the risqué, see [Anon.], *Almanach des Cocus ou Amusements pour le beau Sexe* (Constantinople [probably Paris]: De l'imprimere du Grand Seigneur, 1741). For an early proclamation of the new revolutionary time, see [Par M.J.B.D. Procureur au Châtelet de Paris, B.D.S.L.], *Catéchisme du Curé Meslier. Mis au jour par l'Editeur de l'Almanach des honnêtes gens* (L'An Premier, Du règne de la Raison & de la Liberté, 1790). For the work of an astrologer, see [Anon.], *Almanach des Plaideurs pour l'Anné 1745* (n.p., 1745), Cote 90311 in the Bibliothèque historique de la ville de Paris.

13. UCLA, Young Research Library, MS 1437, box 1, "Diary of Mrs Sherwood, 1788–93," not foliated. Section begins "In 1790 my Grandfather died & my father went over previously to reside in France." As told by her cousin.

14. Ibid., by the same cousin.

15. Vanessa Ogle, *The Global Transformation of Time 1870–1950* (Cambridge, MA: Harvard University Press, 2015), introduction, pp. 1–19.

16. Jeroen Salman, *Populair Drukwerk in de Gouden Eeuw. De Almanak als lectuur en handelswaar* (Zutphen: Walburg Pers, 1999), pp. 136. And see N. W. Lovely, "Notes on New England Almanacs," *New England Quarterly*, vol. 8, no. 2 (June 1935), pp. 264–77.

17. UCLA, Young Research Library, MS 1437, box 8, "Mrs Sherwood's Diaries, 1775–1800," pp. 24–25, typescript based on the original and composed at an older age. She was born in 1775 and is writing in 1835; see p. 40, where she attributes the changes to "the Revolution in the neighboring country."

18. Thomas Hobbes, *Philosophicall rudiments concerning government and society. Or, A dissertation concerning man in his severall habitudes and respects, as the member of a society, first secular, and then sacred. Containing the elements of civill politie in the agreement which it hath both with naturall and divine lawes. In which is demonstrated, both what the origine of justice is, and wherein the essence of Christian religion doth consist. Together with the nature, limits, and qualifications both of regiment and subjection* (London: Printed by J.G. for R. Royston, at the Angel in Ivie-lane, 1651).

19. S. de Vries, *Omstandigh Vervolgh op Joh. Lodew. Gottfrieds Historische Kronyck: or algemeen historische Gedenk-Boeken der woornaemste, uytgeleesenste weereldlycke en kercklycke Geschiendenissen ... tot ... 1697* (Leiden: Pieter van der Aa, 1700). See Hobbes, *Leviathan: of van de stoffe, gedaente, ende magt van de kerckelyke ende wereltlycke regeeringe* (Amsterdam: Wagenaar, 1667); and see Catherine Secretan, intro. [Lambert van Velthuysen] *A Letter on the Principles of Justness and Decency, Containing a Defence of the Treatise de Cive of the Learned Mr Hobbes* (Leiden: Brill, 2013).

The 1651 English title page speaks only of "The Matter, Forme and Power of a Commonwealth Ecclesiasticall and Civil."

20. Hobbes, *Philosophicall rudiments concerning government and society*, p. 17.

21. Ibid., ch. 18, p. 341.

22. Arianne Baggerman, *Een Drukkend Gewicht. Leven en werk van de zeventiende-eeuwse veelschrijver Simon de Vries* (Amsterdam: Rodopi, 1993), pp. 154–70.

23. There is a vast collection of these almanacs in the library of the Stationers' Company, London; see www.stationers.org/archives.html (accessed June 20, 2015).

24. Samuel Clough, *The New England, Almanac for the Year of Our Lord, MDCCIII* (Boston: B. Green, 1703), n.p.

25. J. Salman, *Populair Drukwerk*, p. 163.

26. A. Baggerman, Rudolf Dekker, and Michael Mascuch, eds. *Controlling Time and Shaping the Self: Developments in Autobiographical Writing since the Sixteenth Century* (Leiden: Brill, 2011), pp. 6, 97. The Dutch information appears in the introduction by the editors; for French diaries, see in same volume, Philippe Lejeune, "Marc-Antoine Jullien: Controlling Time," pp. 91–119. For the picture of a Dutch page for note taking, see J. Salman, *Populair Drukwerk*, p. 162 from 1625.

27. [Christopher Sower, printer], *Der Hoch-deutsch americanische Calendar, aus das Jahr der gnadenreichen Geburt unsers Herrn und Heylandes Jesu Christi* (Germantown, PA, 1752), n.p.

28. J. Glover, *Hemelloopkundige Almanak, of Tijdwijzer voor 't Jaar 1797* (Arnhem: J. H. Moeleman, 1797), p. 5. J. Salman, *Populair*, pp. 173–76.

29. *Teliamed, or Conversations between an Indian Philosopher and a French Missionary on the Diminution of the Sea*, translated and edited by Albert V. Carozzi (Urbana, Chicago, and London: University of Illinois Press, 1968). The more common spelling of the title is *Telliamed*. This edition is a reliable re-creation of the original text that was heavily worked over by its editor after Benoît's death. See also the important contributions of Claudine Cohen, *Science, libertinage et clandestinité à l'aube des Lumières: Le transformisme de Telliamed* (Paris: Presses Universitaires de France, 2011); Francine Markovits, ed., *Telliamed* (Paris: Université de Paris Ouest–Nanterre–La Défense, 2011).

30. Miguel Benítez, *Le Foyer clandestine des lumières. Nouvelles recherches sur les manuscrits clandestins* (Paris: Champion, 2013), vol. I, pp. 117–40.

31. Lejeune, "Marc-Antoine Jullien," pp. 96–97.

32. Paolo Quintili, *Matérialismes et Lumières. Philosophe de la vie, autour de Diderot et de quelques autres 1706–1789* (Paris: Champion, 2009), ch. 2.

33. [Anon., but attributed to the abbé Coyer], *Lettre au R. P. Berthier sur le Matérialisme* (Geneva, 1759), pp. 1–19; p. 19 for the quotation. Cf. Franck Salaün, *L'Affreuse Doctrine. Matérialisme et Crise des moeurs au temps de Diderot* (Paris: Editions Kimé, 2014), pp. 163–68, for the complexity of the attribution to Coyer.

34. Morgan Kelly and Cormac Ó Gráda, "Adam Smith, Watch Prices, and the Industrial Revolution," UCD Centre for Economic Research Working Paper Series, 2015; see www.ucd.ie/t4cms/WP15_05.pdf (accessed January 16, 2018).

35. Constantijn Huygens, *Journaal van de Reis naar Venetië,* ed. and trans. by Frans R. E. Blom (Amsterdam: Bert Bakker, 2003).

36. Hans-Jürgen Döpp, *The Temple of Venus: The Sex Museum, Amsterdam* (New York: Parkstone Press, 2001), p. 65. The watch is from the eighteenth century, but the provenance is not given.

37. Roland Racevskis, *Time and Ways of Knowing under Louis XIV: Molière, Sévigné, Lafayette* (Lewisburg, PA: Bucknell University Press, 2003), pp. 40–41.

38. A. Baggerman, Rudolf Dekker, Müichael Mascuch, eds. *Controlling Time and Shaping the Self,* pp. 30–31.

39. Bruno Blondé and Gerrit Verhoeven, "Against the Clocke: Time Awareness in Early Modern Antwerp, 1585–1789," *Continuity and Change,* vol. 28, 2013, pp. 213–44.

40. Constantijn Huygens, *Mijn Leven Verteld ann Mijn Kinderen in Twee Boeken,* ed. and trans. by Frans R. E. Blom (Amsterdam: Prometheus, 2003), vol. 1, p. 191.

41. Hendrick Smeeks, *The Mighty Kingdom of Krinke Kesmes (1708),* ed. by David Fausett, trans. by Robert H. Leek (Amsterdam: Rodopi, 1995), p. 109.

42. Siegfried Kracauer offered an extended meditation on this problem in ch. 6 (with a nod toward J. Herder's similar critique made nearly a century and a half earlier) in *History: The Last Things before the Last,* compiled after the death of the author by Paul Oskar Kristeller (Princeton, NJ: Markus Wiener Publishers, 1969), with a new preface by Kristeller, 1995.

43. Marcel Gauchet, *The Disenchantment of the World: A Political History of Religion,* trans. by Oscar Burge (Princeton, NJ: Princeton University Press, 1997), pp. 55 and 4.

44. Vyvyan Evans, *The Structure of Time: Language, Meaning and Temporal Cognition* (Amsterdam: John Benjamins Publishing, 2003), p. 8.

45. See Edmund Law, *An Enquiry into the ideas of space, time, immensity, and eternity; as also the self-existence, necessary existence, and unity of the Divine Nature: In Answer to a Book lately Publish'd by Mr. Jackson* (Cambridge, UK, 1734), pp. 93–95. Jackson was a follower of Samuel Clarke. Reproduced in a facsimile edition in 1990 by Thoemmes Antiquarian Books.

46. Richard Butterwick, "Catholicism and Enlightenment in Poland-Lithuania," in Ulrich L. Lehner and Michael O'Neill Printy, eds., *A Companion to the Enlightenment in Catholic Europe* (Leiden: Brill, 2010), p. 311.

47. John Spurr, "'A Sublime and Noble Service': John Evelyn and the Church of England," in Frances Harris and Michael Hunter, eds. *John Evelyn and His Milieu* (London: British Library, 2003), pp. 145–64.

48. British Library, ADD. MSS 78441, Mary Evelyn, "Book of several designes and thoughts of mine for the regulating my life upon many occasions. Remember thy Creator in the days of thy youth. Redeeme the Tyme 1683," handwritten title page "Redeeme the Tyme" on bottom above date; f. 4 "Rules for spending my pretions tyme well." Cf. Frances Harris and Michael Hunter, eds., *John Evelyn and His Milieu* (London: British Library, 2003); and in the same volume Gillian Wright, "Mary Evelyn and Devotional Practice," pp. 221–32.

49. ADD. MS 78441, Mary Evelyn, f. 4.

50. ADD. MS 78440, f. 558. For such practices among other pious lay women of the period, see Anne Laurence, "Daniel's Practice: The Daily Round of Godly Women in Seventeenth-Century England," in R. N. Swanson, ed., *The Use and Abuse of Time in Christian History: Papers Read at the 1999 Summer Meeting and the 2000 Winter Meeting of the Ecclesiastical History Society* (Woodbridge, Suffolk, UK: Published for the Ecclesiastical History Society by the Boydell Press, 2002), pp. 173–78; notes the similarities of practices in Anglican households and those with Puritan proclivities.

51. ADD. MS 78441, f. 5.

52. Ibid., f. 6.

53. Ibid., f. 9v. While two diaries will not make a case, we note that her contemporary, the pious Catholic William Blundell, evinces no similar anxiety about time; see Rev. T. Ellison Gibson, ed., *Crosby Records: A Cavalier's Note Book . . . of William Blundell* (London: Longmans, Green, 1880); note the usage "at four of the clock and a half retired to his chamber, 1667," p. 133. A similar lack of concern appears in Joseph Gillow and Anthony Hewitson, eds., *The Tyldesley Diary: Personal Records of Thomas Tyldesley . . . during the Years 1712-13-14* (Preston, UK: A. Hewitson, 1873). Tyldesley was also a Catholic.

54. For example, see British Library, ADD. MSS 61903, dated 1678, Peter Le Neve, f. 9v: "At the new palace yard between 11 & 12 hours by the clock were burnt 3 cart loads of popish vestments, books, beads"; f. 17: "Adjourned till tomorrow 8 a clock"; f. 26v: "adjourned till Monday 9 of ye clock"; or f. 29: "ad. Tuesday 8 clock"; f. 44: "adjourned till Tuesday 8 of the clock." The last is more commonly the phrase that he used. William L. Sachse, ed., *The Diary of Roger Lowe of Ashton-in-Makerfield, Lancashire 1663-74* (London: Longman's, 1938), p. 13, in 1663: "aclock." See also British Library, ADD. MSS 60522—travel journal in Low Countries in 1720, 32 v: "came to Brussels at 7 a clock. Mons about 8 a clock." 67v: "went on board 4 of ye clock."

55. [Anon.], *The Ladies Diary: or, the Woman's Almanack for the Year of our Lord*, 1712, claims to have been published for nine years in 1712 and contains statements like "day breaks at 2 a Clock."

56. Wellcome Trust Library, London, MS 5780, a tour of France "made by my grandfather in 1732 (old style)": "we sett sail for France from Emsworth about

5 o'clock in the morning. We gott clear of the harbour about 8 o'clock and reached the Isle of Wight about noon that day"; f. 1: "about 11 o'clock that morning." But note that in 1731 Thomas Wilson is still using "a clock"; see C.L.S Linnell, ed., *The Diaries of Thomas Wilson, D.D. 1731–27 and 1750* (London: S.P.C.K., 1964), p. 30. A transition may have included "a'clock"; see William Dobson, ed., *Extracts from the Diary of the Rev. Peter Walkden, Nonconformist Minister, for the years 1725, 1729, 1730* (Preston, UK: Dobson, 1866), pp. 3, 12–13. Shakespeare used "a clock"; see *Mr William Shakespeares Comedies, Histories, & Tragedies*, London, 1623, a reprint (London: Lionel Booth, 1864), p. 245, from Act 4, scene 1, *All's Well that Ends Well*; as seen in Early English Books Online, "o'clock" in printed English first appears in Abraham Cowley, *Cutter of Coleman Street*, 1658, Act 3, scene 5.

57. ADD. MSS 78440, "Mary Evelyn Her Book of Sermon notes 1679"; number 108 appears on handwritten title page, n.f. but dated 1683 and a sermon given by Mr. Dalbe.

58. Ibid., November [?], last page in folded volume.

59. British Library, ADD. MS 58219, diary and commonplace book of Sir Robert Southwell; in margin, entry is titled, "Time." Date of 1659 on f. 11.

60. Quoted from Yorkshire Archaeological Society MS 21, diary of Ralph Thoresby (1677–83), pp. 118–19, 1680, in David L. Wykes, "'The Sabbaths ... Spent before in Idleness & Neglect of the Word:' the Godly and the Use of Time in Their Daily Religion," in R. N. Swanson, ed. *The Use and Abuse of Time in Christian History*, p. 214.

61. *Some Remarkable Passages in the Holy Life and Death of the late Reverend. Mr Edmund Trench; most of them drawn of his own Diary*, London, 1693, p. 89. Although educated at Cambridge, Trench did not at first conform, but he counted himself a moderate (p. 55).

62. T. Crofton Croker, ed., *Autobiography of Mary Countess of Warwick* (London: Printed for the Percy Society, 1848), p. 23.

63. Ibid., pp. 23–24.

64. Ibid., p. 25.

65. Ibid., p. 34.

66. "Absolute, true, and mathematical time, of itself, and from its own nature, flows equably without regard to anything external, and by another name is called duration: relative, apparent, and common time, is some sensible and external (whether accurate or unequable) measure of duration by means of motion, which is commonly used instead of true time; such as an hour, a month, a year." From Isaac Newton, *Mathematical Principles of Natural Philosophy*, definition xiii, scholium (Motte translation; New York, 1846), p. 77.

67. Robert Poole, *Time's Alteration: Calendar Reform in Early Modern England* (London: University College London Press, 1998), pp. 108–11. The author contrasts

"Newtonian time" with "natural time" (p. 19). We have taken up the first term as useful but not the second.

68. *Mathematical Principles*, p. 77. For a further discussion, see William Lane Craig, *The Tenseless Theory of Time: A Critical Examination* (Boston: Kluwer, 2000) pp. 42–53.

69. John Whalle, *England's Mercury, or an Ephemeris for the year of Christ 1690* (London: W.H. for the Stationers Company, 1690); acknowledges all the discontent with astrology and astrologers and proceeds to predict the good fortune of William of Orange, and possible death of the French king.

70. Wellcome Library, London, MS 4021. Book is dedicated to Ptolomy redivivus. Diary of an astrologer, Norris Purslow, 1673–1737: in 1694, he opens his shop and "had a watch of my father"; in 1703, he has received "ptolomy in English" and pays money to "our astrological club."

71. John Spurr, *The Restoration Church of England, 1646–1689* (New Haven, CT: Yale University Press, 1991), p. 284.

72. Ibid., p. 286.

73. Lady Warwick, *Autobiography*, p. 36, writing in the 1670s.

74. Jeremy Taylor, *A Choice Manual, Containing What is to be Believed, Practised, and Desired . . . Composed . . . especially of younger persons* (London: J. Grover, 1667), preface, n.p.

75. Ibid., p. 45.

76. Ibid., p. 61. Cf. H. R. McAdoo, *The Spirit of Anglicanism: A Survey of Anglican Theological Method in the Seventeenth Century* (London: Adam & Charles Black, 1965), pp. 57–80.

77. Jeremy Taylor, *The Rule and Exercises of Holy Living . . . The Means and Instruments of obtaining every Virtue, and the Remedies against every Vice, and Considerations serving to the resisting all Temptations*, 11th ed. (London, 1686), pp. 4–5.

78. Ibid.

79. "The Diary of Joseph Ryder," The John Rylands Library, Manchester, UK, May 29, 1733.

80. Ibid., June 16, 1733.

81. Ibid., September 4,1733.

82. Ibid., October 24, 1733; January 10, 1734; March 13, 1736.

83. Ibid., on repentance, July 9, 1735; on concern, March 13, 1736.

84. Ibid., April 14, 1748. These references to time in Ryder's diary supplied most kindly by Matt Kadane. For a definitive account of Ryder, see Matthew Kadane, *The Watchful Clothier* (New Haven, CT: Yale University Press, 2013).

85. Poole, *Time's Alteration*, ch. 1.

86. See Paul Alkon, "Changing the Calendar," *Eighteenth-Century Life*, vol. 7, 1982, pp. 1–18; Poole, ch. 9, notes the many exceptions that had to be made for wages lost, and so on.

87. Florence Maris Turner, ed., *The Diary of Thomas Turner of East Hoathly (1754–65)* (London: John Lane, 1925), p. 14. He does however read among the latitudinarians, the Boyle lecturers and "the New Whole Duty of Man."

88. Ibid., p. 38; but two pages later, "Sadly disordered all day, not having recovered Friday night's debauch."

89. British Library, ADD. MSS 37 921 Windham Papers, ff. 1–13. See Macleod Yearsley, ed., *The Diary of Thomas Yeoman* (London: Watts & Co., 1934), p. 40 (an Anglican choir master): "I got up about Six o clock [*sic*], called my cousen Betsey up to get ready by the time the coach did come. My uncle was very uneasy . . . we being determined to go, ye coach come just as we had done tea and set of att eight o clock . . . arrived at . . . Oxford St about 1 o clock . . . for Brentford at which place we arrived about half past four."

90. Michael A. Mullett, "Catholic and Quaker Attitudes to Work, Rest and Play," in R. N. Swanson, ed., *The Use and Abuse*, pp. 185–98, sees similar attitudes among some English Catholics, but it is not clear how much of this anxiety about work and time comes about in reaction to Protestant criticisms, Protestant conversions into the Catholic fold, and the influence of Jansenism. It is also not clear how time itself was being conceptualized.

91. *Memoirs of the Life of the Reverend Mr. Thomas Halyburton, Professor of Divinity in the University of St. Andrews . . .* (Edinburgh, 1714), p. 13. For a similar odyssey, see *Some Remarkable Passages in the Holy Life and Death Of the late Reverend Mr Edmund Trench; Most of them drawn of his own Diary* (London, 1693), pp. 19–20, where we find him given to reading "smutly poets" and to gluttony, drunkenness, swearing, cursing, and stealing. He did not go with "naughty women." All this occurred while at Cambridge in 1659–60. By p. 68, he has repented.

92. Ibid., p. 16.

93. *Oxford English Dictionary*, 2006, entry under "punctuality" and citing Mrs. Manley's *The Adventures of Rivella* (London, 1714), p. 12. This shift in meaning was first pointed out in Daniel A. Rabuzzi, "Eighteenth-Century Commercial Mentalities as Reflected and Projected in Business Handbooks," *Eighteenth-Century Studies*, vol. 29, 1995–96, n. 56.

94. UCLA, Young Research Library, MS 170/196, n.f., toward the last pages in the diary.

95. For evidence of its normalization, see *The Gentleman and Lady's Palladium, for the Year of our Lord, 1762*, where mechanics and optics are treated in succinct formats and time discussed in terms of relative or absolute, pp. 24–26. The whole tone of these diaries is mathematical and scientific. See also *Fame's Palladium, or Annual Miscellary: being a supplement to the Ladies Diary . . . 1767*, pp. 1–4 on longitude, on Bentley's letters to Newton, pp. 22–26. British Library, ADD. MSS 19211 "Journal began July ye 4th 1764," f. 18, "a drole genius who entertained us with fears

of traveling for fear of losing his Family Watch." He looked at his pocket watch and passed it around in the coach and this occasioned much conversation. For a general discussion, see A. J. Turner, *Of Time and Measurement: Studies in the History of Horology and Fine Technology* (Aldershot, UK: Ashgate, 1993), pp. 22–23, from ch. 1.

96. Rudolf Dekker, "De rafelrand van het zeventiende-eeuwse hofleven in het dagboek van Constantijn Huygens de zoon Roddel en seks," *Mededelingen van de Stichting Jacob Campo Weyerman.* Jaargang 23 (2000); at www.dbnl.org/auteurs /auteur.php?id=huyg007 (accessed July 31, 2015).

97. My guide through this text is Rudolph Dekker, who kindly sent me an advance copy of his *Family, Culture and Society in the Diary of Constantijn Huygens Jr., Secretary to Stadholder-King William of Orange* (Leiden: Brill, 2013); see p. 112 for the absence of religious conversation. To consult the original diary, see www.dbnl.org /tekst/huyg007jour02_01/ (accessed July 31, 2015).

98. Ibid., p. 51. The day was September 18, 1692.

99. [Balduine van der Aa,] *Bibliotheca Magna et Elegantissima Zuylichemiana . . . Librorum . . . D. Constantini Huygens . . . Secretis Guilielmi III* (Leiden: Peter and Balduine van der Aa, 1701), pp. 92, 99 for Bekker; p. 88 for Simon.

100. Dekker, *Family, Culture and Society*, ch. 10.

Chapter Three. Secular Lives

1. Roland Krebs, *Helvétius en Allemagne ou la Tentation du Matérialisme* (Paris: Champion, 2006), pp. 15–48; p. 31 for the letter from Luise Gottsched.

2. UCLA, Young Research Library, MS 170, 18, manuscript notes for a revised edition done by the author, and the quotation appears between pp. 8 and 9.

3. Ibid., MS notes next to pp. 34–36.

4. See Peter Gay, *The Enlightenment: An Interpretation. The Rise of Modern Paganism* (New York: Knopf, 1966), ch. 2; and Timothy D. Walker, "Enlightened Absolutism and the Lisbon Earthquake: Asserting State Dominance over Religious Sites and the Church in Eighteenth-Century Portugal," *Eighteenth-Century Studies*, vol. 48, no. 3, 2015, pp. 307–28.

5. UCLA, Young Research Library, MS 170/3.1, written in the late 1750s, f. 25.

6. Ibid., MS 170/16.6, f. 54; on Sicily, notebook begun in 1766, unfoliated second volume.

7. Ibid., f. 36; f. 58 shows the date as January 19, 1760.

8. Ibid., MS 170/16.4, ff. 31–32.

9. Ibid., MS 170/16.5, ff. 44–48.

10. MS 170/18, p. 69–70 printed text.

11. Ibid., MS 170/16.4, ff. 55–56 on the ruins in Arles; and on St. Peter's in Rome, notebook 6, f. 58 last page before index.

12. Ibid., MS 170/16, notebook 9, unfoliated with discussion of Boerhaave and the decline in the teaching of medicine; ends in 1767. See notes opposite p. 74 for the library.

13. Bibliothèque d'Arsenal, Paris, MS 9528 with a preface dated 1749, Peking, and a dedication dated 1758. Facsimile edition available through Google Books and attributed, in the preface of the original manuscript and in the facsimile edition, to Robert Dodsley—that is, Lord Philip Dormer Stanhope Chesterfield. There is a printed version of the text, [Anon.], *Le Elixir de la morale indienne, ou Economie de la vie humaine* (Paris: Chez Ganeau, 1760); authorized by a royal privilege. See also Harry M. Solomon, *The Rise of Robert Dodsley: Creating the New Age of Print* (Carbondale: Southern Illinois University Press, 1996).

14. See Johann Anton Trinius, *Freydenker Lexicon* (Turin: Bottega d'Erasmo, 1966, with a preface by Franco Venturi), originally published in Leipzig, 1759, pp. 3–7.

15. MS 9528, f. 18.

16. MS 9528, ff. 110–13.

17. John Bray, "The Oeconomy of Human Life: An 'Ancient Bramin' in Eighteenth-Century Tibet," *Journal of the Royal Asiatic Society,* Third Series, vol. 19, no. 4, 2009, pp. 439–58; and James E. Tierney, ed., *The Correspondence of Robert Dodsley 1733–1764* (Cambridge: Cambridge University Press, 1988), pp. 10–11.

18. [Anon.], *Le Elixir de la morale indienne*, f. 34.

19. Tierney, ed., *The Correspondence of Robert Dodsley*, p. 21.

20. Ibid., p. 21.

21. Lynn Hunt, Margaret Jacob, and Wijnand Mijnhardt, *The Book That Changed Europe: Picart and Bernard's Religious Ceremonies of the World* (Cambridge, MA: Harvard University Press, 2010).

22. UCLA, Young Research Library, MS 170/429, 1758, "Journal of a Voyage to Goree in Africa by Samuel Dickenson," ff. 24–25. Dickenson is from Blymhill in Staffordshire.

23. Ibid., f. 28.

24. Ibid., f. 34.

25. Alexander Campbell, *A journey from Edinburgh through parts of North Britain; containing remarks on Scottish landscape; and observations on rural economy, natural history, manufactures, trade, and commerce; interspersed with anecdotes, traditional, literary, and historical* (London: Printed by A. Strahan, for T. Longman and O. Rees, 1802), vol. 1, pp. 19–22.

26. Dickenson, MS/429, "Journal from London to Marseilles by S. Dickenson 1766, 1767, 1768," ff. 45–50; f. 54 for quotation.

27. Ibid., f. 67.

28. Ibid., "Journal Mediterranean Gibraltar," 1760, f. 29.

29. Richard Lovell Edgeworth and Maria Edgeworth, *Memoirs of Richard Lovell Edgeworth, esq. Begun by Himself, and Concluded by his Daughter, Maria Edgeworth* (London: Richard Bentley, 1844). UCLA, Young Research Library, MS 170/650; this copy belonged to the family and contains handwritten material.

30. UCLA, Young Research Library, MS 170/587: Lectures on Chemistry by Doctor Black and Doctor Hope taken by Lovell Edgeworth; Bound Manuscripts Collection, Department of Special Collections. See http://guides.library.ucla.edu /industrialization (accessed June 24, 2018).

31. Roger L. Emerson, *Academic Patronage in the Scottish Enlightenment* (Edinburgh: Edinburgh University Press, 2008), pp. 129–30, 187–88.

32. Science Museum, London, MS 2416, 3 out of 5, ff. 63–64.

33. Ibid., MS 2416, 5 out of 5, ff. 1–2, 21.

34. Ibid., f. 28–29, "Machines have been constructed which greatly alleviate the labour of man & the exertion of brute force."

35. Ibid., ff. 30–31.

36. Science Museum, London, MS 2421, notebook 3.10, "Government, Part I, Of the Origin and Progress of Government." F. 13 for attack on the Tories; f. 17 for the people form a contract to make government and can unmake it; ff. 18–50 on the stages.

37. Ibid., ff. 59 and 67; and f. 79 on luxury and manufacturing laborers are constantly employed; f. 73; f. 75 on manufacturing rendering the higher ranks intelligent and the lower ranks ignorant.

38. Joel Mokyr, *The Enlightened Economy: An Economic History of Britain 1700–1850* (New Haven, CT: Yale University Press, 2009).

39. Isabella Moerloose, *Vrede Tractaet. Gegeven van den Hemel door Vrouwen Zaet. Beschreven door Isabella De Moederloose Weduwe van Domini Laurentius Hoogentoren, In zijn Leven Predikant in Zuit-Beverland* (Amsterdam: Printed by the author, 1695).

40. J. Campo Weyerman, *De Rotterdamse Hermes*, ed. A. Nieuweboer (facsimile of 1721 edition; Amsterdam, 1980), p. 178.

41. All this is recounted in Herman Roodenburg, "Sex, opvoeding en volksgeloof in de zeventiende eeuw. De autobiografie van Isabella de Moerloose," *Tijdschrift voor social geschiedenis*, vol. 9, 1983, pp. 311–42; a translation can be found in *Journal of Social History*, Summer 1985, pp. 517–40.

42. Wilhelm Lütjeharms, *Het Philadelphisch-Oecumenisch Streven der Hernhutters in de Nederlanden in de Achttiende Eeuw* (Zeist: Zendingsgenootschap der Evang. Broedergemeente, 1935), pp. 144–49, citing in particular "te waken tegen de Sociniaansche, Ariaansche en Arminiaansche dwalingen, alsmede die van Van Hattem, Leenhof, Deurhof, Hernhutters en anderen."

43. Eric Jorick and Ad Maas, eds., *Newton and The Netherlands* (Leiden: University of Leiden Press, 2012).

44. See Henk Boom, *Onze man in Constantinopel, Frederick Gijsbert Baron van Dedem (1743–1820)* (Zutphen: Wals Pers, 2012).

45. Antonio de Ulloa, *Historical Account of Voyage to South America. Relación histórica del viage a la América Meridional* (Madrid: A. Marin, 1748).

46. Francisco Bouligny, *Noticia del estado actual del comercio y población de la Nueva Orleans y Luisiana espanola, y los medios de adelantar aquella provincia que presenta a S.M. Carlos por mano de su ministro de Indias el Ilmo* (MS. Biblioteca Del Museo Ultramar, Madrid, 1776); Luis de Sales, *Noticias de la Provincia de Californias, 1794* (Madrid: J. Porrúa Turanzas, 1960); Antonio de Ulloa and Jorge Juan y Santacilia, *Relación histórica del viage a la América Meridional: hecho de orden de S. Mag. para medir algunos grados de meridiano terrestre, y venir por ellos en conocimiento de la verdadera figura, y magnitud de la tierra, con otras varias observaciones astronómicas, y phisicas* (Madrid: A. Marin, 1748); Antonio de Ulloa y de la Torre-Giralt, *Noticia del estado actual del comercio y poblacion de la Nueva Orleans y Luisiana espanola y los medios de adelantar aquella privincia que presenta a S.M. Carlos por mano de su ministro de Indias el Ilmo; Sr. don Joseph de Galvez, Luis de Sales, Noticias de la Provincia de las Californias en tres cartas de un sacerdote, religioso, hijo del Real convento de Predicadores de Valencia a un amigo suyo* (Valencia: Printed by the Orga brothers, 1794): Antonio de Ulloa y de la Torre-Giralt, *Viaje que hicieron a Lima desde Quito don Jorge Juan I don Antonio de Ulloa el año de 1740: Travels to Lima from Quito by Don Jorge and Don Antonio de Ulloa, 1740*, and *Viaje a varias cortes europeas y otras ciudades, con varios encargos del Real Servicio: Travels to Several European Courts and Other Cities*. And see *Noticia y descripcion de los paises que median entre la ciudad y puerto de Veracruz, en el reyno de Nueva España hasta los asientos de Minas, Guanjuato, Pachuca y Real del Monte*.

47. Andrei Zorin, "Feeling across Borders: The Europeanization of Russian Nobility through Emotional Patterns," in David Adams and Galin Tihanov, eds., *Enlightenment Cosmopolitanism* (London: Legenda, 2011), pp. 32–38.

48. *Herders Reisejournal*, intro. by Elizabeth Blochmann (Weinheim: Julius Beltz, 1961), pp. 58–61.

49. Ibid., pp. 67–68.

50. Ibid., pp. 82–87.

51. Almut and Paul Spalding, "Living in the Enlightenment: The Reimarus Household Accounts of 1728–1780," in Martin Mulsow, ed., *Between Philology and Radical Enlightenment: Hermann Samuel Reimarus (1694–1768)* (Leiden: Brill, 2011), pp. 217–18.

52. *Gespräch über eine-unsichtbar-sichtbare Gesellschaft*, in Ion Contiades, ed., *Gotthold Ephraim Lessing, Ernst und Falk; met den Fortsetzungen Herders und Friedrich Schlegels* (Frankfurt am Main: Insel, 1968), p. 69.

53. Frank Hatje, "Jakobiner, Demokraten, Republikaner? Französische Revolution, Aufklärung und deutsches Bürgertum in den Tagebüchern Ferdinand Benekes," *Aufklärung*, vol. 24, 2012, pp. 29–63.

54. Suzanne Necker, "Sur un nouveau genre de Spectateur," in Catriona Seth, ed., *La Fabrique de l'Intime. Mémoires et journaux de femmes du XVIIIe siècle* (Paris: Editions Robert Laffont, 2013), pp. 253–59.

55. See www.metmuseum.org/art/collection/search/205459 (accessed May 20, 2017).

56. Évariste Désiré de Forges Parny, *Poésies érotiques* (n.p. [Paris], 1778).

57. Debray, *Oeuvres d'Évariste Parny*, vol. II (Paris: Debray, 1808), pp. 162–63; and pp. 237–38 for his ode to the lodge. And see the discussion by Jacques-Charles Lemaire, ed., *La Guerre des Dieux (1799)* (Paris: Champion, 2002), pp. 22–27. On Parny and slavery, see Catriona Seth, "Evariste Parny (1753–1814)," Ph. D. dissertation, Université de Paris-Sorbonne (Paris IV), 1995, pp. 107–8; and by the same author, *Évariste Parny (1753–1814). Créole, révolutionnaire, académicien* (Paris: Hermann Éditeurs, 2014), pp. 76–81.

58. Lemaire, *Le Guerre*, p. 79.

59. Ibid., p. 87.

Chapter Four. Paris and the Materialist Alternative: The Widow Stockdorff

1. Raymond Birn, *Royal Censorship of Books in 18th-Century France* (Stanford, CA: Stanford University Press, 2012), pp. 1–20. See also "French censorship was perhaps more arbitrary, capricious, and irrational than any other. The Inquisitors of Spain and Portugal were at least consistent in their malevolence. In contrast, French censors were wholly unpredictable. . . . The bureaucracy that dispensed permissions to print was not only quixotic, but also complex, redundant, and painfully slow. Thus a manuscript could emerge from three years of deliberations with an approval, only to be suppressed upon publication. Sometimes authorities would condemn a book in formal decree, but give verbal *permission tacite* for its sale in the clandestine markets of Paris." From Sue Curry Jansen, *Censorship: The Knot That Binds Power and Knowledge* (New York: Oxford University Press, 1991), p. 79; F. Weil, "Les Livres persecutés en France de 1720 à 1770," *La Lettre clandestine*, vol. 6, 1997, p. 267; and Mogens Lærke, "Introduction," in *The Use of Censorship in the Enlightenment* (Leiden: Koninklijke Brill NV, 2009), p. 15.

2. Nicole Hermann-Mascard, *La Censure des livres à la fin de l'Ancien Régime (1750–1789)* (Paris: Presses Universitaires de France, 1968), p. 42. Cf. Catherine Blangonnet, "Recherches sur les censeurs royaux au temps de Malesherbes (1750–1763)," *Ecole Nationale des Chartres, Positions des thèses soutenues parles élèves de la promotion de 1975* (Paris: Ecole des Chartres, 1975), p. 19. Cf. Anne Goldgar, "The Absolutism of Taste: Journalists as Censors in 18th-Century Paris," in *Censorship & the Control of Print: In England and France 1600–1910,* illustrated ed., ed. Robin Myers and Michael Harris. (New Castle, DE: Oak Knoll Press, 1992), p. 90.

3. Sue Curry Jansen, *Censorship*, p. 79. See also William Hanley, *A Biographical Dictionary of French Censors, 1742–1789 A–B* (Ferney-Voltaire: Centre international d'étude du XVIIIe siècle, 2005), vol. I, p. 386, and Bibliothèque Nationale de France (BnF) Fonds français 21939–21942, 21995–22002, 22014–22016, 22137–22139; and Ernest Coyecque, *Inventaire de la Collection Anisson sur l'histoire de l'imprimerie et la librairie principalement à Paris*, 2 vols. (Paris, 1900; reprint New York: Burt Franklin Bibliography and Reference Series, 1964).

4. Jean-Jacques Rousseau, *Confessions*, trans. by Angela Scholar (Oxford: Oxford University Press, 2008), p. 204. First published in French in 1762.

5. Daniel Droixhe, *Une histoire des Lumières au pays de Liège. Livre, idées, société* (Liège: Fondation Universitaire de Belgique, 2007), chs. 1 and 2.

6. Jonathan Israel, *Radical Enlightenment* (New York: Oxford University Press, 2001), p. 574.

7. For a study of the entire generation of journalist refugees, see Marion Brétéche, *Les Compagnons de Mercure. Journalisme et politique dans l'Europe de Louis XIV* (Ceyzérieu: Champ Vallon, 2015). And for the coterie around Marchand, see Margaret C. Jacob, *The Radical Enlightenment: Pantheists, Freemasons and Republicans* (London: Allen and Unwin, 1981; 2nd ed., Santa Ana, CA: Cornerstone Books, 2006). For an example of the inability of Francophone scholars to integrate the French language press outside their borders, see Suzanne Dumouchel, *Le Journal littéraire en France au dix-huitime siècle: émergence d'une culture virtuelle, preface by Jean-Paul Sermain* (Oxford: Voltaire Foundation, 2016).

8. University Library, Leiden, Marchand MSS 2 Fritsch to Marchand, January 17, 1740.

9. [Anon.], *La vie et l'esprit de Mr. Benoit de Spinosa* ([Amsterdam: Charles le Vier], 1719). *Le Traité* was first published under this title. See library catalogue of UCLA, B3997. L96v 1719 [Barcode: G0000523258], one of the few extant copies. The Toland manuscripts are at the British Library.

10. Their views made their way into *The Persian Letters*. See Ursula Haskins Gonthier, *Montesquieu and England: Enlightened Exchanges, 1689–1755* (London: Pickering & Chatto, 2010), pp. 17–18.

11. David L. Crosby, ed., *The Complete Antislavery Writings of Anthony Benezet 1754–1783: An Annotated Critical Edition* (Baton Rouge: Louisiana State University Press, 2013).

12. Pierre Bayle, *Nouvelles Lettres*, 2 vols. (The Hague: Van Duren, 1739), vol. II, p. 421, letter of January 1, 1705. Typically, Bernard stocked his shops with books he had acquired on credit. For more details about his dealings, see Amsterdam Municipal Archives, notary public J. Hoekebak, No. 5922, December 22, 1711; idem, March 18, 1712, no. 5923.

13. J. F. Bernard, *Réflexions morales satiriques & comiques, sur les Moeurs de notre siècle* (Cologne: Pierre Marteau le Jeune, 1711), ch. 6.

14. Ibid., p. 139.

15. Ibid., ch. 11. And for the identity of Amsterdam, see the 1723 edition, p. 199 and the unpaginated key at the end; and see p. 177 for further praise of the Dutch Republic. See also Jens Häseler and Anthony McKenna, eds., *La vie intellectuelle aux refuges Protestants. Actes de la Table ronde de Münster du 25 juillet 1995* (Paris: Champion, 1999).

16. For a lengthy discussion of *Religious Ceremonies of the World*, see Lynn Hunt, Margaret Jacob, and Wijnand Mijnhardt, *The Book That Changed Europe: Picart and Bernard's Religious Ceremonies of the World* (Cambridge, MA: Harvard University Press, 2010).

17. Montesquieu, *Persian Letters with Related Texts*, trans. with intro and notes by Raymond N. MacKenzie (Indianapolis, IN: Hackett Publishing, 2014), p. 37.

18. Ibid., pp. 83–85, letters 57 and 58.

19. Ibid., p. 87, letter 59.

20. Ibid., p. 41.

21. Montesquieu, *The Spirit of the Laws* (Amherst, NY: Prometheus Books, 2002; text originally published in English ca. 1900, New York: Colonial Press), p. 226; original French edition, 1748.

22. Montesquieu, *Persian Letters*, p. 242, letter 160.

23. Silvia Sebastiani, *The Scottish Enlightenment: Race, Gender, and the Limits of Progress*, trans. by Jeremy Carden (New York: Palgrave-Macmillan, 2013), pp. 26–27.

24. Montesquieu, *Spirit of the Laws*, p. 150.

25. Aurelian Craiutu, *A Virtue for Courageous Minds: Moderation in French Political Thought, 1748–1830* (Princeton, NJ: Princeton University Press, 2012).

26. James Jones Jr., "Montesquieu and Jefferson Revisited: Aspects of a Legacy," *French Review*, Fiftieth Anniversary Issue, vol. 51, no. 4, 1978, pp. 577–85.

27. Annelien de Dijn, "Montesquieu's Controversial Context: *The Spirit of the Laws* as a Monarchist Tract," *History of Political Thought*, vol. 34, 2013, pp. 66–88.

28. Montesquieu, *Spirit of the Laws*, p. 189, and books 11 and 12, in general.

29. Sebastiani, *The Scottish Enlightenment*, p. 34, quoting from Hume's footnote to the 1753–54 edition, "Of National Characters," in *Essays Moral, Political and Literary*, ed. Eugene F. Miller (Indianapolis: Liberty Fund, 1985). For exiting the tunnel, see S. Muthu, *Enlightenment against Empire* (Princeton, NJ: Princeton University Press, 2003).

30. Mr. de Voltaire, *Letters concerning the English Nation* (London: Printed for C. Davis in Pater-Noster-Row, MDCCXLI [1741]). The second edition, with large additions.

31. Voltaire, *Letters*, letter 5.

32. Ibid., letter 7.

33. For a more detailed discussion, see J. B. Shank, *The Newton Wars and the Beginning of the French Enlightenment* (Chicago: University of Chicago Press, 2008).

34. Glenn Roe, "A Sheep in Wolff's Clothing: Émilie du Châtelet and the Encyclopédie," *Eighteenth-Century Studies*, vol. 51, no. 2, 2018, pp. 179–96.

35. Brookliss, *French Higher Education*, p. 366.

36. Adam Smith, *Lectures on Rhetoric and Belles Lettres . . . delivered at the University of Glasgow . . . reported by a student in 1762–63*, ed. by John M. Lothian (London: Thomas Nelson and Sons, 1963), p. 140.

37. Shank, *Newton Wars*, pp. 129–32. And see Ann Thomson, "Toland, Dodwell, Swift and the Circulation of Irreligious Ideas in France: What Does the Study of International Networks Tell Us about the 'Radical Enlightenment'?" in Lise Andries, Frédéric Ogé, John Dunkley, and Darach Sanfey, eds., *Intellectual Journeys: The Translation of Ideas in Enlightenment England, France and Ireland* (Oxford: Voltaire Foundation, 2013), pp. 169–73. And see Margaret C. Jacob, "The Radical Enlightenment: A Heavenly City with Many Mansions," in Steffen Ducheyne, ed., *Reassessing the Radical Enlightenment* (New York: Routledge, 2017), pp. 48–60.

38. Shank, *Newton Wars*, pp. 434–40.

39. [Anon.], *Thérèse philosophe* (The Hague, 1748), p. 23.

40. Archives of the Prefecture of the Police, Paris, Aa/7/592–97.

41. Paula Bertucci, *Artisanal Enlightenment: Science and the Mechanical Arts in Old Regime France* (New Haven, CT: Yale University Press, 2017).

42. For easy access to a portion of the text, see Margaret C. Jacob, *The Enlightenment, Second Edition* (Boston: Bedford Books, 2017), pp. 81–100; p. 85 for the quotation.

43. Margaret C. Jacob, "The Materialist World of Pornography," in Lynn Hunt, ed., *The Invention of Pornography: Obscenity and the Origins of Modernity, 1500–1800* (New York: Zone Books, 1996), pp.157–202.

44. Laurence Macé-Del Vento, "'Lancer la foudre et retirer la main.' Les stratégies clandestines de Voltaire vues par la censure romaine," *La Lettre clandestine*, no. 16, 2008, pp. 165–77, quoted on p. 166, from Rome, Archivio della Congregazione per la Dottrina della Fede (ACDF), Index, Protocolli 1771–73, dossier 17, f. 66r.

45. For the text, see http://du.laurens.free.fr/epitres/epitr_chandel.htm (accessed September 29, 2016).

46. [Anon.], *Nouvelles libertés de Penser* (Amsterdam, 1743); cf. James. O'Higgins, S.J., *Anthony Collins* (The Hague: Nijhoff, 1970), pp. 216–17. Cf. Hans Ulrich Gumbrecht, *Making Sense in Life and Literature, Theory and History of Literature*, vol. 79 (Minneapolis: University of Minnesota Press, 1992), pp. 138–39; here, the author assumes that the writer of *Le Philosophe* must be speaking out of a French context. See the discussion in Jacob, *The Radical Enlightenment, Pantheists, Freemasons and Republicans*, p. 217, and see Margaret C. Jacob, *Living the Enlightenment: Freemasonry and Politics in Eighteenth-Century Europe* (New York: Oxford University Press, 1991).

The evidence for Dumarsais as author is good but not conclusive; see A. W. Fairbairn, "Dumarsais and *Le Philosophe*," *Studies on Voltaire and the Eighteenth Century*, vol. lxxxvii, 1972, pp. 375–95; and Olivier Bloch, ed., *Le Matérialisme du XVIIIe siècle et la litterature clandestine* (Paris: Librairie Vrin, 1982), pp. 179–81, where once again the manuscript is reassigned to a Dutch context.

47. Here, I am working from the electronic version of an English translation by Samuel Wilkinson, of 1820, available at www.gutenberg.org/files/8909/8909 -h/8909-h.htm#link2H_PREF (accessed July 1, 2018), p. 1. *The System of Nature; Or, the Laws of the Moral and Physical World. Translated from the Original French of M. De Mirabaud* (London: Samuel Davison, 1820).

48. Ibid., ch. 1.

49. Ibid., ch. 4.

50. Bibliothèque Mazarin, Paris, MS 1193, pp. 92–93.

51. [Voltaire], *Sermon des cinquante* (Geneva: Cramer, 1762). See Miguel Benitez, "Voltaire and Clandestine Manuscripts," in *The Cambridge Companion to Voltaire*, ed. Nicholas Cronk (Cambridge: Cambridge University Press, 2009), 71–72.

52. Adam Sutcliffe, "Judaism in the Anti-Religious Thought of the Clandestine French Early Enlightenment," *Journal of the History of Ideas*, vol. 64, no. 1, January 2003, pp. 97–117.

53. David Williams, "Voltaire," in Graham Robert Oppy and Nick Trakakis, eds., *The History of Western Philosophy of Religion: Volume 3, Early Modern Philosophy of Religion*, (Oxford: Oxford University Press, 2009), pp. 203–4.

54. See Laure Marcellesi, "Louis-Sébastien Mercier: Prophet, Abolitionist, Colonialist"; at www.dartmouth.edu/~laurewik/publications/2011-studies/mercier.pdf (accessed September 12, 2016).

55. M. Mercier, *De J. J. Rousseau, considéré comme l'un des premiers auteurs de la revolution* (Paris: Buisson, 1791), pp. 1–47.

56. Jean-Jacques Rousseau, *Profession of Faith of a Savoyard Vicar* (New York: Peter Eckler; reprinted by Leopold Classic Library, 1889), p. 19.

57. Ibid., p. 20. Samuel Clarke, *A demonstration of the being and attributes of God* [electronic resource]: *more particularly in answer to Mr. Hobbs, Spinoza, and their followers: Wherein the notion of liberty is stated, and the possibility and certainty of it proved, in opposition to necessity and fate. Being the substance of eight sermons preach'd at the Cathedral-Church of St. Paul, in the year 1704. at the lecture founded by the honourable Robert Boyle* (London: James Knapton, at the Crown in St. Paul's Church-Yard, 1706). The French edition appeared in 1717.

58. Ibid., pp. 31–38.

59. James Miller, *Rousseau: Dreamer of Democracy* (New Haven, CT: Yale University Press, 1984).

60. Rousseau, *Savoyard Vicar*, p. 84.

61. Ibid., pp. 78–79.

62. Ibid., pp. 103–7.

63. C. L. Griswold, "Liberty and Compulsory Civil Religion in Rousseau's *Social Contract*," *Journal of the History of Philosophy*, vol. 53, no. 2, 2015, pp. 271–300.

64. Rousseau, *Confessions*, p. 191. Cf. M. K. McAlpin, "Innocence of Experience: Rousseau on Puberty in the State of Civilization," *Journal of the History of Ideas*, vol. 71, no. 2, 2010, pp. 241–61.

65. McAlpin, "Innocence of Experience," p. 131.

66. Rousseau, *Confessions*, p. 160.

67. Jean-Jacques Rousseau, *The Social Contract*, trans. and intro. by Maurice Cranston (London: Penguin, 1968), p. 49.

68. *Confessions*, p. 168.

69. Rousseau, *The Social Contract*, p. 65.

70. Ibid., p. 68.

71. *Du Contrat social*, in *Œuvres complètes*, ed. by B. Gagnebin and M. Raymond (Paris: Gallimard, 1964), vol. 3, p. 429: "Ce mot de *finance* est un mot d'esclave; il est inconnu dans la Cité. Dans un Etat vraiment libre les citoyens font tout avec leurs bras et rien avec de l'argent."

72. Rousseau, *The Social Contract*, p. 69.

73. Ibid., p. 74. Luc Foisneau, "Governing a Republic: Rousseau's General Will and the Problem of Government," *Republics of Letters: A Journal for the Study of Knowledge, Politics, and the Arts*, vol. 2, no. 1, December 15, 2010; at http://rofl.stanford.edu/node/70 (accessed January 30, 2017).

74. C. L. Griswold, "Liberty and Compulsory Civil Religion in Rousseau's *Social Contract*." *Journal of the History of Philosophy*, vol. 53 no. 2, 2015, pp. 271–300.

75. Library of the Grand Lodge, The Hague, MS 191.E.2, f. 60, spoken in 1800.

76. For example, see [Anon.], *Essai sur la secte des illumines* (Paris, 1789), and repeated almost verbatim in *La Loge rouge devoilée à toutes les têtes couronnées* (new edition, July 1790, probably Paris).

77. See Archives nationales, Paris, MS F 7 6689, documents from the Prefecture of the Police in the 1820s.

78. For a copy of the 1738 encyclical, see www.papalencyclicals.net/Clem12/c12 inemengl.htm (accessed May 16, 2016).

79. See [Anon.], *Les Francs-Maçons ecrasés* (Amsterdam, 1747). See also Harry Carr, ed., *The Early French Exposures* (London: Quatuor Coronati Lodge, 1971), pp. 282–91. See also Margaret C. Jacob, *Living the Enlightenment: Freemasonry and Politics in Eighteenth-Century Europe* (New York: Oxford University Press, 1991), ch. 1.

80. Archives municipals, Strasbourg, Legs Gerschel, box 34, f. 1, "esquisse de la cérémonie de reinstallation."

81. Lenni Brenner, ed., *Jefferson & Madison on Separation of Church and State* (Fort Lee, NJ: Barricade Books, 2004), p. 75, Jefferson to Marquis de Chastellux, September 2, 1785.

Chapter Five. The Scottish Enlightenment in Edinburgh

1. Michael F. Graham, *The Blasphemies of Thomas Aikenhead: Boundaries of Belief on the Eve of the Enlightenment* (Edinburgh: Edinburgh University Press, 2008), pp. 70–75. If lists of offending books were produced, they have not survived in the archives. For banned books almost entirely religious or political in nature, see Appendix 2 in Alastair F. Mann, *The Scottish Book Trade, 1500–1720* (East Linton, UK: Tuckwell Press, 2000), pp. 175–77. See manuscript by Thomas Ruddiman, predecessor of Hume, National Library of Scotland MS 20492; "Visitation to universities, National records of Scotland, parliamentary visitation of universities," 1690, MS PA10/4 and CH12/12/210.

2. Richard B. Sher, *Church and University in the Scottish Enlightenment: The Moderate Literati of Edinburgh* (Edinburgh: University of Edinburgh Press, 1985), p. 27.

3. Alasdair Raffe, *The Culture of Controversy: Religious Arguments in Scotland, 1660–1714* (Woodbridge, UK: Boydell Press, 2012), pp. 57–61.

4. Raffe, *The Culture*, ch. 2.

5. See in general, Michael F. Graham, *The Blasphemies of Thomas Aikenhead: Boundaries of Belief on the Eve of the Enlightenment* (Edinburgh: Edinburgh University Press, 2008). For his particular beliefs, see pp. 102–4, 117–20.

6. British Library, ADD. MS 4295.

7. Mungo Craig, *A Satyr against Atheistical Deism with a Genuine Character of a Deist* (Edinburgh: Robert Hutchison, 1696), p. 10.

8. Cited in Graham, *The Blasphemies*, p. 22.

9. See Paul Monod, Murray Pittock, Daniel Szechi, eds., *Loyalty and Identity. Jacobites at Home and Abroad* (Basingstoke, UK: Palgrave Macmillan, 2010); Bruce Lenman, "The Scottish Episcopal Clergy and the Ideology of Jacobitism," in Eveline Cruickshanks, ed., *Ideology and Conspiracy: Aspects of Jacobitism, 1689–1759* (Edinburgh: John Donald, 1982), pp. 36–48.

10. Graham, *The Blasphemies*, 46–47. On toleration, see [Anon.], *Good News from Scotland: or the Abjuration and the Kirk of Scotland reconcil'd* (n.p., 1712), p. 10, "The Toleration is a hard Chapter."

11. See David D. Wilson, *Seeking Nature's Logic: Natural Philosophy in the Scottish Enlightenment* (University Park: Pennsylvania State University Press, 2009), ch. 1.

12. For a good overview of Scottish clubs in the period, see Roger L. Emerson, *Neglected Scots: Eighteenth Century Glaswegians and Women* (Edinburgh: Humming Earth, 2015).

13. For example, L. Weber, "Predicting the Bankruptcy of England: David Hume's Political Discourses and the Dutch Debate on National Debt in the Eighteenth Century," *Early Modern Low Countries*, vol. 1, no. 1, 2017, pp. 135–55.

14. Archibald Pitcairne, *Babell; A Satirical Poem, on The Proceedings of the General Assembly in the year 1692* (Edinburgh: Maitland Club, 1830), pp. xii–xiii.

15. Ibid., p. 16.

16. [Anon.], *A Modest Examination of a Late Pamphlet entitled Apollo Mathematicus* (n.p., 1696).

17. [A. Pitcairne], *Apollo Mathematicus. Or the Art of curing Diseases by the Mathematics, According to the Principles of Dr. Pitcairne* (n.p., 1695), p. 43.

18. [Anon.], *A Catalogue of the Graduates in the Faculties of Arts, Divinity and Law, of the University of Edinburgh, since Its Foundation* (Edinburgh: Neill and Company, 1858), pp. 137–38.

19. John P. Wright, *Hume's 'A Treatise of Human Nature': An Introduction* (Cambridge: Cambridge University Press, 2009), pp. 4–5.

20. William Robertson, *Reasons of Dissent from the Judgment and Resolution of the Commission, March 11, 1752* (Edinburgh, 1752), pp. iii–iv. And see Richard Sher, *Church and University*, pp. 50–57.

21. John Witherspoon, *Ecclesiastical characteristics: or, the arcana of church policy. Being an humble attempt to open up the mystery of moderation. Wherein is shewn A plain and easy way of attaining to the character of a moderate man, as at present in repute in the church of Scotland* (Glasgow, 1753), pp. 5–22.

22. Essay 12 in the 1777 edition of Hume, *Essays, Moral and Political* (Edinburgh: Printed by R. Fleming and A. Alison, for A. Kincaid Bookseller, 1741–42), vol. 1, pp. Mil 77–78; at http://davidhume.org/texts/emp.html (accessed June 15, 2018).

23. I am indebted here to Richard Sher, *Church and University*, ch. 2.

24. Ibid., p. 87.

25. Quoted in Sher, pp. 87–88, Hume to Elliot, July 2, 1757, in *The Letters of David Hume*, ed. J.Y.T. Greig, 2 vols. (Oxford: Oxford University Press, 1932), vol. 1, p. 255.

26. National Library of Scotland, MS 23159, ff. 89–96, May 2, 1754–January 1, 1755. The last four were in 1758. By 1761, the Society was preoccupied with trying to revive itself (p. 162). See p. 32 for the question about ancient or modern manners and women, November to December 1754, when Hume was very active in the society; indeed, he presided over the December meeting.

27. Ibid., December 18, 1759, p. 149; the question about women was followed by one about whether convents and nunneries were "prejudicial to the population of the country." Also on the same day, another question about whether a nation "sunk in luxury and pleasure can be retrieved."

28. National Library of Scotland, MS 23159, ff. 89–96.

29. Ibid., p. 137; mention of the freemasons' meeting place can be found throughout the minutes—for example, p. 114 and pp. 163–64.

30. Ibid., f. 187, a separate list of questions with "debated" after some of them, including the mutual consent question. For Hume as satirist, see essay 6, "Of Love and Marriage," in the 1777 edition of Hume, *Essays, Moral and Political* (Edinburgh: Printed by R. Fleming and A. Alison, for A. Kincaid Bookseller, 1741–42), vol. 1; at http://davidhume.org/texts/emp.html (accessed June 18, 2018).

31. László Kontler, "Beauty or Beast, or Monstrous Regiments? Robertson and Burke on Women and the Public Scene," in Ferenc Hörcher and Endre Szécsényi, eds., *Aspects of the Enlightenment: Aesthetics, Politics, and Religion* (Budapest: Akadémiai Kiadó, 2004), pp. 238–74.

32. Paul Bator, "The University of Edinburgh Belles Lettres Society (1759–64) and the Rhetoric of the Novel," *Rhetoric Review*, vol. 14, no. 2, 1996, pp. 280–98.

33. National Library of Scotland, MS Adv. 5.1.6, 1761.

34. The 1777 edition of Hume, *Essays, Moral and Political* (Edinburgh: Printed by R. Fleming and A. Alison, for A. Kincaid Bookseller, 1741–42), vol. 1; at http://davidhume.org/texts/emp.html, mil 7 (accessed January 24, 2017).

35. David Hume, *Political Discourses* (Edinburgh: R. Fleming for A. Kincaid and A. Donaldson, 1752), quoting here from the 1777 text, essay one, "Of Commerce"; at http://davidhume.org/texts/pd.html (accessed January 25, 2017).

36. Hume, *Essays, Moral and Political*, vol. 1, pp. Mil 89–90.

37. Hume, *Political Discourses*, p. RA 10; at http://davidhume.org/texts/pd.html (accessed May 23, 2018).

38. David Hume, *Dialogues Concerning Natural Religion* (n.p., 1779), p. D 1.14; at http://davidhume.org/texts/dnr.html (accessed May 24, 2018).

39. Ibid., p. D 2.14.

40. On Hume's epistemology, see James A. Harris, *Hume: An Intellectual Biography* (Cambridge: Cambridge University Press, 2015), pp. 85–102, and pp. 78–81 on his time in France.

41. Hume, *Dialogues Concerning Natural Religion*, p. D 2.21, and p. D 3.7 for the argument about the eye.

42. Ibid., p. D 3.12.

43. Thomas A. Apel, *Feverish Bodies: Enlightened Minds. Science and the Yellow Fever Controversy in the Early American Republic* (Stanford, CA: Stanford University Press, 2016), pp. 25–28.

44. [George Horne], *A letter to Adam Smith, L.L.D. on the life, death and philosophy of his friend David Hume, Esq. By one of the people called Christians* (Oxford, 1777), p. 11, quoting from the 1804 edition (London: Addinson), found in Early America's Historical Imprints; [Samuel Jackson] Pratt, *An apology for the life and writings of David Hume, Esq: with a parallel between him and the late Lord Chesterfield:*

to which is added an address to one of the people called Christians. By way of reply to his *letter to Adam Smith, L.L.D.* (London: Printed for Fielding and Walker, D. Prince, Oxford; T. and J. Merrill, Cambridge; and W. Creech, Edinburgh, 1777); at http://name.umdl.umich.edu/004806357.0001.000 (accessed July 1, 2018).

45. Adam Ferguson, *Analysis of pneumatics and moral philosophy. For the use of* *students in the College of Edinburgh* (Edinburgh: A. Kincaid and J. Bell, 1766), p. 5.

46. Adam Ferguson, *An essay on the history of civil society* (Edinburgh: A. Kincaid and J. Bell, 1767), Part II, sections 1 and 2.

47. Ibid., p. 355.

48. Iain McDaniel, *Adam Ferguson in the Scottish Enlightenment: The Roman Past* *and Europe's Future* (Cambridge, MA: Harvard University Press, 2013), ch. 4.

49. James A. Harris, "Religion in Hutcheson's Moral Philosophy," *Journal of the* *History of Philosophy*, vol. 46, no. 2, April 2008, pp. 205–22.

50. See [Anthony Benezet], *A short account of that part of Africa, inhabited by* *the Negroes. With respect to the fertility of the country; the good disposition of many* *of the natives, and the manner by which the slave trade is carried on. / Extracted from* *divers authors, in order to shew the iniquity of that trade, and the falsity of the arguments* *usually advanced in its vindication. With quotations from the writings of several persons* *of note, viz. George Wallis* [that is, Wallace], *Francis Hutcheson, and James Foster, and* *a large extract from a pamphlet, lately published in London, on the subject of the slave* *trade, second edition* (Philadelphia: W. Dunlap, 1762).

51. Francis Hutcheson, *An essay on the nature and conduct of the passions and affec-* *tions. With illustrations on the moral sense. By the author of the Inquiry into the original of* *our ideas of beauty and virtue* (London: J. and J. Knapton, 1730). Cf. Stephen Darwall, "Hutcheson on Practical Reason," *Hume Studies*, vol. 23, no. 1, April 1997, pp. 73–89.

52. For an interesting discussion of the limits that Smith set on sympathy or pity, see Adam Potkay, "Pity, Gratitude, and the Poor in Rousseau and Adam Smith," in Eve Tavor Wheeler and Roxann Wheeler, eds., *Studies in Eighteenth-Century Cul-* *ture*, vol. 46 (Baltimore. MD: Johns Hopkins University Press, 2017), pp. 163–82. And for Cullen, see his *Clinical lectures, delivered in the years 1765 and 1766, by William* *Cullen, M.D. Taken in short-hand by a gentleman who attended* (London: Printed for Messrs. Lee and Hurst, Paternoster-Row, 1797), pp. 28–39, and David B. Wilson, *Seeking Nature's Logic: Natural Philosophy in the Scottish Enlightenment* (University Park: Pennsylvania State University Press, 2009), pp. 80–81.

53. Hutcheson, *An essay on the nature . . . of the passions*, pp. 29–30.

54. Adam Smith, *The Whole Works* (London: J. Richardson and Co., 1822), vol. 5, p. 79. From *The Principles That Lead and Direct Philosophical Enquiries: Illustrated by* *The History of Astronomy*; unpublished in Smith's lifetime.

55. Adam Smith, *The Whole Works* (London: J. Richardson and Co., 1822), vol. 1, p. 142, from *The Theory of Moral Sentiments* (1759).

56. Adam Smith, *An Inquiry into the Nature and Causes of the Wealth of Nations* (Dublin: Printed for Messrs. Whitestone, Chamberlaine [etc.], 1776), p. 2.

57. Nicholas Phillipson, *Adam Smith: An Enlightened Life* (London: Allen Lane, an imprint of Penguin Books, 2010), p. 201. See E. P. Dennison Torrie and Russel Coleman, *Historic Kirkcaldy: The Archaeological Implications of Development* (Aberdeen: Scottish Cultural Press, 1995), p. 15.

58. For the early innovations, see A. E. Musson and Eric Robinson, *Science and Technology in the Industrial Revolution (with Foreword to the Second Printing, Margaret C. Jacob)* (Reading, UK: Gordon and Breach, 1989; first printing 1969); Margaret C. Jacob, *The Cultural Meaning of the Scientific Revolution* (New York: Alfred Knopf, 1987) and *Scientific Culture and the Making of the Industrial West* (New York: Oxford University Press, 1997); and by the same author, *The First Knowledge Economy* (Cambridge: Cambridge University Press, 2015).

59. Adam Smith, *An Inquiry*, p. 39.

60. Ibid., pp. 158–60.

61. Robert G. W. Anderson and Jean Jones, eds., *The Correspondence of Joseph Black* (Burlington, VT: Ashgate, 2012), pp. 6–15; Phillipson, *Smith*, pp. 279–80.

62. For what Black was teaching, see UCLA, Young Research Library, MS 170/587: *Lectures on Chemistry by Doctor Black and Doctor Hope taken by Lovell Edgeworth*; at http://digital2.library.ucla.edu/viewItem.do?ark=21198/zz0019rp5j (accessed January 19, 2018).

63. Donald Fleming, "Latent Heat and the Invention of the Watt Engine," *Isis*, vol. 43, no. 1, April 1952, pp. 3–5; for an up-to-date account, see Rev. Dr. Richard L. Hills, *James Watt: Volume One, His Time in Scotland, 1736–1774* (Ashbourne, Derbyshire, UK: Landmark, 2002), ch. 2. And from 2012, *Month in Physics History*; at www.aps.org/publications/apsnews/201204/physicshistory.cfm (accessed March 24, 2017).

64. UCLA, Young Research Library, MS 170/587, 1796.

65. Ibid., f. 217.

66. Ibid., ff. 228–29.

67. *Lectures on the elements of chemistry delivered in the University of Edinburgh by the late Joseph Black published from his manuscripts by John Robison* (Philadelphia: M. Carey, 1806), p. xxvii. Robison is to be used with caution. Based on these concepts, in 1679, an associate of Boyle's named Denis Papin built a bone digester, which is a closed vessel with a tightly fitting lid that confines steam until a high pressure is generated. Later designs implemented a steam release valve to keep the machine from exploding.

68. I am indebted here to Charles W. J. Withers, "William Cullen's Agricultural Lectures and Writings and the Development of Agricultural Science in Eighteenth-Century Scotland," *Agricultural History Review*, vol. 37, no. 2, 1989, pp. 144–56.

69. For a selection of his writings, see Andreas Rahmatian, ed., *Lord Kames: Selected Writings* (Exeter, UK: Andrews, 2017).

70. James Hutton, *Abstract of a Dissertation read in the Royal Society of Edinburgh . . . 1785 . . . concerning the Sytem of the Earth, its Duration, and Stability.*

71. Anna Plassart, *The Scottish Enlightenment and the French Revolution* (New York: Cambridge University Press, 2015).

72. J. Keir writing to Watt, November 24, 1797, and found in Eric Robinson and Douglas McKie, eds., *Partners in Science: Letters of James Watt and Joseph Black* (Cambridge, MA: Harvard University Press, 1970), pp. 283–84, and 286–87 on response to his book.

73. Robison, *Proofs of a Conspiracy against all the Religions and Governments of Europe, carried on in the Secret Meetings of Free-Masons, Illuminati and Reading Societies, etc., collected from good authorities* (Edinburgh, 1797; 2nd ed. with postscript, London: T. Cadell & W. Davies, 1797; 3rd ed., Philadelphia: T. Dobson & W. Cobbet, 1798; 4th ed., New York and Dublin: G. Forman, 1798); *Proofs of a Conspiracy,* Western Islands, 1900; *The Illuminati,* taken from "Proofs of a World Conspiracy," Elizabeth Knauss [1930]; *Proof's [sic!] of a Conspiracy,* Ram Reprints, 1964; *Proofs of a Conspiracy,* Boston, Western Islands, "The Americanist Classics," [1967]; *Proofs of a Conspiracy,* Islands Press, 1978; C. P. Book Pub.; Kessinger Publishing; annotated 5th ed. with foreword by Alex Kurtagic, *Proofs of a Conspiracy,* The Palingenesis Project (Wermod and Wermod Publishing Group), 2014.

74. Eric Robinson and Douglas McKie, eds., *Partners,* pp. 286–87, letter from Robison to Watt, January 14, 1798.

75. Ibid., Robison to Watt, July 17, 1798, pp. 293–94, and torture, p. 299, December 15, 1798.

76. Val Honeyman, "A Very Dangerous Place? Radicalism in Perth in the 1790s," *Scottish Historical Review,* vol. 87, issue 2, no. 224, October 2008, pp. 278–305.

77. Anna Plassart, *The Scottish Enlightenment,* pp. 103–7.

Chapter Six. Berlin and Vienna

1. H. C. Erik Midelfort, *Exorcism and Enlightenment: Johann Joseph Gassner and the Demons of Eighteenth-Century Germany* (New Haven, CT: Yale University Press, 2005). There is some question as to whether or not the 1775 execution occurred.

2. F. Andrew Brown, *On Education: John Locke, Christian Wolff, and the "Moral Weeklies"* (Berkeley: University of California Press, 1952).

3. Matthew Kadane, "Original Sin and the Path to the Enlightenment," *Past and Present,* vol. 235, no. 1, 2017, pp. 105–40.

4. Christian Thomasius, *Essays on Church, State, and Politics* (Kindle Edition, Liberty Fund, 2007), Kindle locations 250–254, quoting from *On the History of Natural Law until Grotius.* Christian Thomasius, *Essays on Church, State, and Politics* (Indianapolis, IN: Liberty Fund, 2007), ed. by Ian Hunter, Thomas Ahnert, and Frank Grunert.

This essay on the history of natural law was published as the foreword to the first German translation of Grotius's *De jure belli ac pacis* (The right of war and peace), which appeared under the title *Drei Bücher vom Recht des Krieges und des Friedens* in 1707. For a modern edition, see *The Rights of War and Peace*, 3 vols., ed. by Richard Tuck (Indianapolis, IN: Liberty Fund, 2005). Here reproduced with the translation in Thomasius, *Essays on Church, State, and Politics* (Indianapolis, IN: Liberty Fund, 2012).

5. Thomasius, *On the History of Natural Law*, loc. 261.

6. Ibid., loc. 317.

7. Ibid., loc. 492.

8. See Petra Schellenberger, "Sozinianismus und deutsche Frühausfklärung," in Karol Bal, Siegfried Wollgast, and Petra Schellenberger, eds., *Frühaufklärung und Polen* (Berlin: Akademie Verlag, 1991), pp. 113–35.

9. For a fuller discussion of Thomasius and his pupils, see Martin Mulsow, *Enlightenment Underground: Radical Germany, 1680–1720* (Charlottesville: University of Virginia Press, 2015; original German edition, 2002).

10. Ibid., pp. 80–92.

11. Margaret C. Jacob, *The Radical Enlightenment: Pantheists, Freemasons and Republicans* (London: George Allen & Unwin, 1981; second edition, Santa Ana, CA: Cornerstone Books, 2006).

12. Ibid., pp. 277–79, Gaspar Fritsch to Marchand, September 7, 1737.

13. A portion of the text can be found in Margaret C. Jacob, *The Enlightenment: A Brief History with Documents* (Boston: Bedford Books, second edition, 2017), pp. 81–100. There is one copy of the original 1719 edition at UCLA and at the Bibliothèque Mazarin in Paris.

14. *The Radical Enlightenment*, pp. 184–85.

15. University Library, Leiden, Marchand MSS 2, January 9, 2011, and April 31, 1712; cf. Jacob, *The Radical Enlightenment*, pp. 184–85.

16. Johann Gottfried Herder, *God, Some Conversations*, trans. and ed. by Frederick H. Burkhardt (New York: Bobbs-Merrill, 1940), pp. 112–13.

17. Michiel Wielema, "Abraham van Berkel's Translations as Contributions to the Dutch Radical Enlightenment," in Sonja Lavaert and Winfried Schröder, eds., *The Dutch Legacy: Radical Thinkers of the 17th Century and the Enlightenment* (Leiden: Brill, 2017), pp. 204–26.

18. Mulsow, *Enlightenment Underground*, pp. 154–55.

19. Matteo Favaretti Camposampiero, "Bodies of Inference: Christian Wolff's Epistemology of the Life Sciences and Medicine," *Perspectives on Science*, vol. 24, no. 3, May–June 2016, pp. 362–79. For a list of his major works, see "Siglenverzeichnis Der Zitierten Werke Christian Wolffs," *Aufklärung*, vol. 23, 2011, pp. 6–8.

20. C. I. Gerhardt, ed., *Briefwechsel zwischen Leibniz und Christian Wolff* (Hildesheim: Georg Olms, 1963).

21. John Robert Holloran, "Professors of Enlightenment at the University of Halle, 1690–1730," Ph.D. dissertation, University of Virginia, 2000, pp. 18–19.

22. Moses Mendelssohn, *Morning Hours or Lectures on the Existence of God*, 1785, and found in *Last Works*, trans., intro., and commentary by Bruce Rosenstock (Urbana: University of Illinois Press, 2012), lecture 9, p. 69.

23. Martin Gierl, *Pietismus und Aufklärung. Theologische Polemik und die Kommunikationreform des Wissenschapt am Ende des 17. Jahrhunderts* (Göttingen: Vandenhoeck & Ruprecht, 1997), ch. 11.

24. For an early example of their lexiconic approach to freethinking, see Johann Anton Trinius, *Freydenker Lexicon* (Turin: Bottega d'Erasmo, 1966, with a preface by Franco Venturi), originally published in Leipzig, 1759.

25. Holloran, p. 141. For Lange's assist, see J. Lange, *Modesta disquisitio novi philosophiae systematis de Deo, mundo et homine, et praesertim de harmoni commercii inter animam et corpus praestabilita* (Halle: Waisenhaus, 1723).

26. Derek Beales, "Was Joseph II an Enlightened Despot?" in Ritchie Robertson and Edward Timms, eds., *The Austrian Enlightenment and Its Aftermath*, Austrian Studies 2 (Edinburgh: Edinburgh University Press, 1991), pp. 1–21.

27. Peter Horwath, "The Altar of the Fatherland: Wilhelm Friedrich von Meyern's Utopian Novel *Dya-Na-Sore*," in Robertson and Timms, eds., *Austrian Enlightenment*, pp. 43–58.

28. Thomas Ahnert, "Newtonianism in Early Enlightenment Germany, c. 1720 to 1750: Metaphysics and the Critique of Dogmatic Philosophy," *Studies in History and Philosophy of Science Part A*, vol. 35, no. 3, September 2004, pp. 471–91.

29. Thomas Broman, "Metaphysics for an Enlightened Public: The Controversy over Monads in Germany, 1746–1748," *Isis*, vol. 103, no. 1, 2012, pp. 1–23.

30. Helga Brandes, "The Literary Marketplace and the Journal, Medium of the Enlightenment," in Barbara Becker-Cantarino, ed., *German Literature of the Eighteenth Century: The Enlightenment and Sensibility* (Rochester, NY: Boydell & Brewer, 2005), pp. 79–102.

31. Francis Lamport, "Lessing, Bourgeois Drama, and the National Theater," in Barbara Becker-Cantarino, ed., *German Literature*, pp. 156–82.

32. See [Samuel Formey], *La Belle Wolfienne: avec deux Lettres Philosophiques* (The Hague: Veuve de Charles Le Vier, 1741). Published by the widow of Charles Le Vier, one of the original "brothers" in the 1710 group.

33. [Anon.], *Gedichte und Lieder verfasst von den Brüder der Loge zur wahren Eintracht* (Vienna: Wappler, 1783), p. 23, and cited in Ewan West, "Masonic Song and the Development of the *Kunstlied* in Enlightenment Vienna," p. 82 in Robertson and Timms, eds., *Austrian Enlightenment*.

34. Joseph P. Steilka, "Gottlieb von Leon and His *Rabbinische Legenden*," in Robertson and Timms, eds., *Austrian Enlightenment*, pp. 59–87.

35. Johann Pezzl, *Faustin: oder das philosophische Jahrhundert* (Vienna: Neuauflage, 1783). Cf. Ritchie Robertson, "Johann Pezzl (1756–1823): Enlightenment in the Satirical Mode," in Jeffrey D. Bruson and Ulrich L. Lehner, eds., *Enlightenment and Catholicism in Europe: A Transnational History* (Notre Dame, IN: University of Notre Dame Press, 2014), pp. 227–45.

36. Cited in R. William Weisberger, *Speculative Freemasonry and the Enlightenment: A Study of the Craft in London, Paris, Prague, and Vienna* (New York: Columbia University Press, 1993), p. 138, from the *Journal für Freymaurer*, vol. II, 1785, part I, pp. 193–94.

37. [Anon.], *Almanach des Francs-Maçons* (The Hague: Van Laak, 1788), p. 32.

38. The best essay on this opera is Dorothy Koenigsberger, "A New Metaphor for *The Magic Flute*," *European Studies Review*, vol. 5, 1975, pp. 229–75. Also useful, but does not acknowledge Koenigsberger's work, see Nicholas Till, *Mozart and the Enlightenment: Truth, Virtue and Beauty in Mozart's Operas* (New York: W. W. Norton, 1992).

39. Jane K. Brown, "Classicism and Secular Humanism: The Sanctification of *Die Zauberflüte* in Goethe's 'Novelle,'" in Elizabeth Krimmer and Patricia Anne Simpson, eds., *Religion, Reason, and Culture in the Age of Goethe* (Rochester, NY: Camden House, 2013), pp. 120–36.

40. For an overview of the period, see Elizabeth Krimmer and Patricia Anne Simpson, eds., *Religion, Reason, and Culture in the Age of Goethe.*

41. Francis Lamport, "'Solcher Väter giebt es keinen mehr': Paternal Authority in Lessing's Tragedies," in Ritchie Robertson, ed., *Lessing and the German Enlightenment* (Oxford: Voltaire Foundation, 2013), pp. 139–57. For the Diderot translation, see H. B. Nisbet, *Gotthold Ephraim Lessing: His Life, Works, and Thought* (Oxford: Oxford University Press, 2013), p. 274.

42. For the life of Elise, see Almut Spalding, *Elise Reimarus (1735–1805): The Muse of Hamburg* (Würzburg: Köigshausen & Neumann, 2005).

43. *Third Fragment from the Work of Hermann Samuel Reimarus* (Drittes Fragment; Durchgang der Israeliten durchs Rote Meer, G. Koehn trans.); at www.gkoehn.com /miscellaneous-translations/ (accessed July 16, 2017). Hermann Samuel Reimarus, *Fragments*, ed. by Charles H. Talbert (Philadelphia: Fortress Press, 1970).

44. Henry Chadwick, ed., with intro., *Lessing's Theological Writings* (Stanford, CA: Stanford University Press, 1957), pp. 24–29.

45. Chadwick, ed. "The Religion of Christ," 1780, p. 106.

46. H. B. Nisbet, *Gotthold Ephraim Lessing*, pp. 572–74, 582–83.

47. For an accessible text, see Ion Contiades, ed., *Gotthold Ephraim Lessing, Ernst und Falk; met den Fortsetzungen Herders und Friedrich Schlegels* (Frankfurt am Main: Insel, 1968), p. 48, fifth dialogue "Falk: In des hat freilich die freimaurerei immer und aller Orten sich nach der Bürgerlichen Gesellschaft schmiegen und biegen müssen, den diese war stets die stärkere. So mancherlei die bürgerliche Gesellschaft

gewesen, so mancherlei Formen hat auch die Freimaurerei an zunehmen sich nicht entbrechen können."

48. Ibid., p. 193.

49. Ibid., p. 46.

50. David Hill, "Enlightenment as Historical Process: *Ernst und Falk* and *Die Erziehung des Menschengeschlechts,"* in R. Robertson, *Lessing and the German Enlightenment*, pp. 227–44. Cf. Nisbet, pp. 594–95.

51. *Gespräch über eine-unsichtbar-sichtbare Gesellschaft*, in Ion Contiades, ed., *Gotthold Ephraim Lessing, Ernst und Falk; met den Fortsetzungen Herders und Friedrich Schlegels*, p. 69.

52. Johann Gottfried Herder, *God, Some Conversations*, trans. and ed. by Frederick H. Burkhardt (New York: Bobbs-Merrill, 1940), p. 190.

53. Allan Arkush, *Moses Mendelssohn and the Enlightenment* (Albany: State University of New York Press, 1994) pp. 114–121.

54. Moses Mendelssohn, *Jerusalem and Other Jewish Writings*, trans. and ed. by Alfred Jospe (New York: Schocken Books, 1969), p. 61.

55. Moses Mendelssohn, *Morning Hours, or Lectures on the Existence of God*, 1785, and found in *Moses Mendelssohn, Last Works*, trans., intro, commentary by Bruce Rosenstock (Urbana: University of Illinois Press, 2012), p. 4.

56. Schmuel Feiner, "The 'Happy Time' of Moses Mendelsohn and the Transformative Year of 1782," in Richard I. Cohen, Natalie B. Dohrmann, Adam Shear, and Elchanan Reiner, eds., *Jewish Culture in Early Modern Europe: Essays in Honor of David B. Ruderman* (Pittsburgh, PA: University of Pittsburgh Press, 2014), pp. 282–93.

57. Mendelssohn, *Morning Hours*, p. 3.

58. Ibid., p. 22.

59. Ibid., p. 23.

60. Ibid., Lecture 8, p. 61.

61. Bruce Rosenstock, trans., *Moses Mendelssohn, Last Works, To the Friends of Lessing: A Supplement to Mr. Jacobi's Correspondence Concerning the Doctrine of Spinoza*, 1786, p. 148.

62. Johann Gottfried Herder, *God, Some Conversations*, trans. and ed. by Frederick H. Burkhardt (New York: Bobbs-Merrill, 1940), p. 158.

63. Nisbet, *Lessing*, pp. 568, 634–37.

64. Toshimasa Yasukata, *Lessing's Philosophy of Religion and the German Enlightenment: Lessing on Christianity and Reason* (Oxford: Oxford University Press, 2002), pp. 138–39.

65. John H. Zammito, "'The Most Hidden Conditions of Men of the First Rank': The Pantheist Current in Eighteenth-Century Germany 'Uncovered' by the Spinoza Controversy," *Eighteenth-Century Thought*, vol. I, 2003, pp. 335–68. Cf. Tom Spencer, "Personal Impersonalism in Herder's Conception of the Afterlife," in

Elizabeth Krimmer and Patricia Anne Simpson, eds., *Religion, Reason, and Culture in the Age of Goethe*, pp. 56–78.

66. J. Herder, *Essay on the Origin of Language*, pp. 121–37 in F. M. Barnard, trans., ed., and intro., *J. G. Herder on Social and Political Culture* (Cambridge: Cambridge University Press, 1969), originally, Berlin, 1772.

67. Ibid., p. 141.

68. Ibid., p. 150.

69. Ibid., p. 177.

70. J. Herder, *Ideas for a Philosophy of the History of Mankind* (1784–91) in F. M. Barnard, trans., ed., and intro., *J.G. Herder on Social and Political Culture*, pp. 272–74.

71. Ibid., p. 284.

72. Ibid., p. 275.

73. Ibid., pp. 274–75.

74. Ibid., p. 280.

75. Ibid., p. 281.

76. Ibid., p. 286–87. Cf. Sankar Muthu, *Enlightenment against Empire* (Princeton, NJ: Princeton University Press, 2003), pp. 226–38.

77. Ibid., p. 311.

78. Johann Gottfried Herder, *God, Some Conversations*, trans. and ed. by Frederick H. Burkhardt, pp. 97–105; second conversation. See also John Zammito, Karl Menges, and Ernest A. Menze, "Johann Gottfried Herder Revisited: The Revolution in Scholarship in the Last Quarter Century," *Journal of the History of Ideas*, vol. 71, no. 4, 2010, pp. 661–84.

79. Kant, *Werke, Akademie Ausgab* (Berlin: Walter de Gruyter, 1902), vol. 8, pp. 58–66. For an earlier written and equally critical review of the *Ideas*, see ibid., vol. 8, pp. 45–55.

80. Sonia Sikka, "On the Value of Happiness: Herder Contra Kant," *Canadian Journal of Philosophy*, vol. 37, no. 4, December 2007, pp. 515–46.

81. Immanuel Kant, *Idea for a Universal History from a Cosmopolitan Point of View* (1784), trans. by Lewis White Beck, from Immanuel Kant, *On History* (Indianapolis, IN: Bobbs-Merrill, 1963); theses 1–4.

82. Ibid., theses 7–8.

83. Ibid., thesis 8.

84. Cited in Muthu, *Enlightenment against Empire*, p. 183.

85. Peggy Kamuf, ed., *A Derrida Reader: Between the Blinds* (New York: Columbia University Press, 1991), p. 340, translated from *Glas* (Paris: Galilee, 1974).

86. Lea Ypi, "Revolution in Kant and Marx," *Political Theory*, vol. 42, no. 3, 2014, pp. 262–87.

87. Pauline Kleingeld, "Kant's Second Thoughts on Colonialism," in Katrin Flikschuh and Lea Ypi, eds., *Kant and Colonialism: Historical and Critical Perspectives*

(Oxford: Oxford University Press, 2014), pp. 43–67. In the same volume, see the essay "Commerce and Colonialism," pp. 99–127.

88. Quoting from Stefan Majetschak, ed., *Vom Magus im Norden und der Verwegenheit des Geistes. Ein Hamann Brevier* (Munich: Deutscher Taschenbuch Verlag, 1988), p. 204, and cited in Manfred Kuehn, "Kant's Critical Philosophy and Its Reception—The First Five Years (1781–86)," p. 633, in Paul Guyer, ed., *The Cambridge Companion to Kant and Modern Philosophy* (Cambridge: Cambridge University Press, 2006), pp. 630–64.

89. Quoted by John Christian Laursen, "From Libertine Idea to Widely Accepted: The Human Right to Sexual Satisfaction: A Research Program for the Study of the Idea from Carl Friedrich Bahrdt to the Present," in Lorenzo Bianchi, Nicole Gengoux, and Gianni Paganini, eds., *Philosophe et Libre Pensée: Philosophy and Free Thought XVIIe et XVIIIe Siècles* (Paris: Honoré Champion, 2017), pp. 492–510.

Chapter Seven. Naples and Milan

1. Vinzenzo Ferrone, *The Intellectual Roots of the Italian Enlightenment: Newtonian Science, Religion, and Politics in the Early Eighteenth Century*, trans. by Sue Brotherton (Amherst, NY: Humanities Press, 1995), first edition in Italian 1982; now Humanity Press, an imprint of Prometheus Books, pp. 1–7; letter cited on p. 279, n. 21.

2. Harold Samuel Stone, "Epicureanism and Historical Writing: A Study of Vico and Giannone," Ph.D. dissertation, University of Chicago, 1981, pp. 39–80; for the Hebrews, pp. 110–12; for Boyle, p. 12.

3. Margaret C. Jacob, *The Newtonians and the English Revolution, 1689–1720* (Ithaca, NY: Cornell University Press, 1976), pp. 187–92.

4. Ferrone, *Intellectual Roots*, p. 11.

5. See Franco Venturi, *Italy and the Enlightenment: Studies in a Cosmopolitan Century*, ed. and intro. by Stuart Woolf, trans. by Susan Corsi (New York: New York University Press, 1971), ch. 10.

6. See Geoffrey Symcox, "From Commune to Capital: The Transformation of Turin, Sixteenth to Eighteenth Centuries," in Robert Oresko, G. Gibbs, and H. M. Scott, eds., *Royal and Republican Sovereignty in Early Modern Europe* (Cambridge: Cambridge University Press, 1997), pp. 242–71.

7. Pietro Giannone, *The civil history of the kingdom of Naples. In two volumes. Vol. I. Wherein is contain'd, The History of that Kingdom (comprizing also the general Affairs of Europe) under the Romans, Goths, Greeks, Dongobakds, Normans, and the Princes of the House of Suevia, 'till the Death of the Emperor Frederick II. in the Year 1250. With the History of the Civil, Canon, and Feodal Laws; the Ecclesiastical Polity; the Succession of the Popes, and by what subtle Arts the pontificate gain'd upon the Regale. Where the Author clearly demonstrates, That the Temporal Dominion and Power exercis'd by the*

Popes, has been altogether owing to the Ignorance, and Connivance of, or Concessions extorted from Secular Princes during the dark Ages, &c. Written in Italian, by Pietro Giannone, Civilian and Advocate in Naples; and publish'd Anno 1723. Translated into English, by Captain James Ogilvie. Vol. 2. Trans. into English by Captain James Ogilvie (London, 1729). *Eighteenth Century Collections Online,* Gale Publishing, University of California, Los Angeles, August 17, 2017. For the academic culture of the 1780s, see Vincenzo Ferrone, "The Accademia Reale delle Scienze: Cultural Sociability and Men of Letters in Turin of the Enlightenment under Vittorio Amedeo III," *Journal of Modern History,* vol. 70, no. 3, September 1998, pp. 519–60.

8. Stone, "Epicureanism," pp. 301–15.

9. Chiara Continisio, "Governing the Passions: Sketches on Lodovico Antonio Muratori's Moral Philosophy," *History of European Ideas,* vol. 32, no. 4, 2006, pp. 367–84. On his impact in the Veneto, see Ferrone, *Intellectual Roots,* pp. 99–105.

10. Till Wahnbaeck, *Luxury and Public Happiness: Political Economy in the Italian Enlightenment* (Oxford, UK: Clarendon Press, 2004), pp. 55–60.

11. Chiara Continisio, "Governing the Passions."

12. Alberto Radicati, *Christianity set in a true light, in XII discourses, political and historical. By a pagan philosopher newly converted* (London: Printed for J. Peele, at Locke's Head, in Pater-Noster-Row; and sold by the booksellers of London and Westminster, 1730), pp. xiv–xvi. *Eighteenth Century Collections Online:* Range 8298.

13. [Anon.], *A Parallel between Muhamed and Sosem, the great deliverer of the Jews. By Zelim Musulman: in a letter to Nathan Rabby* (London: J. Harbert, 1732). Sosem is Moses.

14. [Anon.], *A Philosophical Dissertation upon Death. Composed for the Consolation of the Unhappy. By a Friend to Truth* (London: W. Mears, 1732), back pages. Cf. Sergio Ferrarese, "Whose Life? Whose Body? Sovereignty and the Early Modern Subject in Radicati's Philosophical Dissertation upon Death," *Italian Studies,* vol. 69, no. 3, 2014, pp. 328–39.

15. *A Philosophical Dissertation,* pp. 5, 8–9, 10–11. For more background on Radicati, see Margaret C. Jacob, *The Radical Enlightenment: Pantheists, Freemasons and Republicans* (London: George Allen & Unwin, 1981), pp. 172–81.

16. Franco Venturi, *Italy and the Enlightenment: Studies in a Cosmopolitan Century,* ed. with intro. by Stuart Woolf (New York: New York University Press, 1972), ch. 3.

17. Paola Bertucci, "Designing the House of Knowledge in Eighteenth-Century Naples: The Ephemeral Museum of Ferdinando Spinelli," in Jim Bennett and Sofia Talas, eds., *Cabinets of Experimental Philosophy in Eighteenth-Century Europe* (Leiden: Brill, 2013), pp. 119–36.

18. Albert Meier and Heide Hollmer, eds., *Johann Gottfried Herder. Italienische Reise. Briefe und Tagebuchaufzeichnungen 1788–1789* (Munich: Deutscher Taschenbuch Verlag, 1988), p. 536, Hildebrand to Herder, September 29, 1789.

19. On musical life, see Harold Acton, *The Bourbons of Naples (1734–1825)* (London: Prion Books, 1957), ch. 2.

20. Wahnbaeck, *Luxury and Public Happiness*, pp. 59–62.

21. Elvira Chiosi, "Academicians and Academies in Eighteenth-Century Naples," *Journal of the History of Collections*, vol. 19, no. 2, November 1, 2007, pp. 177–90.

22. David Garrioch, "Lay-Religious Associations, Urban Identities, and Urban Space in Eighteenth-Century Milan," *Journal of Religious History*, vol. 28, no. 1, February 2004, pp. 35–49. For the lodges in the Neapolitan context, see Vinzenzo Ferrone, *The Politics of Enlightenment: Constitutionalism, Republicanism, and the Rights of Man in Gaetano Filangieri*, trans. Sophus A Reinert (London: Brill, 2012), ch. 4.

23. I have found the following to be particularly helpful: Annalisa Rosselli, "The Role of the Precious Metals in *Della Moneta* by Ferdinando Galiani," in Riccardo Faucci and Nicola Giocoli, eds., *Della Moneta by Ferdinando Galiani: A Quarter Millennium Assessment, History of Economic Ideas*, vol. 9, 2001/3, pp. 43–60.

24. Wahnbaeck, *Luxury and Public Happiness*, pp. 66–69.

25. J. Robertson, "The Enlightenment above National Context: Political Economy in Eighteenth-Century Scotland and Naples," *Historical Journal*, vol. 40, no. 3, 1997, pp. 667–97.

26. Galiani, *On Money*, trans. Peter R. Toscano (Chicago: University of Chicago Press, 1977), pp. 6–7.

27. Quoted in Francis Steegmuller, *A Woman, a Man, and Two Kingdoms, The Story of Madame d'Epinay and the Abbe Galiani* (New York: Knopf, 1991), pp. 86–89.

28. H. Acton, *The Bourbons of Naples* (London, Methuen, 1956), pp. 156–57; 177–80.

29. Paola Bertucci, "The Invisible Woman: Mariangela Ardinghelli and the Circulation of Knowledge between Paris and Naples in the Eighteenth Century," *Isis*, vol. 104, no. 2, June 2013, pp. 226–49.

30. Paula Findlen, "Science as a Career in Enlightenment Italy: The Strategies of Laura Bassi," *Isis*, vol. 84, no. 3, 1993, pp. 441–69; and Gabriella Berti Logan, "The Desire to Contribute: An Eighteenth-Century Italian Woman of Science," *American Historical Review*, vol. 99, no. 3, June 1994, pp. 785–812.

31. Franco Venturi, *The End of the Old Regime in Europe, 1768–1776*, trans. by R. Burr Litchfield (Princeton, NJ: Princeton University Press, 1989, a translation from the Italian of 1979), ch. 4.

32. Ferrone, *The Politics*, pp. 16–19.

33. The letter can be found in E. Lo Sardo, *Il mondo nuovo e le virtù civili. L'epistolario de Gaetano Filangieri (1772–1788)* (Naples: Fridericiana editrice universitaria, 1999), pp. 236–38, and quoted in Vincenzo Ferrone, *The Politics of Enlightenment*, p. 13.

34. Ferrone, *The Politics of Enlightenment*, ch. 4.

35. H. Acton, *The Bourbons*, pp. 178–80.

36. Ibid., pp. 232–34.

37. *The Science of Legislation, from the Italian of Gaetano Filangieri*, trans. by R. Clayton (London: Thomas Ostell, 1806), pp. 94–95.

38. Ibid., p. 304. Cf. Maria Silvia Balzano, Gaetano Vecchione, and Vera Zamagni, "Contemporary of Every Age: Gaetano Filangieri between Public Happiness and Institutional Economics," MPRA Paper No. 84538, February 2018; at https://mpra .ub.uni-muenchen.de/84538 (accessed February 15, 2018).

39. MPRA Paper No. 84538, p. 112.

40. Ibid., p. 156.

41. Ferrone, *The Politics of Enlightenment*, p. 103.

42. Maarten Bosker, Steven Brakman, Harry Garretsen, Herman De Jong, and Marc Schramm, *The Development of Cities in Italy 1300–1861*, CESIFO Working Paper No. 1893, Category 10: Empirical and Theoretical Methods, January 2007; at cesifo1_wp1893.pdf (accessed September 14, 2017).

43. As quoted in Till Wahnbaeck, *Luxury and Public Happiness. Political Economy in the Italian Enlightenment* (Oxford, UK: Clarendon Press, 2004), p. 141, citing Verri, *Pensieri sullo stato politico del Milanese nel 1790*.

44. Philippe Audegean, "La critique des corps intermédiaires à Milan et à Naples. 'Distinguer mes pas des siens,'" *Revue française d'histoire des idées politiques*, no. 35, *Débats et polémiques autour de L'Esprit des lois* (1er semestre 2012), pp. 61–71.

45. See Franco Venturi, *Italy and the Enlightenment: Studies in a Cosmopolitan Century*, ed. and intro. by Stuart Woolf, trans. by Susan Corsi (New York: New York University Press, 1971), pp. 155–57.

46. C. Beccaria, *On Crimes and Punishments*, trans. by David Young (Indianapolis, IN: Hackett, 1986), p. 7.

47. Ibid., p. 14.

48. Ibid., pp. 7–10.

49. Ibid., p. 12.

50. Ibid., pp. 13–18.

51. Franco Venturi, *Italy and the Enlightenment*, pp. 52–62.

52. Beccaria, *On Crimes*, p. 21.

53. Ibid., pp. 21–23; p. 26 for judgment of one's peers; p. 39 for the idea that punishments should be the same.

54. Archives generals du royaume, Brussels, Conseil privé, A124, 576B, April 28, 1781; in Antwerp, Mr. Stocker "est condamné a mort que ses juges se proposent de faire secretement dans la prison ou il es detenu." The government in Brussels, representing the Austrians, thought differently and wanted him taken to the border and exiled.

55. Beccaria, *On Crimes*, ch. 16.

56. Ibid., pp. 51–53.

57. Ibid., pp. 51–53.

58. Alexander I. Grab, "The Politics of Subsistence: The Liberalization of Grain Commerce in Austrian Lombardy under Enlightened Despotism," *Journal of Modern History*, vol. 57, no. 2, June 1985, pp. 185–210.

59. For a biased account of Beccaria's moderate stance, see Philip Jenkins, "Varieties of Enlightenment Criminology: Beccaria, Godwin, de Sade," *British Journal of Criminology*, vol. 24, no. 2, April 1984, pp. 112–30.

60. Luigi Delia, "La peine de mort dans l'*Encyclopédie* et ses suppléments," *Revue Française d'Histoire des Idées Politiques*, no. 35, *Débats et polémiques autour de "L'Esprit des lois"* (1er semestre 2012), pp. 93–107.

61. Pietro Verri, *Réflexions sur l'économie politique. Ouvrage traduit de l'italien* (Lausanne: J. H. Pott & Co., 1773), pp. 40–43. *The Making of the Modern World*; at http:// find.galegroup.com/mome/infomark.do?&source=gale&prodId=MOME&us erGroupName=uclosangeles&tabID=T001&docId=U3601598879&type=multipage &contentSet=MOMEArticles&version=1.0&docLevel=FASCIMILE (accessed September 23, 2017). Gale Publishing, Document Number: U3601598879.

62. Till Wahnbaeck, *Luxury and Public Happiness*, p. 151; see also Raymond Abbrugiati, *Études sur le Café 1764–1766. Un Périodique des Lumières* (Aix-en-Provence: Publications de l'Université de Provence, 2006).

63. See the whole of John D. Bessler, *The Birth of American Law: An Italian Philosopher and the American Revolution* (Durham, NC: Carolina Academic Press, 2014). Cf. Lynn Hunt, *Inventing Human Rights* (New York: Norton, 2007), pp. 102–5.

Chapter Eight. The 1790s

1. [Anon.], *Modern Propensities; or, an essay on the Art of Strangling, etc. . . . with Memoirs of Susannah Hill and A Summary of her Trial at the Old-Bailey . . . 1791, On the Charge of Hanging Francis Kotzwarra . . .* (London, ca. 1791); in the possession of the Lewis Walpole Library of Yale University, #791 0 22. The organizing theme in the opening of this chapter first appeared in Lynn Hunt and Margaret Jacob, "The Affective Revolution in 1790s Britain," *Eighteenth Century Studies*, vol. 34, 2001, pp. 491–521. Credit for the argument should be shared with Lynn Hunt.

2. Jane Judge, "Provincial *Manifestes*. Belgians Declare Independence, 1789–1790," *De Achttiende Eeuw*, vol. 47, 2015, pp. 127–45.

3. Wayne Franklin, ed., *The Selected Writings of Thomas Jefferson* (New York: W. W. Norton, 2010), TJ to Joseph Priestley, March 21, 1801, p. 284.

4. John Catanzariti, ed., *The Papers of Thomas Jefferson*, volumes 24–28 of 39 vols. (Princeton, NJ: Princeton University Press, 1950–), vol. 24, p. 761, December 21, 1792. The term used for the Enlightenment is *les lumières*.

5. William Hamilton Reid, *The Rise and Dissolution of the Infidel Societies in this Metropolis: including the origin of modern deism and atheism . . . ,* (London:

J. Hatchard, 1800), pp. v, 6–8, and found in Victor E. Neuburg, ed., *Literacy and Society* (London: Woburn Books, 1971).

6. For a good summary of approaches currently taken to the history of the Revolution, see Francesco Benigno, "Plus jamais la même; à propos de quelques interpretations récentes de la Révolution française," *Annales: Histoire sciences socials,* vol. 71, no. 2, 2016, pp. 319–46.

7. As quoted in Mark Storey, *Robert Southey: A Life* (New York: Oxford University Press, 1997), p. 9; from a manuscript letter of October 1, 1997, now in the Bodleian.

8. Richard Price, "A Discourse on the Love of our Country," in D. O. Thomas, ed., *Price, Political Writings* (Cambridge: Cambridge University Press, 1991), p. 195.

9. William Jones, *A Letter to John Bull, Esq. from his second cousin Thomas Bull* (London: Norman and Carpenter, 1793; first edition, 1792), p. 5.

10. On the comings and goings of these circles, see New York Public Library, Phorzheimer Collection, MSS 2164–71, on Dyer and Priestley, the Hays sisters, and Mary Wollstonecraft.

11. Ibid., MSS 2164, Dyer cautioning Mary Hays about revealing Priestley's identity as the author of a pamphlet answering Evanson, December 2, 1792, and Misc 2142; and see Mark L. Reed, *Wordsworth: The Chronology of the Early Years, 1770–1799* (Cambridge, MA: Harvard University Press, 1967), pp. 163–64, when Wordsworth, Frend, Dyer, and Godwin are present for tea on February 27, 1795.

12. William Godwin, *An Enquiry Concerning Political Justice, and Its Influence on General Virtue and Happiness* (London: G.G.J. and J. Robinson, 1793), vol. 2, pp. 844–52. Cf. Pamela Clemit, "Godwin, *Political Justice*," in Clemit, ed., *The Cambridge Companion to British Literature of the French Revolution in the 1790s* (Cambridge: Cambridge University Press, 2011), pp. 86–100.

13. British Library, ADD. MS 35 345, George Burnett, Dec 1803 to Thomas Poole, f. 69; "the enchantment of pantisocracy threw a gorgeous light over the objects of life; but it soone disappeared and has left me in the darkness of ruin!"

14. George Dyer, *A Dissertation on the Theory and Practice of Benevolence* (London, 1795), pp. 3–5. Cf. Kaz Oishi, "Coleridge's Philanthropy: Poverty, Dissenting Radicalism, and the Language of Benevolence," *Coleridge Bulletin,* New Series, no. 15, Spring 2000, pp. 56–70.

15. George Dyer, *Poems* (London, 1800), preface, p. xxxvii; and vol. 2, pp. 88–91, for the ode. This copy was owned by Southey and can be found at the Huntington Library, San Marino, CA.

16. Margaret C. Jacob, *Strangers Nowhere in the World: The Rise of Cosmopolitanism in Early Modern Europe* (Philadelphia: Penn Press, 2006), pp. 139–43.

17. Huntington Library, MS 31 201, Mrs. Larpent's Diary, writing on December 2, 1796. The previous month, she heard conversations on the education of women.

18. Huntington Library, Southey-Rickman correspondence, Box 10, R to S. January 4, 1800, and January 30, 1800; on Pantisocracy, "a thing never to be ashamed of." Box 11, R to S, November 4, 1809.

19. Huntington Library, HM MS 10836 to Charlotte Smith to Sarah Farr Rose, June 15, 1804. On her being a democrat, see Judith Phillips Stanton, ed., *The Collected Letters of Charlotte Smith* (Bloomington: Indiana University Press, 2003), p. 39.

20. [Anon.], *The Cabinet, by a Society of Gentlemen* (London: J. March, 1795), vol. 1, pp. 178–85; on slavery, pp. 77–80.

21. For her sympathy, see Charlotte Smith, *The Emigrants, a Poem, in Two Books* (London: T. Cadell, 1793). On her politics, see Angela Keane, *Women Writers and the English Nation in the 1790s* (Cambridge: Cambridge University Press, 2000), ch. 4.

22. Judith Thompson, ed., *John Thelwall: Selected Poetry and Poetics* (New York: Palgrave Macmillan, 2015), p. 89, writing in 1792 for *Universal Magazine*.

23. John Rylands University Library, Deansgate, Manchester, Wedgwood Correspondence (1758–1804), MS 1109, ff. 94–96, Wedgwood to Erasmus Darwin, July 1789, "I know you will rejoice with me in the glorious revolution which has taken place in France. The politicians tell me that as a Manufacturer I shall be ruined if France has her liberty but I am willing to take my chance I that respect—nor do I yet see that the happiness of one Nation includes in it the misery of its next neighbor."

24. Birmingham City Library, Birmingham Archives and Collections, MS 3219/ 6/2/W/164, May 15, 1791.

25. Ibid., April 9, 1791.

26. See August von Kotzebue, *The Natural Son* (London: R. Phillips, 1798), p. 21 for the baron, and p. 14 for the Jew.

27. Barry Murnane, "Radical Translations: Dubious Anglo-German Cultural Transfer in the 1790s," in Maike Oergel, ed., *(Re-)Writing the Radical: Enlightenment, Revolution, and Cultural Transfer in 1790s Germany, Britain, and France* (Boston: De Gruyter, 2012), pp. 44–48.

28. Anne Plumptre, *Something New*, ed. by Deborah McLeod (Peterborough, Ont.: Broadview Press, 1966).

29. New York Public Library, Phorzheimer Collection, MS MIS. 2164, August 25, 1793.

30. Gary Kelly, *Women, Writing, and Revolution 1790–1827* (New York: Oxford University Press, 1993), p. 108, citing her articles in *Monthly Magazine*, vol. I, June 1796, pp. 386–87.

31. A. F. Wedd, ed., *The Love-Letters of Mary Hays (1779–80)* (London: Methuen, 1925), p. 238.

32. Judith Thompson, ed., *John Thelwall: Selected Poetry and Poetics*, publishing for the first time, from the Derby MS, comp. 1805–28, "Visions of Philosophy," pp. 168–69.

33. New York Public Library, Phorzheimer Collection, MISC. 921–95, July 25, 1807, Coleridge speaking of Edward Seward.

34. Wayne Franklin, ed., *The Selected Writings of Thomas Jefferson* (New York: W. W. Norton, 2010), TJ to his daughter, Martha, March 28, 1787, pp. 247–48.

35. [Anon.], *The Cabinet*, vol. 2, pp. 36–49, with excerpts from Helvètius.

36. [William Vaughan], *The Catechism of Man* (London: D. I. Eaton, 1794), p. 214, and found in Gregory Claeys, ed., *Political Writings of the 1790s*, vol. 4 (London: William Pickering, 1995).

37. F. M Grimm, *Historical and Literary Memoirs and Anecdotes, selected from the Correspondence of Baron de Grimm and Diderot . . . , 1770–1790* (London: H. Colburn, 1814).

38. Henry Yorke, *Thoughts on Civil Government: Addressed to the Disenfranchised Citizens of Sheffield* (London: D. I. Eaton, 1794), p. 244, and found in Gregory Claeys, ed., *Political Writings of the 1790s*, vol. 4.

39. W. Wyn James, "Welsh Ballads and American Slavery," first published in *Welsh Journal of Religious History*, vol. 2, 2007, pp. 59–86; now at http://www.cardiff .ac.uk/special-collections/subject-guides/welsh-ballads/slavery (accessed February 22, 2017). See also Geraint H. Jenkins, ed., *A Rattleskull Genius: The Many Faces of Iolo Morganwg* (Cardiff: University of Wales Press, 2005).

40. William Hamilton Reid, *The Rise and Dissolution of the Infidel Societies in This Metropolis*, p. 26.

41. Jon Mee, *Dangerous Enthusiasm: William Blake and the Culture of Radicalism in the 1790s* (Oxford, UK: Clarendon Press, 1992), pp. 18–23.

42. Jennifer Mori, *Britain in the Age of the French Revolution 1785–1820* (Harlow, UK: Pearson, 2000), ch. 4. And see Cathryn A. Charnell-White, "Networking the Nation: The Bardic and Correspondence Networks of Wales and London in the 1790s," in Mary-Ann Constantine and Dafydd Johnston, eds., *"Footsteps of Liberty and Revolt": Essays on Wales and the French Revolution* (Cardiff: University of Wales Press, 2013), pp. 143–68.

43. Roger L. Emerson, "Politics and the Glasgow Professors, 1690–1800," in Andrew Hook and Richard B. Sher, eds., *The Glasgow Enlightenment* (East Lothian, Scotland: Tuckwell Press, 1995), pp. 21–39, esp. pp. 32–33.

44. Birmingham City Library, Watt MSS, JWP, C4/C18A, Gregory Watt's exercise book, 1793.

45. Jan Golinski, *The Experimental Self: Humphry Davy and the Making of a Man of Science* (Chicago: University of Chicago Press, 2016), pp. 160–62, and see ch. 3 for dandyism. See Birmingham City Library, JWP MS C2/28, memoir of the life of Gregory Watt with mention of his visit to Cornwall, where he stayed with Mrs. Davy. For the radicalism of this circle and its being spied upon, see Clive Emsley, "The Home Office and Its Sources of Information and Investigation 1791–1801," *English Historical Review*, vol. XCIV, July 1979, pp. 533–34.

46. See National Library, Ireland, MS 16685, juvenile poetry by Moore.

47. Louis Crompton, *Byron and Greek Love: Homophobia in 19th-Century England* (Berkeley: University of California Press, 1985), pp. 91–93.

48. Jeffery Vial, *Lord Byron and Thomas Moore* (Baltimore, MD: Johns Hopkins University Press, 2001), pp. 6–13. On their view of Southey, see Jonathan David Gross, *Byron: The Erotic Liberal* (Oxford, UK: Rowman & Littlefield, 2001), pp. 162–64.

49. Gross, *Byron*, pp. 127–28.

50. For a recent biography, see Linda Kelly, *Ireland's Minstrel: A Life of Tom Moore: Poet, Patriot and Byron's Friend* (London: I. B. Taurus, 2006), particularly ch. 2.

51. William Hamilton Reid, *The Rise and Dissolution of the Infidel Societies in this Metropolis* . . . (London, 1800), reprinted in Victor E. Neuburg, ed., *Literacy and Society* (London: Woburn Press, 1971), pp. 39 and 79 for the quotations.

52. *The Anti-Jacobin*, January 1, 1798, London, p. 61, a letter from a "batchelor" who recounts, "One little friend of mine, married to a pretty widow, and who used to declaim much on the infamy of the times, and the great evil of a standing army, I found, secretly feared in a certain weak quarter, the advances of an Irish Cornet of Horse." A cornet holds the standard for a horse company.

53. [William Drennan], *The Letters of Orellana, an Irish Helot* (Dublin: J. Chambers and T. Heery, 1785), letter one.

54. Ultán Gillen, "Radical Enlightenment and the Revolution in Late Eighteenth-Century Ireland," in Steffen Ducheyne, ed., *Reassessing the Radical Enlightenment* (London: Routledge, 2017), pp. 240–58.

55. Theobald Wolfe Tone, *An Argument on Behalf of the Catholics of Ireland* (Belfast: Reprinted by the order of the Society of United Irishmen, 1791), p. 12.

56. Richard Sher, *The Enlightenment and the Book: Scottish Authors and Their Publishers in Eighteenth-Century Britain, Ireland, & America* (Chicago: University of Chicago Press, 2006). Cf. Matthew Crow, *Thomas Jefferson, Legal History, and the Art of Recollection* (Cambridge: Cambridge University Press, 2017), p. 89.

57. Justin Roberts, *Slavery and the Enlightenment in the British Atlantic, 1750–1807* (New York: Cambridge University Press, 2013).

58. Lenni Brenner, ed., *Jefferson and Madison: On Separation of Church and State* (Fort Lee, NJ: Barricade Books, 2004), Jefferson to Jean Nicholas dé Meunier, June 2, 1786, p. 79.

59. The anecdote about Paine trying to get a drink opens Seth Cotlar, *Tom Paine's America: The Rise and Fall of Transatlantic Radicalism in the Early Republic* (Charlottesville: University of Virginia Press, 2011). See also Margaret C. Jacob, "Sociability and the International Republican Conversation," in Gillian Russell and Clara Tuite, eds., *Romantic Sociability: Social Networks and Literary Culture in Britain, 1770–1840*

(Cambridge: Cambridge University Press, 2002), pp. 24–42. For Jefferson's comment, see Wayne Franklin, ed., *Thomas Jefferson* (New York: W. W. Norton, 2010), TJ to Thomas Paine, June 19, 1792, p. 272, writing to Paine in Paris from Philadelphia.

60. Elihu Palmer, *An enquiry relative to the moral & political improvement of the human species. An oration, delivered in the city of New-York on the fourth of July, being the twenty-first anniversary of American independence* (New York, 1797). Eighteenth-Century Collections Online, Gale Publishing, pp. 10–11.

61. See Douglas Anderson, *The Radical Enlightenments of Benjamin Franklin* (Baltimore, MD: Johns Hopkins University Press, 1997).

62. James Delbourgo, *A Most Amazing Scene of Wonders: Electricity and Enlightenment in Early America* (Cambridge, MA: Harvard University Press, 2006).

63. For Franklin and freemasonry, see the most recent account in J. A. Leo Lemay, *The Life of Benjamin Franklin: Printer and Publisher 1730–1747* (Philadelphia: Penn Press, 2006), vol. 2, ch. 3. Nicholas Hans, "Franklin, Jefferson, and the English Radicals at the End of the Eighteenth Century," *Proceedings of the American Philosophical Society*, vol. 98, no. 6; *Studies for the Library of the American Philosophical Society*, December 23, 1954, pp. 406–26.

64. Cited in Gordon S. Wood, "The American Enlightenment," in Gary L. McDowell and Johnathan O'Neill, eds., *America and Enlightenment Constitutionalism* (New York: Palgrave Macmillan, 2006), ch. 6, p. 159.

65. Harry Alonzo Cushing, ed., *The Writings of Samuel Adams* (New York: Octagon Books, 1968), letter to G.W., November 13, 1765.

66. Ibid., letter to John Smith, December 19, 1765, draft version, p. 55.

67. Ibid., vol. 4, 1790, p. 349.

68. Ibid., vol. 4, 1794, pp. 357–58, also citing Montesquieu.

69. Wayne Franklin, ed., *Thomas Jefferson* (New York: W. W. Norton, 2010), TJ to Richard Price, August 1785, writing from Paris, pp. 226–27.

70. Ibid., Thomas Jefferson to John Jay, July 19, 1789, p. 263.

71. Ibid., TF to James Madison, September 6, 1789, pp. 263–67; on the experiment, TJ to John Tyler, June 28, 1804, p. 299.

72. W. Daniel Wilson, "Goethe and Schiller, Peasants and Students, Weimar and the French Revolution," in Maike Oergel, ed., *(Re-)Writing the Radical. Enlightenment, Revolution and Cultural Transfer in 1790s Germany, Britain and France* (Berlin: De Gruyter, 2012), pp. 61–71.

73. Wilson, "Goethe and Schiller," p. 69.

74. Ernst Wangermann, *From Joseph II to the Jacobin Trials: Government Policy and Public Opinion in the Habsburg Dominions in the Period of the French Revolution* (Oxford: Oxford University Press, 1959; reprinted 1979, Westport, CT: Greenwood Press). Cf. R. S. Agin, "The Debate on Judicial Torture in Austrian Lombardy," *Studies in Eighteenth-Century Culture*, vol. 46, 2017, pp. 95–106.

75. Heather Morrison, "Making Degenerates into Men by Doing Shots, Breaking Plates, and Embracing Brothers in Eighteenth-Century Freemasonry," *Journal of Social History*, vol. 46, no. 1, 2012, pp. 48–65.

76. Elena Brambilla, "Entre Eglise et Etat. Les réformes de l'instruction pubique en Lombardie (1765–1790)," in Bruno Bernard, ed., *Lombardie et pays-bas autrichiens. Regards croisés sur les Hapsbourg et leurs Réformes au XVIIIe Siècle, Études sur le 18e siècle*, vol. 36 (Brussels: Éditions de l'Université de Bruxelles, 2008), pp. 111–24.

77. Wangermann, *From Joseph II to the Jacobin Trials*, p. 90.

78. Manjusha Kuruppath, *Staging Asia: The Dutch East India Company and the Amsterdam Theatre, 1650–1780* (Leiden: Leiden University Press, 2016), p. 151.

79. Margaret C. Jacob, *The Radical Enlightenment: Pantheists, Freemasons and Republicans* (London: George Allen & Unwin, 1981). And see also Gert Oostindie, "Dutch Decline during 'The Age of Revolutions,'" in Gert Oostindie and Jessica V. Roitman, eds., *Dutch Atlantic Connections, 1680–1800: Linking Empires, Bridging Borders* (Leiden: Brill, 2014), pp. 309–38.

80. This is discussed in greater detail in Margaret C. Jacob, *Living the Enlightenment: Freemasonry and Politics in Eighteenth-Century Europe* (New York: Oxford University Press, 1991), ch. 7.

Epilogue

1. Anthony Page, *John Jebb and the Enlightenment Origins of British Radicalism* (Westport, CT: Praeger, 2003), pp. 100–102.

2. Margaret C. Jacob, "In the Aftermath of Revolution: Rousset de Missy, Freemasonry and Locke's *Two Treatises of Government*," in *L'Eta dei Lumi; festschrift in honor of Franco Venturi* (Naples: Jovene, 1985), vol. 1, pp. 487–521. And see Holly Brewer, "Slavery, Sovereignty, and 'Inheritable Blood': Reconstructing John Locke and the Origins of American Slavery," *American Historical Review*, vol. 122, October 2017, pp. 1038–78.

INDEX

Note: Page numbers in italic type indicate illustrations.

A NOTE ON THE TYPE

This book has been composed in Arno, an Old-style serif typeface in the classic Venetian tradition, designed by Robert Slimbach at Adobe.

CPSIA information can be obtained
at www.ICGtesting.com
Printed in the USA
LVHW031152180321
681794LV00002B/2